MUHAMMADU

BUHARI

MUHAMMADU BUHARI

The Challenges of Leadership in Nigeria

JOHN N. PADEN

ROARING FORTIES PRESS
Berkeley, California

Roaring Forties Press
1053 Santa Fe Avenue
Berkeley, CA 94706

www.roaringfortiespress.com

Published under the same title in 2016 by Huda Huda Publishers, Zaria, Nigeria.

All photographs are official government photographs or in the archives of the Buhari family.

Cover design and interior design by Nigel Quinney

Library of Congress Cataloging-in-Publication data has been applied for.

ISBN 978-1-938901-64-5 (print)
ISBN 978-1-938901-66-9 (Kindle)
ISBN 978-1-938901-67-6 (ePub)
ISBN 978-1-938901-68-3 (pdf)

This book is dedicated to the unity of Nigeria

Contents

Foreword

General Theophilus Y. Danjuma (rtd.)

Former Chief of Army Staff, Nigerian Army (1975–79)
Defence Minister (1999–2003)

It is my singular delight and privilege to write the foreword to this remarkable biography of Muhammadu Buhari. Since we left the Army, Muhammadu and I have maintained a cordial relationship and have regularly visited each other. He has never failed to honor the invitations I have sent him.

The author illuminates a number of Muhammadu Buhari's key qualities, some of which few Nigerians were aware of before they elected him their president. It may come as no surprise to learn that he was appointed head boy of his school, nor that the school had identified him as someone with great potential for leadership in his chosen career. Competitiveness was another quality that Muhammadu demonstrated in school. He won a merit-based competition for a summer scholarship in Britain, and his time in Britain engendered his appreciation of how advanced societies are organized and governed.

Nigerians may be more surprised to discover that school was the training ground where Muhammadu Buhari developed his remarkable tenacity. His determination to persevere in pursuit of his goals was demonstrated for all to see in his quest for the presidency. Despite losing three elections, he stayed the course, eventually triumphing in his fourth bid.

The military was not his first career choice, but it was the military that helped to mold his outstanding character and his competitive spirit. In the course of his brilliant military career, Muhammadu earned a reputation as an officer of great personal discipline, competence, and valor, driven by a deep sense of patriotism and an abiding concern for the welfare of his troops. It is now evident that these qualities have helped him enormously, sharpening his capacity to adapt to the needs of his country and to make a seamless transition from an autocratic leader to a democratic one. His acceptance of three defeats at the polls, as well as his acceptance of his losses at various judicial levels, including the Supreme Court, is testimony to this profound and remarkable transformation.

As a military head of state, his asceticism and integrity enabled him to pursue a relentless war against indiscipline and corruption. The unremitting manner with which the war was fought created a wide gap between himself and the military machine, on the one hand, and the powerful civilian elite, on the other hand, which led to his premature overthrow. One hopes that this experience, coupled with his period in detention, have taught him useful and enduring lessons about how to cope with the demands and pressures of his young presidency.

He fought an election campaign with two cardinal issues in sharp focus: corruption and insecurity. Together, these issues have threatened to truncate our nascent democratic practice while jeopardizing the national unity that Muhammadu and I fought hard and successfully to preserve.

As a democratically elected president, he has used the institutions provided by the Constitution to combat, with great success, the Boko Haram menace ravaging the northeast of our country. He has also used those institutions to unearth encrusted layers of corruption, tackling the problem with a vigor and determination never before witnessed in any of our previous regimes, civilian or military.

The shuttle diplomacy undertaken by President Buhari has helped Nigeria to rid itself of the pariah status achieved by our corruption-ridden country internationally; in time, the president's diplomacy will be rewarded by the return of the resources looted from our country and laundered in international financial centres.

In addition to exploring these issues, the author narrates the president's relentless efforts to revive the economy, especially the petroleum industry, and to redirect the nation's economy toward agriculture, livestock rearing, and the mining of solid minerals. In government, he has brought accountability in military procurement practices, and has implemented the Treasury Single Account.

As he has made progress in these areas, problems in other areas have suddenly reared their ugly heads and clearly demand presidential attention. The need for socioeconomic justice in the Niger Delta region has never been more urgent. Effective policing of our communities is likewise a critical need if we are to stamp out cases of kidnappings; prevent clashes between herdsmen, farmers, and cattle rustlers; and calm the nerves of followers of various faiths and members of a number of ethnic communities, who feel insecure in certain environments.

A whole chapter is devoted, as it should be, to reconstruction in the northeast, where what the author describes as a "Buhari-Danjuma approach" is being taken. As reconstruction moves forward, attention should be paid to the social and infrastructural needs of the area by following the model of the now defunct Petroleum Trust Fund, which the current president oversaw very successfully as its founding chairman.

The author, whose deep and abiding interest in Nigerian politics, politicians, and society has spanned over half a century, provides us with a fascinating, informative, and revealing book—a book that needs to be updated at the end of Muhammadu Buhari's presidency.

I recommend the book to Nigerians and others interested in Nigeria's quest for inspiring leadership and a political system in which the transfer of power from a ruling party to an opposition party can always occur peacefully.

— July 15, 2016

* * *

Biographical Note: *General Theophilus Y. Danjuma was born on December 9, 1937, in Takum in northeast Nigeria. He joined the Nigerian Military Training Center, Kaduna, in 1960, and Mons Cadet Training School, Aldershot, United Kingdom, in 1961. Like Buhari, he served in the Civil War and remained in the military thereafter. He retired from the Nigerian Army in October 1979, having reached the rank of lieutenant general. He has since served on numerous federal government commissions and been active in the Nigerian business community. He holds the traditional titles of Abonta of Wukari, Ochiagha of Obowu, Etiti, Imo State, and Jarman Zazzau. He has been a major bridge between his Christian community and the various Muslim communities in northern Nigeria, and is a lifelong friend and colleague of Buhari. He also served in the cabinet of President Obasanjo as minister of defence from 1999 to 2003.*

Preface and Acknowledgments

This book was conceived in late September 2015, six months after the presidential victory in Nigeria of Muhammadu Buhari. I was encouraged by two longtime friends and colleagues: Mamman Daura, a senior adviser to Buhari, and Abba Kyari, who had just been appointed by President Buhari to be his chief of staff.

It had become clear to me that the international community was still scratching its collective head and asking, "Who is Muhammadu Buhari?" As Buhari engaged with world leaders, I encountered this question constantly. Some people with long memories thought back to Buhari's time as military head of state in 1984–85, but they had little sense of what had happened in the intervening thirty years. So, with the encouragement of friends, I decided to write a biography of Nigeria's new president—a biography short enough that it would be read by a wide variety of people, including policymakers, journalists, and others too busy to pore over a lengthy volume. In addition, the book may be a reminder to Nigerians of how Buhari emerged to become a national leader, and the qualities he brings to the challenges of leadership.

Buhari has been a friend of mine for more than thirty years. We first met in Kaduna in the early 1980s, and we have remained in touch. He was the keynote speaker in 2005 at the Brookings Institute launch of my book *Muslim Civic Cultures and Conflict Resolution: The Challenge of Democratic Federalism in Nigeria.* He also participated in the Arewa House (in Kaduna) launch of my 2008 book *Faith and Politics in Nigeria.* I met with him privately during his visit to Washington, DC, in July 2015, and have chatted with him in several long sessions subsequently. This biography is thus a personal perspective as well as an attempt at objective history.

This book is based largely on public sources, but has benefited enormously from the full cooperation of President Buhari himself. I have had access to the private notes Buhari dictated in 2012 at a time when he was considering a future autobiography. In that sense, this book is an "authorized biography," although it is in no way an "official biography." There has never been any hint of Buhari imposing his perspectives, or those of his colleagues, on the organization or content of this book. Having lived through much of the past fifty years of Nigerian history, I am fully aware of the range of critiques of Buhari and his policies, ranging from "dictator" to "charismatic savior."

As well as drawing on my personal ties with its subject, this biography also reflects my academic interests. Buhari's electoral victory marks the first time in Nigerian history that an opposition candidate has won the presidency. My own teaching and research interests over the years have focused on comparative political leadership, as well as conflict resolution. Hence, this book has a special focus on leadership issues, and on some of the ways in which leadership responds to existential challenges.

My academic colleagues will note that I have not used footnotes in this book, other than to give references for direct quotations or for material of exceptional salience. I have sought to synthesize a wide variety of materials rather than write an academic treatise. I have also tried to provide a cultural and political perspective on the current challenges of the Buhari presidency.

For the sake of timeliness, I did not conduct the sort of intensive field research I had undertaken when preparing my 800-page biography of the charismatic 1960s politician Ahmadu Bello, which was published in 1986. I have been witness to "the Nigeria Project"—as the quest for a prosperous and unified state of Nigeria is often termed—since I did my doctoral research on religion and political culture in the old city of Kano, beginning in 1964. This was before the trauma of the Civil War and military involvement in Nigeria's leadership affairs. (I am grateful to the late emir of Kano, Ado Bayero, for his support, encouragement, and friendship over the years. We miss him.)

I have returned to Nigeria on many occasions, including once to teach at Ahmadu Bello University and once to serve as founding dean at Bayero University, Kano, in 1975–76. More recently, I have been working with scholars at the Centre for Peace Studies at Usmanu Danfodiyo University, Sokoto (UDUS). Over the years, I have worked with Nigerian students, colleagues, and friends from all points on the political and religious spectrum.

In August 2014, I was invited to participate in Nigeria's Interfaith Initiative for Peace (IIP) in Abuja. This conference included about five hundred "peace delegates" from throughout Nigeria, and was sponsored by Cardinal John Onaiyekan and Sultan Sa'ad Abubakar III, both of whom are longtime friends. At the time, many people feared that the upcoming electoral cycle would result in interfaith violence, and efforts were under way to provide channels of communication and create "shock absorbers" able to defuse potential conflict. (I was surprised and delighted when the Sultan introduced me to the conference by saying, "Our next speaker is a Nigerian with a slightly different skin color.")

The challenges of working across various identity divides has been an abiding concern of academics and practitioners in Nigeria. My own views on this matter are clear. My last three books on Nigeria are all dedicated "to the unity of Nigeria," as is this biography. In a real sense, Nigeria is a reflection of the diversity that characterizes our twenty-first-century world. Building bridges across such identities will be a precondition to coping with the challenges of economic development and political cooperation. Many worst-case scenarios are lurking in the wings, including precipitous descents into violence and turmoil. In the endeavor to avoid going over the brink, leadership is essential.

This book looks at the theme of leadership under trying circumstances, from civil war to the predations of a petro-state. It is divided into three parts, each consisting of eight chapters: part I examines the challenges of personal and military leadership, following Buhari's life and career from his birth in 1942 through the presidential elections in 2015; part II explores the challenges of presidential leadership after Buhari's election in 2015 through to the end of that year; and part III assesses the challenges of presidential leadership from January through May 2016, when Buhari completed his first year in office. (The time line that follows this preface summarizes Buhari's evolution as a national leader, from his birth in 1942 to the end of his first year in office as elected president.)

This book, of course, cannot provide a definitive assessment of that year; such judgments require a longer-term perspective. But what this book does offer is as evenhanded and well-informed a perspective as is possible, and thus gives both Nigerians and foreign friends of Nigeria an opportunity to reflect on the progress that has been made and that still needs to be made in addressing the country's multifaceted challenges.

There are many people I could thank for giving me access to the dynamics of one of the most dynamic countries on earth. For insights into the early period, I would especially like to thank two of my academic colleagues who have not only contributed to strengthening higher education but also served in the Buhari cabinet in the 1980s: Dr. Mahmud Tukur, who served as Buhari's minister of commerce and industries, and Dr. Ibrahim Gambari, who served as minister of foreign affairs.

I also want to thank two contemporary colleagues who (like Dr. Tukur) have read drafts of this biography and made useful suggestions: Dr. M. S. Barkindo, former group managing director of the Nigerian National Petroleum Corporation (NNPC), and during 2015–16 a visiting scholar at George Mason University, Fairfax, Virginia, before being elected secretary general of the Organization of Petroleum Exporting Countries (OPEC) on June 2, 2016; and former US ambassador to Nigeria, Dr. John Campbell, currently with the Council on Foreign Relations. They brought deep insights into the Nigerian domestic situation, as well as a keen understanding of international realities.

I am especially grateful to General Theophilus Y. Danjuma for writing the foreword to this book. He has long represented a military tradition in Nigeria of commitment to national unity and of being willing to reach out across the religious aisle in northern Nigeria to strengthen the Nigeria Project. He has long been a friend and senior colleague of President Buhari, as well as a comrade in arms.

My deepest thanks go to Mamman Daura, a longtime friend and one who has encouraged Buhari to keep going on so many fronts. Mamman's gentle spirit, keen intellect, and sense of integrity, plus his willingness to work to keep faith with the Nigeria Project, even during tough times, are an inspiration to us all.

In the near future, I will be handing off my research library to many Nigerians and international colleagues in the academic community. I have donated approximately four thousand books and papers on Nigeria and Africa to the George Mason University Library in Arlington, Virginia. All author royalties from this current book will go directly to the establishment of a Nigerian research and reading room at George Mason University, a public university with a clear global vision. A future generation of Nigerians and others will, I hope, get some sense of the backstory of the Nigeria Project by acquiring a fuller sense of the past as it affects the future. The success of this project will affect not only Africa but also the wider international community.

Time Line,
December 1942–May 2016

Events in Buhari's Life		Events in Nigeria's History
	Colonial Era	
Born in Daura	1942	Under British colonial rule
Attends local schools in Katsina	until 1961	Independence in 1960
	First Republic (1960–66)	
Nigerian Military Training College	1961–63	
Mons Officer Training, UK	1962–63	
Commissioned Second Lieutenant	1963	
Mechanical transport course, UK	1964	
	1964–65	Nigerian elections
	Military Rule (1966–79)	
Leads troops in battle	1967–70	Civil War
First trip to Mecca	1970	
Marries Safinatu Yusuf	1971	
Infantry headquarters	1971–72	Postwar reconstruction
Sent to India for training	1972–73	
Acting director, Transport, Army	1974–75	
Governor, North-East State	1975	Palace coup against Gowon
Federal Commissioner for Petroleum	1976	Gen. Murtala Mohammed, (1975–76)
Sent to US for military training	1979–80	Gen. Olusegun Obasanjo, head of state (1976–79)
	Second Republic (1979–83)	
Continues US military training	1979–80	President Shehu Shagari (1979–83)
Gen. Officer Commanding (4th Div.)	1980–81	
Gen. Officer Commanding (2nd Div.)	1981	Petroleum economy expands
Gen. Officer Commanding (3rd Div.)	1981–83	
	Military Rule (1983–85; 1985–99)	
Becomes head of state	Dec. 31, 1983	Palace coup against Shagari
Removed in coup	Aug. 25, 1987	Gen. Babangida, head of state
In detention	1985–88	
Returns to Daura	1988	
Divorces	1988	
Marries Aisha Halilu	1989	
	1993	Third Republic aborted
Chair of Katsina Foundation	1991–99	Gen. Abacha, head of state (1993–98)
Chair of Petroleum Trust Fund	1996–99	Gen. Abubakar returns civilian rule (1999)

Fourth Republic (1999–present)

Leaves Petroleum Trust Fund	May 1999	Pres. Obasanjo installed
Enters politics	April 2002	
Defeated for president	2003	Obasanjo reelected
Defeated for president	2007	Umaru Yar'Adua elected (dies in May 2010)
	2010	Vice President Jonathan succeeds
Defeated for president	2011	Goodluck Jonathan elected
Elected president	March 2015	First time opposition party wins
Inaugurated	May 29, 2015	Buhari becomes president on APC ticket

Buhari's First Seven Months in Office, June–December 2015

Domestic Vision and Team Building

Settles into Abuja, transition report prepared	June	International oil prices drop
Replaces service chiefs	July	Boko Haram fight continues
Announces federal cabinet	Sept.–Oct.	EFCC takes firm action
Installs cabinet, with portfolios	November	Massive corruption unveiled

Key International Links and Partnering

Trips to Niger, Cameroon, Chad	July	International partners help
Trip to Washington, DC	July	
Trips to South Africa, Ethiopia	Dec.–Jan. 2016	
Trips to Ghana, France	September	
United Nations (New York)	September	
Additional meetings with Cameron, Merkel, etc.	Throughout	

Buhari's Next Five Months in Office, January–May 2016

International Links and Partnering

The UAE and Gulf connection	Throughout	Economic stress continues
Saudi Arabia and anti-ISIS coalition	Throughout	Boko Haram pushed back
US and counterterrorism summit	March–April	Crackdown on corruption
China and economic links	April	International partners help
London and Anticorruption Summit	May	

Domestic Policies

Counterinsurgency	Throughout
Anticorruption	Throughout
Economic recovery	Throughout
Political change	Throughout

THE THIRTY-SIX STATES OF CONTEMPORARY NIGERIA

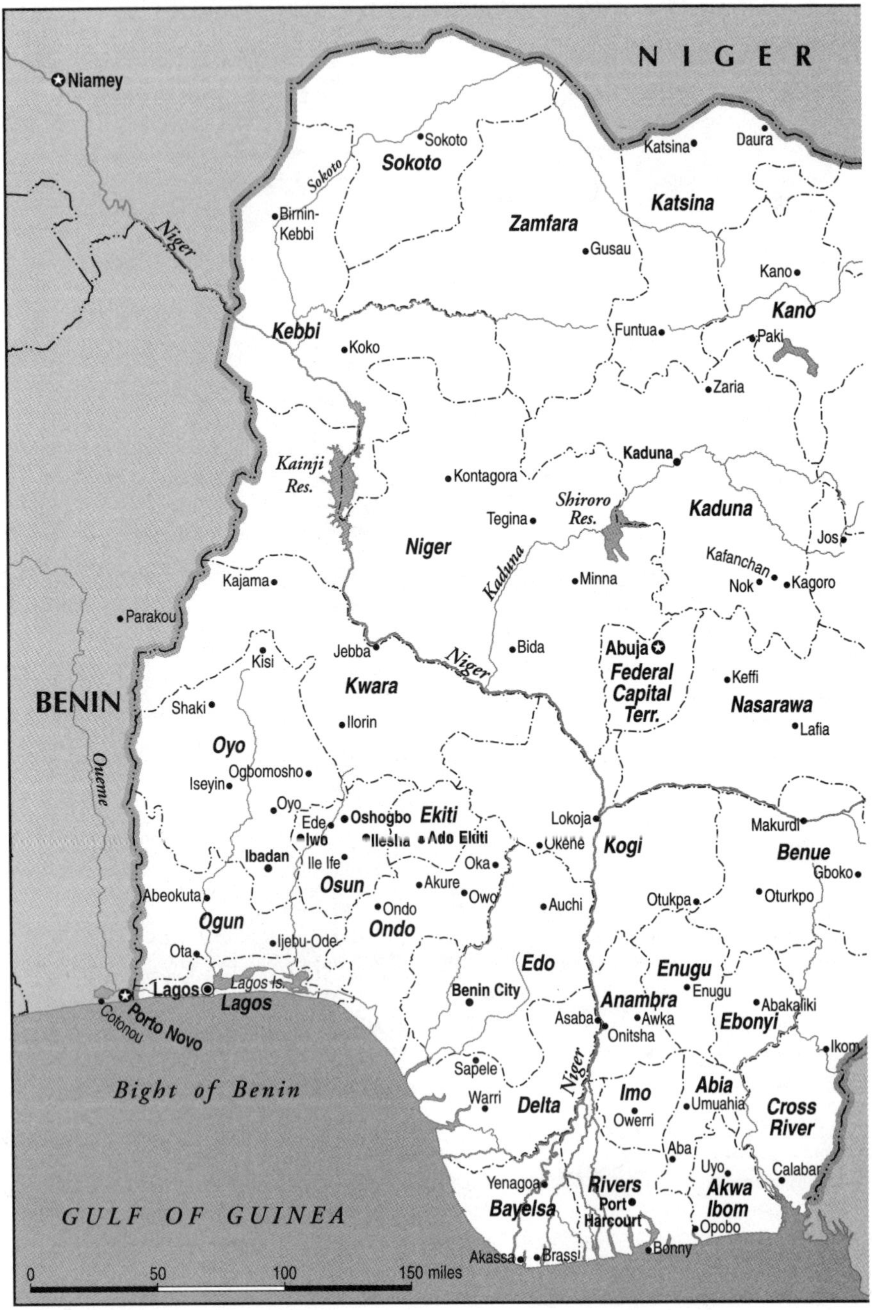

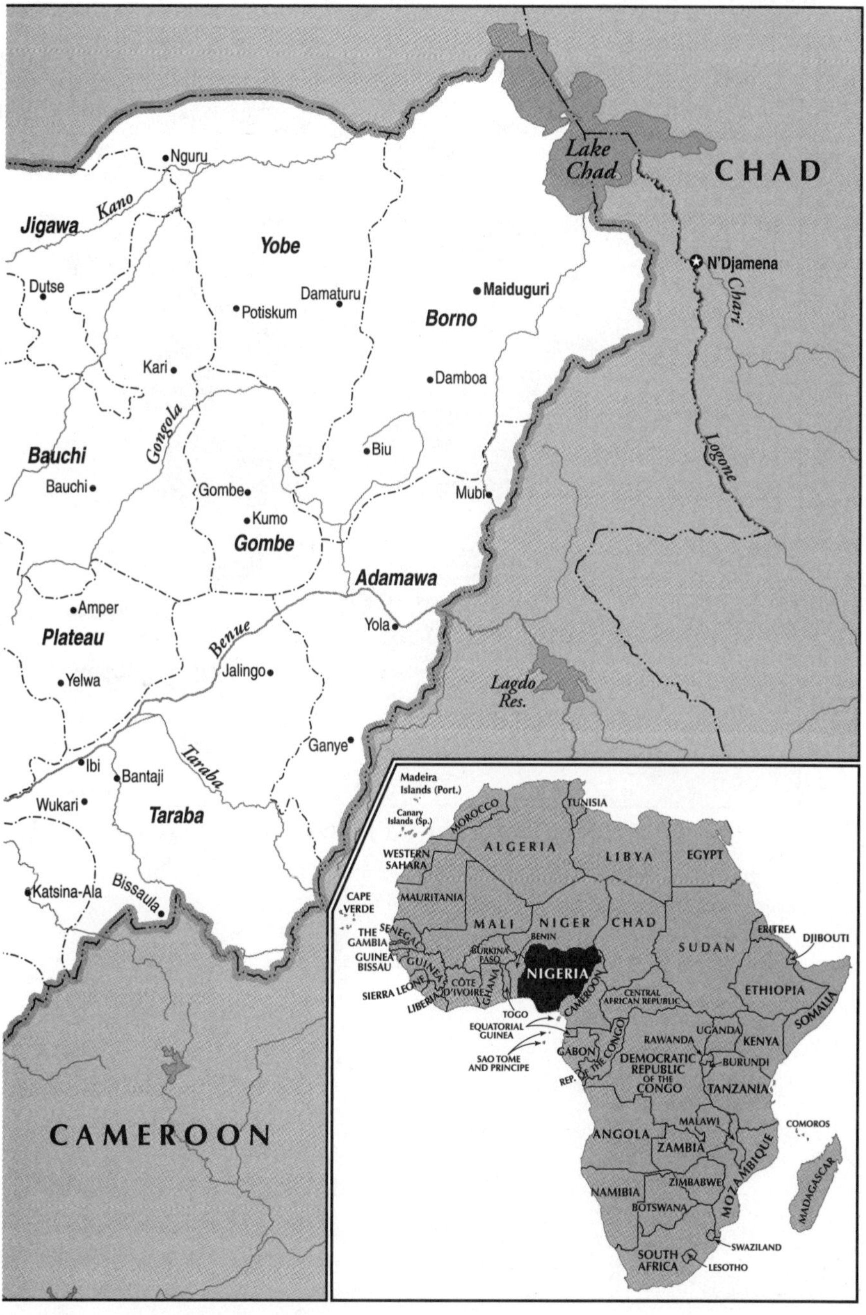

Nguru
Kano
Jigawa
Yobe
Dutse
Damaturu
Potiskum
Maiduguri
Borno
Kari
Damboa
Gongola
Biu
Bauchi
Bauchi
Gombe
Mubi
Kumo
Gombe
Adamawa
Amper
Plateau
Yola
Benue
Jalingo
Yelwa
Ganye
Taraba
Ibi
Bantaji
Wukari
Taraba
Katsina-Ala
Bissaula
Lake Chad
CHAD
N'Djamena
Chari
Logone
Lagdo Res.
CAMEROON
Madeira Islands (Port.)
Canary Islands (Sp.)
MOROCCO
TUNISIA
ALGERIA
LIBYA
EGYPT
WESTERN SAHARA
CAPE VERDE
MAURITANIA
MALI
NIGER
CHAD
SUDAN
ERITREA
DJIBOUTI
THE GAMBIA
SENEGAL
BENIN
BURKINA FASO
GUINEA BISSAU
GUINEA
NIGERIA
SIERRA LEONE
LIBERIA
CÔTE D'IVOIRE
GHANA
TOGO
CAMEROON
CENTRAL AFRICAN REPUBLIC
ETHIOPIA
SOMALIA
EQUATORIAL GUINEA
SAO TOME AND PRINCIPE
GABON
REP. OF THE CONGO
RAWANDA
UGANDA
KENYA
DEMOCRATIC REPUBLIC OF THE CONGO
BURUNDI
TANZANIA
COMOROS
ANGOLA
MALAWI
ZAMBIA
MOZAMBIQUE
MADAGASCAR
ZIMBABWE
NAMIBIA
BOTSWANA
SWAZILAND
SOUTH AFRICA
LESOTHO

THE SIX GEOPOLITICAL ZONES OF CONTEMPORARY NIGERIA

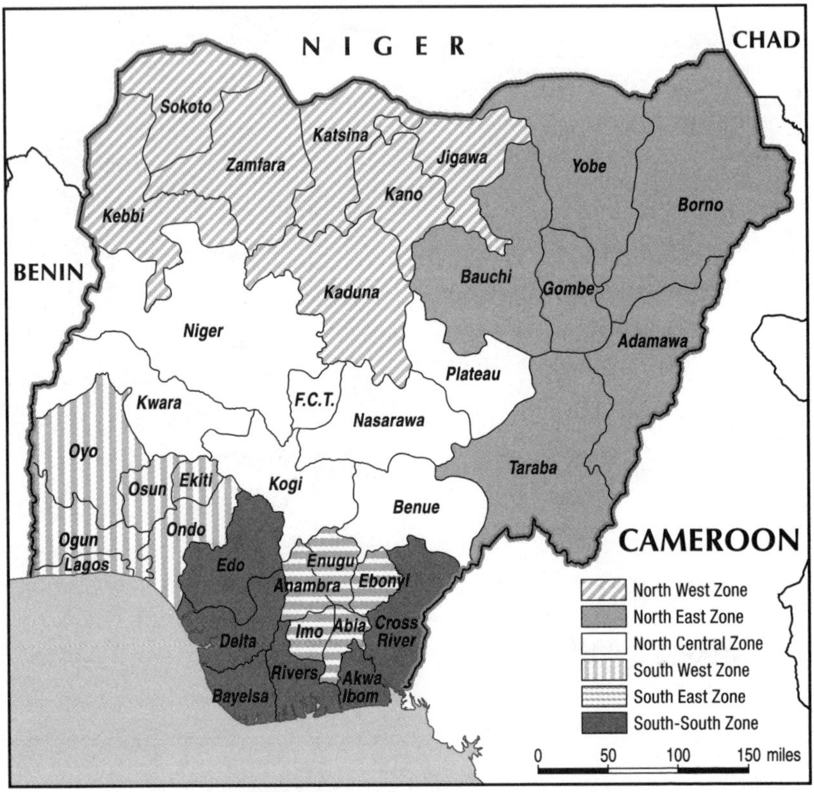

Note: The Federal Capital Territory (F.C.T.) is not part of the North Central zone.

Introduction

The "Nigeria Project," as the quest for a prosperous and unified state of Nigeria is often termed, is a work in progress. With over 180 million people, Nigeria is one of the largest countries in the world. In this globalized age, it is also possible to find thousands or even hundreds of thousands of Nigerians in many of the major urban centers of the world, from Guangzhou to London, from Washington, DC, to Mecca, and from Dubai to Atlanta.

If we are to understand the Nigeria Project and to help it overcome the many obstacles in its path, we need to answer several basic questions. How did such a large country emerge over time? What are its geographic and demographic components? What tensions and fractures exist within it, and how can they be defused and remediated? Leadership is clearly the key to the success of the Nigeria Project and the achievement of national unity. Without such unity, economic prosperity and human security will always be in jeopardy.

Muhammadu Buhari has been a key player in this drama. To assess his contribution, it is necessary to review the cultural and historical context of his early life and its salience to the present situation.

Historically, the Sahel zone in West Africa was a lateral transmission belt for the movement of peoples. Perhaps the largest ethnolinguistic group in the Sahel has been the Fulani—known by many different names—who stretched from Senegal to Sudan. A dominant feature of the Fulani was their cattle culture and, in recent centuries, the Islamic learning of some of their clans.

The other major linguistic group located in what is now northern Nigeria (and the Republic of Niger) has been the Hausa. (In the pre-Jihad period, which culminated in the establishment of the Sokoto Caliphate in 1804, the Hausa were termed "Habe.") Their origins go back to the mythical legend of the seven true Hausa states: Daura, Kano, Zazzau (Zaria), Katsina, Gobir, Rano, and Birom.

Legend has it that a man from Iraq named Bayajidda came across the Sahel to Daura, killed the snake in the local well, and married the local queen. Their seven sons set up the seven city-states. Thus, Daura has special significance as the fountainhead of Hausa culture. From around the fifteenth century, Islam spread to Hausaland from across the Sahara, although many accommodations to pre-Islamic customs prevailed, especially in the rural areas.

The Islamic reform movement of the early nineteenth century brought these two groups—Fulani and Hausa—together. The other major ethnolinguistic group in northern Nigeria, the Kanuri, was based in Borno in the northeast and resisted the reform movement.

With the imposition of colonial rule in West Africa by European powers, especially after the Berlin Conference of 1884–85, peoples were coalesced into "states." Nigeria was created in 1914 by the British with the amalgamation of the colonies of Southern Nigeria and Northern Nigeria.

In the twentieth century, the Fulani and Hausa in Nigeria tended to blend together into the "Hausa-Fulani," forming by far the largest ethnic group in contemporary Nigeria. Today, the Hausa-Fulani account for about 30 percent of the population. (Recently, there has been a trend to disaggregate this term, and for "Hausa" and "Fulani" to self-identify separately, even though the historical mixture in many cases had already occurred.) Farther south are the Yoruba and the Igbo, accounting for about 20 percent and 17 percent of the population, respectively. Numerous smaller groups make up the remaining one-third of Nigeria's people. Indeed, with as many as four hundred distinct ethnolinguistic groups, Nigeria ranks as one of the most diverse countries in the world. The Nigeria Project is the story of how such diversity can be blended into a nation.

Nigeria was, and remains, the largest political entity in Africa, with a population approximately twice the size of Egypt's and three times the size of South Africa's.

As Nigeria's independence movement gathered momentum after World War II, culminating in the end of British colonial rule in 1960, pressure grew to split up this large state. Nigeria's Civil War of 1967–70 was fought to prevent secession in the southeast, and proved to be the turning point in efforts "to keep Nigeria one" —a popular government slogan at the time.

Nigeria also ranks as the largest country in the world that is approximately half Muslim and half Christian. The last Nigerian census to ask about religious identity issues was conducted in 1963. It found that Muslims formed 50 percent of the population, Christians 40 percent, and traditionalists 10 percent. In the wake of the Civil War, military leaders decided that the politically correct estimate of Muslim/Christian ratios would be 50/50 for purposes of appointments. Religious identity questions have not been included in subsequent census exercises.

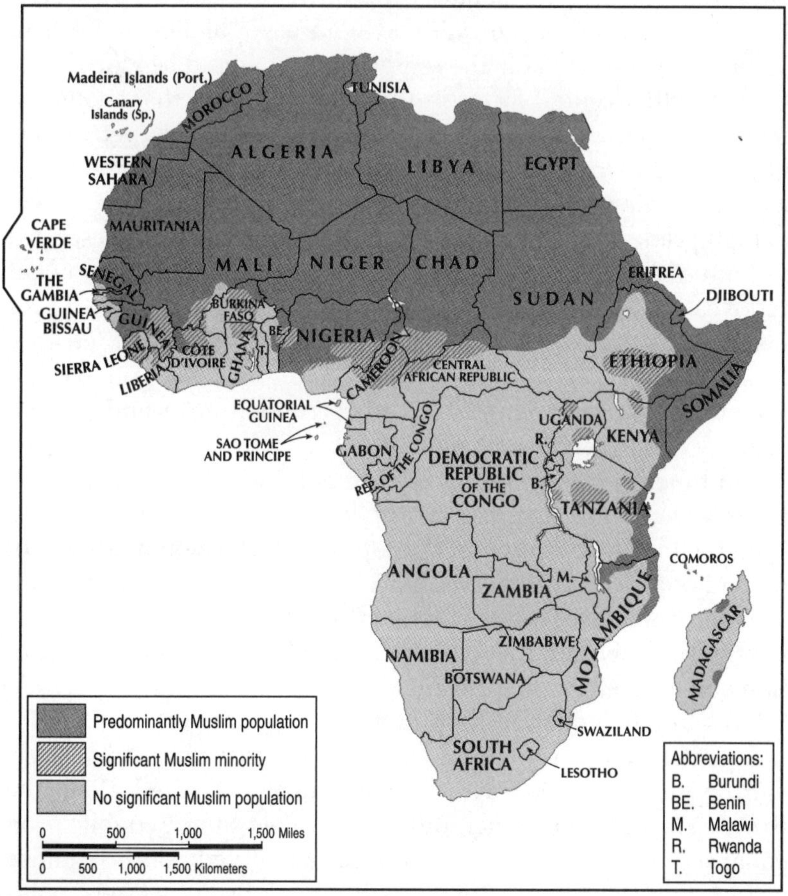

ISLAM IN AFRICA

Nonetheless, birth rate data (from as recently as 2008) clearly indicate that Muslims form a significant majority. Birth rates are approximately twice as high in the far north, which is overwhelmingly Muslim, as in those parts of the south that are predominantly Christian. Nigeria's Muslims are Sunni and follow Maliki law. There are only a few so-called Shi'ites, most of them in the Zaria region who self-identified as Shi'ite after the Iranian Revolution in 1979.

With most Nigerian Muslim peoples living in the north and southwest, and with most Christians in the south and southeast, political leaders have struggled to find ways of balancing access to power and resources in a way that is inclusive. Whether these efforts succeed or fail will have consequences for the whole world. Nigeria is not too big to fail, and with a population more than seven times that of Syria, the refugee fallout would be global.

One other central factor in the Nigeria Project that should be mentioned is the country's evolution into an oil and gas petro-state. Nigeria is a member of the still-salient Organization of the Petroleum Exporting Countries (OPEC), and one of the major producers of high-grade crude oil in the world. This status has been described as both a blessing and a curse. On the one hand, the government receives considerable revenue from the oil and gas industry; for instance, resources were available to relocate the capital territory from Lagos in the south to Abuja in the center of the country. On the other hand, the temptations of corruption have undermined stability and international credibility.

In times of political crisis or instability, the Nigerian military has intervened and assumed power. In some ways, the military has been the major institution in the country, the bastion of a sense of nationhood. The military fought a civil war in which perhaps two million people died in the federal effort "to keep Nigeria one." In later years, however, the military has not been immune to corruption and even ethnic favoritism.

A central element in keeping the Nigeria Project on track for future generations is political leadership. Nigeria began its sovereign existence in 1960 with a government organized along the British Westminster model. But the so-called First Republic soon collapsed, crumbling in 1966 with an attempted coup by junior officers and the killing of many northern and southwestern political and military leaders.

After the ensuing Civil War, a period of military rule continued until 1979, with the inception of the civilian-based Second Republic, which followed a US-style presidential model and was based on a three-tiered federal structure with specified states and local government areas. The Second Republic lasted through 1983. The onrush of oil revenues was creating chaos, the inclusiveness of the government was shrinking, austerity and food shortages were growing, and the price of oil was falling. Senior military officers stepped in and took over.

This military era lasted until 1999, when the Fourth Republic was established, largely based on the model of the Second Republic. (The so-called Third Republic was aborted by the military in June 1993, for a variety of reasons, to be discussed later.) Elections for president in the Fourth Republic occurred every four years: in 1999, 2003, 2007, 2011, and 2015. Elections for the National Assembly and for the governors and legislators of the country's thirty-six constituent states occurred at approximately the same times.

The main challenge for the country's leadership throughout these cycles of military and civilian rule was to hold the country together. But how the government sought to hold Nigeria together varied according to the nature of the government. Although military rule could be based on *power*, civilian governments had to be based on *legitimacy*. The most obvious way of achieving legitimacy was through elections that had to be seen as free and fair. An additional source of legitimacy was conferred by the broadly inclusive character of the coalitions that contested for power. Military heads of state are not encumbered by democratic checks and balances, and hence can appear to be more decisive in addressing perceived challenges. Civilian heads of state may attempt to address basic challenges but are constrained by constitutional limits.

Only two elected presidents of Nigeria have also served as military heads of state: Olusegun Obasanjo (from Ogun State in the southwest) and Muhammadu Buhari (from Katsina State in the northwest). In many ways, Obasanjo is extremely well known, both in Nigeria and in the world. He has written his memoir, and much has been written about him. President Muhammadu Buhari, elected president in 2015, is less well known, at least internationally.

Buhari is a remarkable man and politician for a variety of reasons. Among these is the fact that, despite having been an unelected military head of state in the mid-1980s, during the Fourth Republic, he committed himself to playing by the rules of democratic constitutionalism. He ran for president in 2003, 2007, and 2011, and, according to official results, lost to the incumbents. In 2012, it appeared to many in Nigeria, and perhaps to Buhari himself, that his political career was over. He was a three-time loser in a system where incumbents had never lost an election to a challenger.

Buhari settled down at his home in Kaduna, in the north of the country, and started to dictate an autobiography. By August 2012, he had three hundred pages of draft notes. (These drafts have not yet been published but were made available to the author of this biography.)

But he put those drafts aside when he was encouraged to run for a fourth time in 2015. And he has yet to return to writing his autobiography, because, amazingly, he not only ran but also won. For the first time in Nigerian history, an incumbent president was beaten in an election by a challenger. Buhari's success owed much to a combination of grassroots popularity in the north and coalition building with parties in the southwest and elsewhere.

Literally, millions of ordinary people came out to see and hear Buhari on the campaign trail. His ability to connect with ordinary Nigerians has been phenomenal. The international community also responded favorably to Buhari's well-deserved image as a committed reformist who would embark on far-reaching changes across many different sectors of the country.

Whether he can maintain the level of support—and of respect—he has enjoyed depends on whether he can address issues of insurgency, corruption, economic development, and political change. In his first year as president, he has combatted radical insurgents in the northeast, tackled corruption in the oil industry and throughout government, sought to put economic development back on track, and reengaged with the international community. He has also tried to put a team together that exemplifies the "change" promised during the election campaign.

Buhari is trying to be a *transformational* president—that is, a president who changes the political culture in Nigeria and improves ethical standards in government. As military head of state he was a young man in in hurry. As president, now in his seventies, he has taken a "slow but steady" approach. This study of his life describes his paths to leadership and looks in detail at his first year as president.

This book traces Buhari's rise from his early beginnings in a far northern cattle culture, to his military career just as the Civil War was brewing, to his battlefield experiences in the war, to his postwar efforts (including as military head of state) to deal with the Wild West expectations of an emerging petro-state, his three-year detention by fellow officers, and his eventual engagement with the politics of civilian rule.

The focus on Buhari's first year as president is intended to illustrate the challenges of leadership in dealing with the insurgency by violent extremists, with the corrosive cancer of corruption, with the need for economic recovery and diversification at a time of extremely low oil prices, and with the need to manage identity politics to foster national unity. At the same time, Buhari has tried to reengage with the international community, both in West Africa and throughout the continent, as well as with Europe, the United States, the Middle East, China, and numerous international organizations, such as the United Nations.

It has been a privilege and pleasure to have known Buhari for more than three decades and to have witnessed the quiet passion he brings to his commitment to the Nigeria Project.

PART I

CHALLENGES OF PERSONAL AND MILITARY LEADERSHIP, 1942–2015

PREPARATION FOR LEADERSHIP

Chapter 1

Early Foundations for Leadership

Muhammadu Buhari was born in Daura in Katsina State in the far north of Nigeria on December 17, 1942. He was the twenty-third child of his father, Adamu, who had three wives. Adamu died when Muhammadu was four. The boy was raised by his mother, Zulaihat. He attended primary school in Daura and Mai'adua, went on to Katsina Middle School in 1953, and then went to Katsina Provincial Secondary School from 1956 to 1961. After secondary school, he entered the Nigerian Military Training College.

How did these early life experiences shape Buhari's later career and personality? This chapter explores this question by focusing on four aspects of his early life, with particular attention given to how leadership values were instilled. The four aspects are family networks and values; schooling and leadership values; the decision to join the military; and officer training and leadership.

Family Networks and Values

Northern Nigeria in 1942 was far away from the fighting in Europe, and the British colonial empire was still eighteen years away from handing over power to the fledging Nigerian government. The colonial system in the north was based on a system of "indirect rule," in which, for the most part, a preexisting system of emirate government was left in place.

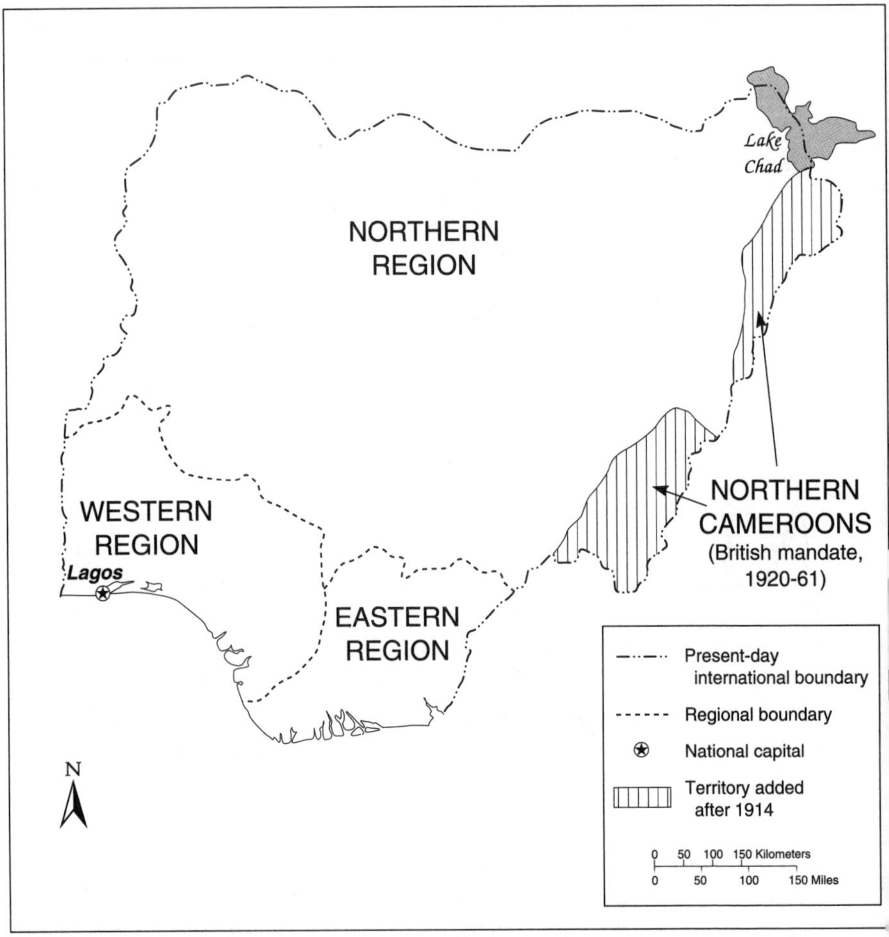

REGIONS OF NIGERIA IN THE COLONIAL AND EARLY INDEPENDENCE ERAS

Daura was one of the smaller emirates, on the far northern border of Nigeria, just next to what became the Niger Republic, which at that time was ruled by the French. The Berlin Conference in the 1880s had drawn a more or less horizontal straight line between Niger colony and colonial Nigeria, thus reifying the French and British spheres of influence. In the process, historic ties and even extended families were divided along this border.

Many family ties in the historic town of Daura reflected the extensive precolonial cultures within the Sahel zone, which stretches from Senegal in the west all the way to Sudan in the east. This zone separated the great Sahara Desert from more lush vegetation farther south. But it was also a corridor along which ideas spread and trade flourished, often cemented by marriage links. It was a zone which saw its share of warfare, with losers often migrating to more welcoming locations.

The two great empires along the Nigerian side of this line were the Sokoto Caliphate in the west—of which Daura was a part—and the Borno Caliphate in the east. Kanem-Borno had been an Islamic polity for more than a thousand years, with a dominant Kanuri-speaking population.

The Sokoto Caliphate was established in the early nineteenth century under the leadership of Muslim reformers Usman Dan Fodio, Abdullahi Dan Fodio, and Muhammad Bello, who were from a scholarly Fulani clan. In the process, the reformers conquered the Hausa-speaking states (called "Habe" states in the preconquest era), including Daura, one of the most ancient of Habe city-states. Over time, many of the Fulani clans married into the Hausa communities. Many Fulani assimilated the Hausa language and culture, and often lost the use of Fulfulde, their original language. By the mid-twentieth century, the term "Hausa-Fulani" reflected this reality, and has been used ever since.

Within the Fulani community, there were not only clan distinctions but also, since the establishment of the Sokoto Caliphate, three major demographic categories, which had cultural and linguistic significance: rural pastoralists, who kept the use of Fulfulde, and who may or may not have spoken Hausa as a lingua franca; settled farmers, often with livestock, who tended to use Hausa as a first language; and city dwellers, who spoke Hausa as first language, having lost the use of Fulfulde. Many in this latter group were engaged in emirate administration or Islamic scholarship.

A third major ethnolinguistic group was (or is still) to be found in northern Nigeria, the Kanuri. The Kanuri were located in Borno in the northeast corner of Nigeria. They have had a long-term, generally cordial relationship with Hausa-Fulani, and they were never conquered during the early-nineteenth-century reform movement, based in Sokoto. Indeed, some of the Hausa states (pre-Jihad) relied on Borno for protection.

At the time of Buhari's birth in 1942, Daura was a small town of perhaps ten thousand persons. His father was Fulani, settled

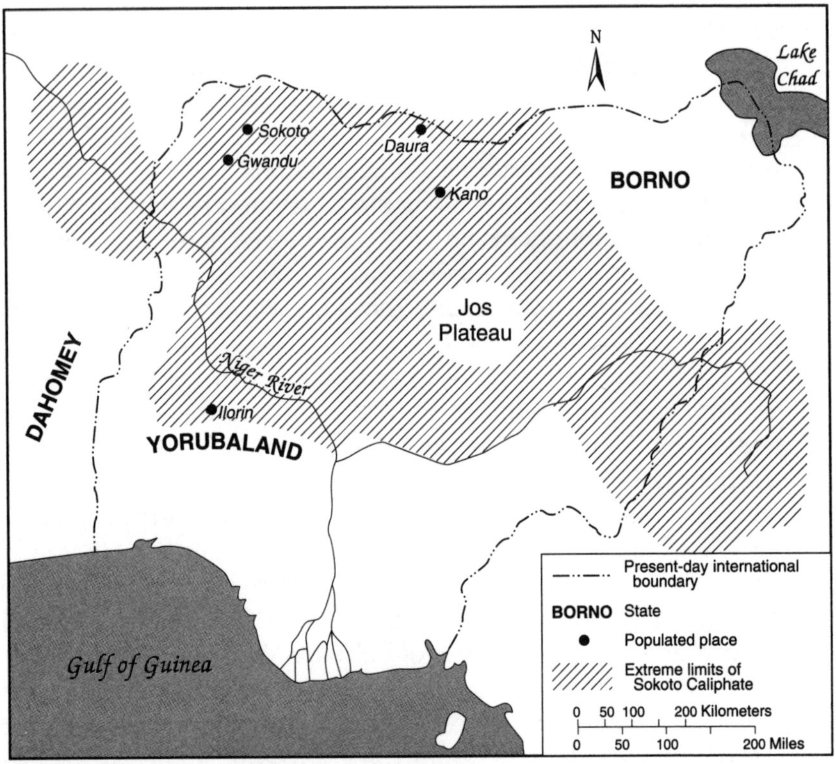

THE SOKOTO CALIPHATE, MID-NINETEENTH CENTURY

on a family farm, with extensive livestock, especially cattle, sheep, and goats. Buhari's great-grandfather, Yusuf, was the founder and chief of several settlements, including Dumurkol, Buhari's father's village, just five miles northwest of Daura. Because this was a time of transition, toward the end of the colonial era, some of Buhari's relatives were in emirate administration under the British system of indirect rule.

Buhari's mother was a mixture of Hausa and Kanuri. Her grandfather, Won Rabbe, had fled Borno during a political upheaval and came to Daura in the nineteenth century. The Fulani had forced the Habe emir into exile in what later became Niger Republic, where the emir met Won Rabbe and gave his son the daughter of a Hausa dignitary to marry. This meant that Buhari's mother was Kanuri on her father's side and Hausa on her mother's side. (For details on Daura, see M. G. Smith, *The Affairs of Daura: History and Change in a Hausa State, 1800–1958* [Berkeley: University of California Press, 1978]. For details on the reign of Emir Musa, 1904–11, see p. 296.)

An agreement was also made by the Habe emir to set up a guardianship to take care of Buhari's mother in the future. When Buhari's father died, Waziri al-Hasan—the son of Emir Musa—became the guardian of Zulaihat and her six children, including her youngest, Muhammadu. This played a major role in the upbringing of Buhari.

This extensive kinship network also affected the future of Buhari in another important way. His senior brother was the father of Mamman Daura, who was three years older than Buhari, although technically his nephew. Mamman would become a lifelong inspiration and confidant to Buhari. He was especially critical in encouraging Buhari to pursue lifelong education.

Like many boys at that time and place, Buhari went to Qur'anic school before going to primary school. He was not enthusiastic about these studies. Early each morning, he would get up and have to fetch firewood for his teacher for the evening Qur'anic readings. There were also several hours of Qur'anic lessons in the morning, at a time when Buhari would rather be outside playing.

Indeed, as had always been the case for many Fulani boys, the outdoors was his real classroom. Buhari spent much of his time helping with the cattle, even drinking from the same pond as they did. He enjoyed nature in all its fullness, from observing scampering rabbits to noticing the seasons come and go. When he did attend school, his love of nature and knowledge of animals made the science courses more interesting to him.

Schooling and Leadership Values

In part because of his love of the outdoors, Buhari was a reluctant student in his early years. He would often skip school altogether, although this always resulted in beatings with a cane by the schoolmaster. Only with the encouragement of Waziri al-Hasan and Mamman Daura did he eventually settle down and take his studies seriously.

The early years of schooling were conducted in Hausa; thereafter, English was used. Buhari began to do very well in English, mathematics, and Arabic, as well as general studies. Buhari also became involved in cross-country running, in which persistence and endurance were key.

Buhari would spend nine years at boarding school, and fortunately he had good teachers. The loss of his father at an early age was compensated for by British teachers who treated each student as if he was their own child. Buhari has often said that in the early days of his schooling, the British sent their best teachers out to northern Nigeria, not their worst. An American Peace Corps teacher in the school also impressed Buhari and the other boys with his love of biology.

Most important, the simple student dress code meant that students looked much the same, except for an occasional student with a wristwatch. The British teachers made a point of disregarding the status of the fathers of the boys. Every boy had to make it on his own.

This point became even clearer when Buhari was eighteen years old and entered a merit-based competition, sponsored by the Elder Dempster shipping line, for selected secondary students to spend a summer holiday in Britain. At that time, many of the northern elites were sending their sons to the prestigious Barewa College, and it was not clear that Buhari had a chance against such competition.

Buhari had been class monitor in second form. He was house prefect in fifth form. In sixth form, he was house captain and head boy of the school. His performance in his studies was excellent. But his leadership potential was outstanding. He was chosen for the summer scholarship to visit in Britain.

In retrospect, this was a life-changing experience for Buhari. After disembarking from his ship in the port of Liverpool, his first impression was that British life was extremely orderly. Moreover, there seemed to be a social compact that enforced unwritten rules of society. This was a society that seemed to work. The model of an orderly society, where people observed the rules, would make a lasting impression. It would also influence his decision to go into the military.

The Decision to Join the Military

At the time that Buhari was finishing secondary school, he was considering becoming a medical doctor. But the only path open to him was in pharmacology at the Nigerian College of Arts, Sciences, and Technology in Zaria. That path would take many years of advanced study to complete.

Meanwhile, the Emir of Katsina, whose emirate adjoined Daura Emirate, was encouraging bright young men to go into the military and train to become officers. His own son, Hassan Katsina, had become a military officer. (Hassan would play a key role stabilizing the situation in the north of the country after a bloody attempted coup led by southeastern officers in January 1966.) When Buhari was considering his options in 1960, Hassan Katsina would often take the secondary school boys out for night hikes and to sleep under the stars. Buhari enjoyed the great sense of adventure of these nighttime ventures into nature.

In addition to considering the military because of the example set by Hassan Katsina, Buhari recognized that officer training provided a pathway to further education. Yet another impetus was provided by Mamman Daura, who strongly encouraged his "younger uncle" to consider officer training and higher education.

Buhari, who was now nineteen years old, had to take several exams even to be considered for officer training. He was able to pass English, mathematics, and general knowledge, plus he met the physical requirements. Still, the competition was nationwide, and only about seventy boys would be selected for officer candidate school. Of these, only half would be commissioned.

The competition was thus stiff, but Buhari was among those selected. One of the key qualities needed in the military was "leadership." Buhari would prove himself time and again to possess that rare gift.

Officer Training and Leadership

Buhari joined the Nigerian Military Training College (NMTC) in Kaduna in 1961, at age nineteen. Basic training lasted seven months, at which point cadets were sent abroad for further training. (This practice prevailed until the college was upgraded in 1964 to become the Nigerian Defence Academy.) From 1962 to 1963, Buhari was sent to officer training at Mons Officer Cadet School in Aldershot, England. In January 1963, Buhari was commissioned as second lieutenant.

In 1961, when Buhari entered the NMTC, Nigeria had been a sovereign country for only a few months, having gained its independence in October 1960. The British were still dominant in education, especially military training, and such training was more about imparting values than about teaching skills or physical conditioning. Skills such as map reading were not ignored, and long marches with heavy backpacks were used to build physical endurance. But, above all, officer training was about values.

The military training in Kaduna was similar to what Buhari would encounter in Aldershot. Nigerian officer training was not a watered-down version for the ex-colony, but the real thing. The Spartan lifestyle, whether in barracks or in the field, was intended to produce toughness of mind and body. This was a total conditioning process. If a student got married, he was sent home. The discipline of school was relentless and was enforced through drill and repetitive writing assignments.

What were the values that military school tried to instill? In retrospect, they seem like something from an old-time war film, and may be hard to grasp from a twenty-first-century perspective. The key was discipline, whether in the daily routine of activities or in the attention paid to academic studies in mathematics, English, or general knowledge. Discipline also meant knowing the hierarchy of command, and respecting it scrupulously.

The purpose of such discipline in the training of officers was to prepare them to fight and (if necessary) die for their country. There was no room for compromise. British training staff did not care who your father was. If you could not handle discipline, you were sent home. Half of Buhari's class of 1961 did not make it.

Other values included team work, bonding with peers, honor and integrity, hard work, duty, and especially honesty. Any hint of corruption or cheating was not tolerated. If you did not pay your food and drink bills in the mess hall, you were punished or even sent home. All of these explicit values were combined in the goal of producing leaders. Indeed, officer training was all about leadership. Careful records were kept on each student, and such records followed them throughout their careers. Superior officers were responsible for junior officers under their watch.

One of the other values encouraged in military training, which was also a skill, was the ability to "appreciate" complex situations and recognize how context matters. This was necessary for both tactical and strategic purposes. The capacity to integrate complex data, ranging from weather conditions to the morale of the enemy, could be the difference between life and death.

The final value that was encouraged was raw courage. Officers were meant to lead their men into battle, and not hesitate when fear took over. This quality was also necessary to ensure good morale among the troops. No one would follow an officer perceived to be a coward.

All these values of military training did not come from a textbook, but from experiential learning. Teamwork and comraderie were encouraged through sports, which all students were expected to play. Long night hikes through unfamiliar terrain were meant to encourage bonding and resourcefulness. Leadership was encouraged through class monitors who were responsible for their classmates.

All of these values would soon be tested by reality. The first test for Buhari came when he was sent to the Congo as a junior officer in the UN peacekeeping mission. Many others from Nigeria including Olusegun Obasanjo, also served in the UN mission. This assignment did not involve a shooting war but it required the ability to manage complex cultural and political situations in order to prevent a civil war. This nine-month experience prepared Buhari for what was to come next in Nigeria.

Chapter 2

Fighting for National Unity

This chapter reviews key aspects of Buhari's leadership development during the Civil War. The chapter begins with an overview of his early career, then sketches the contours of the Civil War, and concludes by examining Buhari's role and experiences during the Civil War. The fight for national unity during the Civil War was the defining experience for Buhari in his early career, and significantly shaped his leadership style.

An Overview of Buhari's Early Career

Buhari's first assignment as a junior officer was in Abeokuta (Ogun State), where he served as platoon commander of the Second Infantry Battalion. In November 1963, he was sent back to NMTC in Kaduna to take a platoon commander's course. Then, in 1964, he went back to Britain for a mechanical transport officers course. In 1965, Buhari returned to Nigeria to take charge of the Second Infantry Battalion, and subsequently became brigade major, Second Sector, First Infantry Division. This promotion came just as civil war was approaching.

The attempted coup in January 1966 staged by junior officers mainly from the Eastern Region not only involved the assassination of the federal prime minister and key northern and southwestern political and military leaders but also led to the collapse of the First Republic. The countercoup and subsequent Civil War to prevent the secession of "Biafra" (a new name coined by the secessionists in the southeast) was traumatic—indeed, it has proved to be the major trauma in Nigerian history.

The Civil War, which lasted from 1967 to 1970, profoundly impacted the military culture of Nigeria. Officers and enlisted men were fighting and dying to "keep Nigeria one"—in the words of a federal slogan at the time. Many Nigerian officers came to see themselves as the guardians of Nigeria, and in the heat of battle developed a strong sense of nationalism. At the same time, leadership skills were tested as never before.

When the Civil War began, Buhari was brigade major of the Third Infantry. When it ended, he became brigade major and commandant of the Thirty-First Infantry Brigade. In 1971–72, he served as assistant adjutant general, First Infantry Division Headquarters. In 1973, he was sent to Wellington, India, to attend the Defence Services Staff College and further develop his leadership skills.

During 1974–75, Buhari became acting director of transport and supply at the Nigerian Army Corps Supply and Transport Headquarters. In August 1975, General Murtala Muhammad appointed Buhari to be governor of North-Eastern State, which comprised what are now the six separate states of Borno, Yobe, Adamawa, Gombe, Bauchi, and Taraba. Then, in March 1976, General Olusegun Obasanjo appointed Buhari to be federal commissioner for petroleum and natural resources. The Nigerian National Petroleum Corporation (NNPC) was created in 1977 by merging the Nigeria National Oil Company (NNOC) with the Ministry of Petroleum. Buhari was appointed chairman of the new corporation.

Buhari moved up to serve as military secretary, Army Headquarters, in (1978–79), and was a member of the Supreme Military Council during this same period. In 1979, Colonel Buhari was selected to go to the United States for further military training. He attended the US Army War College in Carlisle, Pennsylvania The residence program lasted ten months, followed by two years of distance learning. He received a master's degree in strategic studies, class of 1980.

On his return to Nigeria, Buhari earned the following assignments: general officer commanding (GOC), Fourth Infantry Division (August 1980–January 1981); GOC, Second Mechanised Infantry Division (January–October 1981); and GOC, Third Armed Division (October 1981–December 1983). At the time, he was the only officer to have commanded three of the Nigerian Army's four divisions.

On December 31, 1983, senior officers took over the struggling civilian government in a palace coup. Major General Buhari was selected by fellow officers to became head of state (as discussed in chapter 3).

Three Years of Civil War

On May 30, 1967, Colonel Odumegwu Ojukwu, military governor of the First Republic Eastern Region, declared the independence of the Republic of Biafra. In part, this step was a result of frustrations building since the 1966 attempted coup and the subsequent backlash against persons from the Eastern Region. The Supreme Commander of the Nigerian Armed Forces, Lieutenant Colonel Yakubu Gowon, responded by placing an embargo on Biafra, although the embargo did not at first include oil, which at the time was not a major issue. On July 6, federal troops advanced into Biafra. On August 9, Biafran forces swept through the Mid-West Region and headed toward Lagos. The war had begun in earnest.

To the junior officers on the federal side, however, the war had begun earlier, in January 1967, with the breakdown of the "peace talks" between Ojukwu and Gowon at Aburi, in Ghana, reflecting the growing tensions in Nigeria. Buhari was just a lieutenant, but it was clear to him and his comrades that they would have to fight. The war would continue until January 15, 1970.

As the shooting war began, the Biafran sweep through the Mid-West toward Lagos, sent a strong message to the federal officers that Ojukwu did not intend just to carve out Biafra from the southeast; he had designs on the whole country. The details of the Civil War can be viewed from many perspectives, both international and domestic.

The international community had to choose sides between the belligerents, and did so in a fashion that reflected in part the colonial competition between Britain and France. The United Kingdom, the United States, and the Soviet Union—plus Egypt, Saudi Arabia, Niger, Chad, and others—supported the federal side. Support for Biafra came from, among other countries, France, Portugal, Gabon, Ivory Coast, and Haiti.

Many of the officers leading the federal side—including Mohammed Shuwa, Murtala Mohammed, Benjamin Adekunle,

Olusegun Obasanjo, Theophilus Danjuma, and Ibrahim Babangida—would be tested in battle. Most were at the level of colonel or lieutenant colonel, because many of the higher-ranking northern officers had been killed in the January 1966 attempted coup. Military casualties were heavy—the toll reaching somewhere between 25,000 and 50,000 deaths on each side. Civilian deaths were far higher, climbing to perhaps 2 or 3 million in all, most of whom perished from disease and hunger.

In the fog of war, it was often difficult to determine the overall dynamics of the many localized battles. And as the war dragged on, it was sometime unclear who was winning the war overall. Not until federal forces captured the city of Onitsha in late 1969 did the tide shift decisively to the federal side.

When the war finally ended in January 1970, Ojukwu fled to Ivory Coast. General Gowon and other leaders on the federal side made extraordinary efforts to pursue a "no victor, no vanquished" policy. Putting this bold policy of national reconciliation into practice included returning lands and homes taken before the war to Igbos, reintegrating Igbos into the Army, and allowing Biafran military officers to take retirement with full benefits.

Reconstruction after the war would require a major effort to rebuild national unity, and would take many years. Meanwhile, mid-ranking federal officers, many with well-earned battlefield promotions, would take responsibility for running the entire country.

Buhari's Role and Experiences during the Civil War

This first full generation of Nigerian military officers—those trained after independence in 1960—have shaped the destiny of postindependence Nigeria. The names of Danjuma, Gowon, Babangida, Buhari, Obasanjo, Abacha, and others each feature prominently in chapters in the Nigeria Project. They all knew each other, and worked closely at various times. (At other times, they would have serious differences.) But it was the Civil War that gave them common cause.

The northern and southwestern federal officers often knew their counterparts on the Biafran side. They had been to school together and trained together. But the northern and southwestern officers had taken to heart the need to defend the unity of Nigeria.

And northern officers, such as Buhari, recognized that if the southeast were allowed to secede, the southwest would probably follow suit, leaving the north cut off from the coastal ports and lifelines to the outside world.

Buhari was among the first of the junior officers to be sent into battle. He served until the end of the war. Buhari fought at Awka, and later commanded a brigade at Makurdi. He also had to defend areas between Enugu and Abakaliki. He learned to distinguish the types of weapons being fired at his men by the sounds of the gunfire. On one occasion, while marching with his men toward Ogoja, Buhari ran into a group of rebels, and the federal soldiers suffered serious casualties. On another occasion, a rebel sniper killed someone standing next to Buhari.

Many in Buhari's battalion were casualties from typhoid and hepatitis. Finding supplies of clean drinking water was a problem. The rainforest of the southeast was very different from the dry savannah of the north, and often Buhari would lead his men with machetes as they cut their way through thick vegetation. Buhari emphasized the importance of seemingly unimportant matters, such as the need for his men to keep their socks dry lest they be crippled by fungus. The health of his men was of critical importance, as was his own.

During the war, Buhari did not observe fasting during the month of Ramadan, nor did many of his Muslim soldiers. To have done so would have resulted in physical weakness and a death sentence on the battlefield. He believed that Islam is not only tolerant and peaceful, but also capable of accommodating a variety of human circumstances.

Throughout the war, Buhari made it clear to his men that they were not fighting the Igbos. Indeed, some of the men in his battalion and even some of his superior officers were Igbos. Buhari insisted that all his men were fighting "the rebels."

The full scope of Buhari's engagement in the three-year war is beyond the scope of this study. The key facts as far as this book is concerned are that Buhari risked his life to defend the unity of Nigeria, that he showed himself to be resourceful and flexible, that he cared about the well-being of his men, and that he repeatedly demonstrated his leadership abilities, being promoted from lieutenant to captain and then to major.

Looking back on the war, Buhari has commented that it could have gone either way. Luck, he has noted, played no small part in the outcome. But far more than luck was required to rebuild a nation after such a civil war; what was most needed was real leadership.

CHALLENGES OF MILITARY LEADERSHIP

Chapter 3

Buhari's Emergence as a National Leader

This chapter examines (1) the coup of July 1975; (2) Buhari's leadership assignments after the Civil War; (3) his further training abroad and return to Nigeria; (4) the military coup of December 1983; and (5) the military and reforms. The chapter begins, however, with an overview of Buhari's role during this period. In particular, it traces his emergence as a national leader.

After the war, when he was twenty-eight, Buhari married. He had wanted to marry sooner, but the war had broken out and he was not sure he would survive it. He did not want to leave a widow struggling to bring up a young family. Now, he started to build his first house in Kaduna. His friend Shehu Yar'Adua gave him advice on a bank loan. But Buhari could not afford the mortgage payments, so he built the house and then rented it out.

In 1970, Buhari also made his first pilgrimage to Mecca. It was a profound experience and reinforced his view that Islam is a religion of peace. It is also a religion that sees the worth in every person. The simple uniform cloth wrapper worn on hajj made it clear that rich and poor were all the same in the eyes of God. This experience reinforced Buhari's view that material things are less important than living a good life. Most important to Buhari, he believed that nobody is above the rules.

In 1972, Buhari received an opportunity to go to India for advanced officer training. He was attached to an armored division. Up to this point, he had traveled abroad professionally only to the United Kingdom and Congo. India was an eye-opening experience for Buhari. He was especially shocked by the caste system, which was still strong at that time. He was also shocked that India could spend millions of dollars on a nuclear device while millions of people suffered in abject poverty.

Meanwhile, in Nigeria after the war, at the national level a federal policy of "no victors, no vanquished" meant that many former Biafran officers were reintegrated into the Nigerian Army. The next phase would be for Nigeria to rebuild itself from the devastation of the war and prepare for a return to civilian rule.

The Coup of July 1975

When General Gowon seemed reluctant to move forward on a military-to-civilian handover, he was removed in a palace coup in August 1975 and replaced by General Murtala Muhammad. This coup included senior officers such as Buhari, Shehu Yar'Adua, Abdullahi Muhammad, Joseph Garba, Ibrahim Taiwo, and Ibrahim Babangida.

There were several reasons for the coup: Corruption had been settling in and nothing was being done to tackle it. Governors were becoming "emperors," and political gridlock was increasing. The situation seemed likely to get only worse. Plus, Joe Garba had some personal reasons. General Danjuma initially discouraged the coup, but when he learned that Buhari and Yar'Adua were involved, he agreed to it.

Early in 1976, Murtala Muhammad was assassinated by rogue Middle Belt region officers in a failed coup attempt. This was led by General Iliya D. Bisalla, Lieutenant Colonel Bukar Dimka, and others. Buhari had known Dimka since he was under Buhari's command in Abakaliki during the war. Buhari remembers him as having gone off frequently to sleep with a girlfriend in Ogoja while his men were still fighting. In short, he was a weak leader. General Theophilus Danjuma dispatched Ibrahim Babangida to apprehend Dimka, and the crisis of Murtala's assassination was nipped in the bud.

Murtala Muhammad was replaced by his second-in-command, General Olusegun Obasanjo. Then, on the strong recommendation of General Danjuma, Obasanjo selected General Shehu Yar'Adua as his second-in-command, thereby preserving the political balance between the north and the south, which was beginning to be seen as vital in the struggle to consolidate the unification of the country.

In March 1976, Obasanjo appointed Buhari as federal commissioner of petroleum and natural resources. The senior officers who had survived the Civil War, including Obasanjo, Babangida, Danjuma, Abacha, Yar'Adua, and Buhari, would all have roles to play in the next phase of the Nigeria Project.

Postwar Leadership Assignments

In the immediate aftermath of war, Buhari's two major postwar leadership assignments, apart from strictly military ones, were as governor of North-Eastern State and as federal commissioner of petroleum and natural resources, including as chairman of the Nigerian National Petroleum Corporation. These experiences would put him at the heart of national policymaking.

In August 1975, Buhari was appointed governor of North-Eastern State by Murtala Muhammad. At the time, the state included Bauchi, Borno, and Gongola, which themselves became states in February 1976. (Later, in 1991, Yobe State was created from Borno, and Gongola was split into Adamawa and Taraba states. In 1996, Gombe State was created from Bauchi State.) In short, this was a vast area, which later became the North East zone during the Fourth Republic. Buhari was assigned to make improvements in the social, economic, and political life of the area.

Buhari's experience in the northeast would become especially useful in two subsequent episodes. The first was the occupation of some Nigerian islands in the Lake Chad area in 1983 by Chadian forces dispatched by President Hissene Habre, who had come to power in Chad the preceding year (and who remained in power until his ouster in 1990). This episode occurred during the Nigerian civilian presidency of Shehu Shagari. Buhari moved his troops from Jos into the area and retook the islands. The second episode was during the Boko Haram insurgency of the Fourth Republic, discussed in chapter 7.

Buhari's second major postwar leadership assignment was in the country's rapidly expanding oil industry. He served as federal commissioner of petroleum and natural resources during 1976–79, an experience that would contribute directly to the success of his efforts in the 1990s as chairman of the Petroleum Trust Fund (PTF) and his efforts as president, beginning in 2015, to regain control of the industry. Petroleum was the lifeblood of Nigeria, and Buhari had gained experience in understanding and managing an industry that subsequently had attracted an international reputation for corruption, especially during the government of President Goodluck Jonathan.

During Buhari's tenure as federal commissioner of petroleum and natural resources, he oversaw the building of two dozen large petroleum depots, in areas as diverse as Lagos, Maiduguri, and Gusau. He constructed pipelines connecting Bonny Terminal to Port Harcourt. He signed contracts to set up refineries in Kaduna and Warri, with pipeline links to the Escravos Terminal in the Delta.

Buhari represented Nigeria at OPEC meetings held in Western Europe and became acquainted with many of the leading international players in that world. Yet as a cabinet minister, he had to attend meetings in Lagos as well. Buhari's perspective on OPEC was to try to generate revenues that would benefit the Nigerian people. This was a period of rapidly changing events.

Buhari's first OPEC meeting was in spring 1976 in Geneva, where security tensions were high in light of the fact that the terrorist Carlos the Jackal had kidnapped key OPEC ministers in Vienna the previous year. In the aftermath of the Arab refusal to sell oil to Europe and the United States following the Yom Kippur War of 1973, there was a global recession. Nigeria had helped break the Arab boycott by increasing production, a move that was appreciated in London and Washington, DC, but not in the Arab world.

When an opportunity came for Buhari to return to his military career by going to the United States for graduate studies—he had been recommended by General Danjuma, chief of army staff (COAS), one of Buhari's closest associates—Obasanjo was at first reluctant to let him go, given his key role in the petroleum industry. Eventually, Obasanjo relented and took over the petroleum ministry himself. Buhari headed for Carlisle, Pennsylvania, and the US Army War College.

Further Training Abroad and Return

The United States started giving Nigeria senior officer training opportunities in the mid-1970s. The first year, Lieutenant General Mohammed Inuwa Wushishi, one of the most experienced federal Civil War officers, had gone, and the Americans were sufficiently pleased by the results to ask for new nominations. Buhari left on June 1, 1979, for a year in Carlisle.

The first culture shock for Buhari was that the Americans used technology, especially computers, far more than did the British. The American regimen also involved more intellectual work and fewer long outdoor hikes than was the case in the United Kingdom or India. In the United States, one worked from 8 a.m. to 5 p.m. every day, with piles of homework on the weekends and even over the Christmas holidays.

In the background, President Jimmy Carter was trying to deal with the Iran hostage crisis. Some of the students in Buhari's class were absent for long periods, and it became clear later that they were engaged in computer gaming the Iran situation. The American television was full of news about the Iranian revolution. The differences between the Shi'a world and the Sunni world were entering the consciousness of American foreign policy analysts.

In 1979, while Buhari was away, General Obasanjo handed over power to an elected civilian government. When Buhari returned to Nigeria in the summer of 1980, Shehu Shagari was president and the Second Republic was under way. Buhari had never met Shagari and had no opinion of him. When they did meet, they got along very well. Buhari respected the office of the president and believed in civilian control of the military.

Buhari had done extremely well in the US Army War College, and on his return was made GOC, Fourth Division, Lagos. Six months later, Buhari was posted as GOC of the Second Division in Ibadan. Four months later, he was appointed GOC of the Third Division in Jos. By all accounts he had the respect of his soldiers and cared about their families. He was seen as consistently fair at courts-martial.

It was during this period, in 1983, that the Chad crisis emerged in the Lake Chad area. Several Nigerian areas had been occupied by Chadian soldiers. President Shagari was reluctant to use armed force. Despite Shagari's orders to avoid military action, Buhari led his troops to the contested zone and reclaimed the lost territory for Nigeria. He was dedicated to the preservation of Nigeria at all costs, even if it might jeopardize his own career. Buhari supported the principle of civilian control of the military, but he was prepared to set aside that principle when the territorial integrity of Nigeria was at stake.

By 1983, Buhari had become the only person to have commanded three of the four divisions of the Nigerian Army. He was well regarded by all of the senior military officers, as well as enlisted men. The stage was set for the next convulsion in Nigerian politics: the toppling of Shagari.

The Military Coup of December 1983

During the twenty-month period between December 31, 1983, and August 27, 1985, Buhari served as military head of state in Nigeria. This period still remains controversial in terms of interpreting what transpired within the military leadership, with a wide range of opinions voiced by those who lived through those times. Yet ordinary Nigerians seemed to appreciate Buhari's efforts to rein in corruption, which was rampant.

The basic facts of the senior officer coup in December were as follows. The gentle former teacher who had served as president since 1979—Shehu Shagari of Sokoto State—was reelected in late summer 1983 in an election widely acknowledged to have been massively rigged by civilian politicians. Riots broke out in the southwest and southeast (e.g., in Ondo, Oyo, and Anambra), as well as in other parts of the country.

Shagari's northern-based National Party of Nigeria (NPN) won majorities or pluralities in six of seven emirate states (all except Kano, which voted for the opposition People's Redemption Party [PRP]). The NPN also won in Benue, Rivers, and Cross River. The Unity Party of Nigeria (UPN) won in some of the Yoruba areas. The Nigerian People's Party (NPP) won in some of the Igbo areas. The Great Nigeria People's Party (GNPP) won in the Borno areas but lost Gongola to the NPN. In short, only the NPN had a national base in terms of electoral victories, but its incursions into the south were regarded as suspect.

Moreover, the oil wealth was coming onstream, which benefited the incumbent party, the NPN. There was no evidence that President Shagari had knowingly awarded crude oil contracts to his ministers or party men, or that he himself had benefited. Yet it appeared that some federal ministers, some state governors, and many others who had access to power had acquired sudden wealth.

With little or no accountability for oil revenues pouring into government coffers, and with state governors being able to approve international loans, there was no way to begin to know the amount of debt being run up by the nouveau riche of Nigeria. The price of oil was going down, but expectations in Nigeria were going up, especially among this class of new rich.

Furthermore, government contracts were being sold and resold for high markups, with little to show in the way of results. A gold rush mentality gripped the country, virtually unrestrained by fiscal discipline. The senior officers of the military, almost without exception, were appalled. The junior officers were making ominous noises about intervening to stem the tide of corruption.

After the turmoil of the summer elections, senior officers too began considering intervention, contemplating a preemptive coup to stabilize the situation. The details of the planning for and the implementation of the coup have been recorded by Buhari in his draft autobiographical notes, and also by others. But such insider notes are not available publicly at this time. (Presumably, after his final retirement from politics, these will be updated and published.)

Major General Buhari was serving as GOC, Third Armored Division, with headquarters in Jos. During spring 1983, even before the presidential election, junior officers began to approach Buhari about launching a coup. He cautioned against such a step.

The prospect of a junior officer coup, which would be bloody, was palpable in Nigeria, given the experience next door in Ghana. Jerry Rawlings, a flight lieutenant in the Ghana Air Force, had led a coup in 1979 that set up the Armed Forces Revolutionary Council (AFRC) and conducted a "housecleaning exercise." The AFRC tried and executed General Akufo, General Acheampong, and General Afrifa, all former heads of state. Many other Ghanaian generals and air marshals were also executed on the grounds of corruption.

Senior officers in Nigeria prevailed on Buhari to lead a coup and he agreed, on condition that there would not be bloodshed. It was planned to be a stabilizing exercise.

The new capital in Abuja was still being built, although "the Villa"—where the President resided—was partly completed. Hence, Lagos still served as national capital. During the days between Christmas and New Year's, President Shagari was in the Villa, in the midst of a vast construction site that must have looked like a moonscape. Normally, Shagari had a brigade of 500 soldiers guarding him in Lagos, but only took 100 to 120 with him to Abuja.

When the coup took place, Shagari fled but was located on a farm in Nasarawa, along with a handful of national security operatives. Brigadier General Ibrahim Bako and his troops were sent by Buhari to remove Shagari from Group Captain Usman Jibrin's farm. Apparently, Shagari had been on his way to Cameroon but had been persuaded by Usman not to run. On his way back to Abuja, Bako was mistakenly killed by coup makers. He was the only casualty of the coup. (It should be noted that some interpretations of this killing suggest it was not a mistake and was instead part of internal political battles within the military.)

In the early hours of January 1, 1984, General Sani Abacha went on the radio to announce that Shagari had been arrested and was in custody. He then handed the microphone to Buhari, who made the following announcement.

> In pursuance of the primary objective of saving our great nation from total collapse, I, Major General Muhammadu Buhari of the Nigerian Army, after due consultation amongst the services of the Armed Forces, have been formally invested with the authority of the head of the Federal Military Government and Commander in Chief of the Armed Forces of the Federal Republic of Nigeria. It is with humility and a deep sense of responsibility that I accept this challenge and call to national duty.
>
> As you must have heard in the previous announcement, the Constitution of the Federal Republic of Nigeria of 1979 has been suspended, except those sections of it which are exempted in the Constitution. The change has been necessary in order to put an end to the serious economic predicament and crisis of confidence now afflicting our nation. Consequently, the Nigerian Armed Forces have constituted themselves into a Federal Military Government comprising a Federal Executive Council, a National Council of States, a Federal Executive Council at the

> centre and state executive councils. Names to be these councils will be announced soon.

The announcement listed the critical problems facing Nigeria, including issues of mismanagement, a lack of checks and balances, financial indiscipline, elections that were not "free and fair," "rigging and thuggery," dependence on "external borrowing," and "corruption and indiscipline." "We deplore corruption in all its facets," Buhari declared. "This government will not tolerate kick-backs, inflation of contracts, and over-invoicing of imports. Nor will we condone forgery, fraud, embezzlement, misuse and abuse of office and illegal dealings in foreign exchange and smuggling."

Buhari continued:

> Arson has been used to cover up fraudulent acts in public institutions. I am referring to the fire incidents that gutted the P&T buildings in Lagos, the Anambra State Broadcasting Corporation, the Republic Building at Marina, the Federal Ministry of Education, the Federal Capital Development Authority Accounts at Abuja, and the NET Building. Most of these fire incidents occurred at a time when Nigerians were being apprehensive of the frequency of fraud scandals and the government incapacity to deal with them. Corruption has become so pervasive and intractable that a whole ministry has been created to stem it. Fellow Nigerians, this is the moment of truth.

Buhari went on to say that "an accurate picture of the financial situation is yet to be determined." He promised to pay "workers who have not received their salaries in the past eight months or so." And he vowed that "the economy will be given a new impetus and a better sense of direction. Corrupt officials and their agents will be brought to book."

Clearly, the senior military officers had thrown down the gauntlet to those who had presided over—and profited from—the Second Republic. It remained to be seen how well those officers could implement their promises and meet the enormous challenges of Nigeria at the early stages of its evolution into a petro-state.

The Military and Reforms

On taking power, the military soon found that things were even worse than they had anticipated. There were literally no foreign reserves. Payments for imported rice had been made to merchants but the ships docking in Nigeria were filled with sand, not rice. There was no accounting of the amount of money in circulation. In many cases, laws were in place but were not being implemented.

Shagari and Vice President Alex Ekwueme were put in detention, although Buhari insisted that they be treated with respect. Tribunals were set up around the country to try cases of corruption. Military officers chaired the tribunals. The most obvious cases involved public officials who had large mansions or other lavish expenses but could not account for their wealth. Some fled the country before they could be detained.

Setting up the new government involved deciding who the service chiefs would be. Ibrahim Babangida was made COS Army, Augustus Aikhomu was made chief of naval staff, and Ibrahim Alfa was made chief of air staff. In terms of ministerial appointments, Domkat Bali became minister of defence and chairman of Chiefs of Service. Onaolapo Soleye became minister of finance; Abdullahi Ibrahim became minister of education; Mamman Vatsa became minister of the Federal Capital Territory (Abuja); and Tam David-West became minister of petroleum. Tunde Idiagbon was chosen as chief of staff.

Other key civilians were appointed to the cabinet, including Dr. Rilwan Lukman (Mines, Power, and Steel); Dr. Mahmud Tukur (Commerce and Industries); Dr. Ibrahim Gambari (Foreign Affairs); and Dr. Bukar Shaib (Agriculture and Forestry). The key was to get people who were experienced and competent. Buhari insisted that everyone in his administration declare their assets before they join it and later, after they left it.

On May 7, Buhari announced the national budget. This included a ban on hiring new federal workers; a raise in interest rates; a halt to capital projects; a prohibition on borrowing by state governments; a 15 percent cut from Shagari's 1983 budget; an adjustment of import duties; and cuts in imports. By October, 200,000 civil servants had been let go.

A number of decrees were promulgated that later came to be regarded as draconian. Decree Number 2 allowed persons deemed as security threats to be detained for up to three months. Decree Number 4, "Protection Against False Accusations," in some ways was similar to the tough slander laws in the United Kingdom.

Decree Number 20 dealt with "ship bunkering" (i.e., oil theft at sea) and drug trafficking.

The drug trafficking decree was controversial in some circles because it carried the death penalty. Buhari was criticized by one of the prominent Islamic scholars in the north, Sheikh Abubakar Gumi. The two met face to face and, as Buhari recalled in a later tribute to Gumi:

> When I first came to Kaduna, Sheikh Abubakar Mahmud Gumi was the first person I met in the Kawo State House. His concern, then, was the execution of three cocaine pushers among whom was a Muslim and two non-Muslims, and those who told him about the issue were not fair to me as a person and as Head of State and Government. He was very agitated when he saw me. I greeted him and he asked me: "Why do you kill people?" I told him I was leading a government that was not democratic. It's a Military Government and a Federal Government that comprised all the components of the country, and the decision to execute three people was the decision of the Federal Government, not mine. The law then stated those who push cocaine should be executed. I asked him: "Sheikh, with all due respect, do you know what cocaine is?" Typical of him, he was honest and said no. Then I said, "Likewise me," but I learnt that it was like a dried cassava flour that people get hooked to, and they become destroyed and people are using Nigeria as a transit point to Europe and America to sell this thing and it is destroying people, including Nigerians. I told him that the materials used to make cocaine were not indigenous to Nigeria; it was not like Indian hemp that was found in all parts of Nigeria, so, the pushers here just do it to make money at the expense of the people. So, the Federal Government then decided that whoever was caught involved in cocaine pushing should be executed. I cannot recall his reaction but I satisfied myself when I told him these things. (Zakari Muhammad, *The Selfless Reformer: Sheikh Abubakar Gumi* [Kaduna, Nigeria: Zakmohd Media Ventures, 2011])

One of the other controversial policies of the Buhari administration was the so-called War against Indiscipline (WAI), launched on March 20. Nigerians were forced to line up in queues at bus stations, airports, and other public places. This requirement might be enforced by soldiers or police with whips known in the north as *bulala* and often used in schools to impose discipline. Civil servants who showed up late for work might be forced to do "frog jumps"—an exercise beloved by military trainers.

Major Muhammadu Buhari in civvies after the Civil War.

A wartime picture of a group of military officers in Awka at the frontline. Buhari is fourth from right. In the middle front row is Chief of Army Staff Major General Hassan Usman Katsina. The picture was taken in November 1969.

Being greeted by the Shehu of Borno, Umar el-Kanem, in August 1975, shortly after Buhari was appointed military governor of North-Eastern State.

Colonel Buhari receiving his medallion from the commandant of the United States War College, Carlisle, Pennsylvania, for completing a senior officers course in 1980.

Accepting a souvenir from the commandant of the United States War College in 1980.

Fatima, President Buhari's eldest surviving daughter, with her children.

Overall, during the twenty months of Buhari's term as head of state, around five hundred persons were jailed for corruption, often for long terms. Many of these were high-ranking civilian former governors and politicians. Others were businessmen. Although these measures were clearly popular at a grassroots level, those jailed had networks that would ultimately undo the Buhari administration.

Buhari was determined to pay all the government's overdue debts, foreign and domestic. He was also determined not to devalue the naira, because the leading Nigerian export was oil, which was denominated in US dollars.

Buhari's most significant economic measure, however, had to be kept a secret, even from his military colleagues in the cabinet, until it was announced. (The only cabinet member who knew was Chief of Staff Tunde Idiagbon.) It was the decision to issue new currency.

The old currency, in principle, was nonconvertible, but millions of ill-gotten currency was stashed abroad, and domestically much of the corruption money was hidden under mattresses and in attics. At a secret location abroad, the new currency was printed. It was returned to Nigeria in C-130s and taken to the Central Bank.

People had two weeks to convert old currency for new. Up to N400,000 could be traded at any bank, with no questions asked. Above that amount, currency could be exchanged but the original source of funds had to be demonstrated. This process was a direct attack on the corruption that had flourished during the Second Republic. But it may also have been a tipping point for those who were willing to strike back at Buhari. Many in the military had links to businessmen feeling the effects of Buhari's anticorruption measures, and splits in the military were already appearing.

By the time Buhari had concluded a nationwide tour in 1985, rumors were spreading of a palace coup being organized by some in the military leadership with fingers in the business world. The sense of instability was made worse by a decline in oil prices. Buhari dispatched his oil minister, Tam David-West, with a letter to Sheikh Zaki Yamani of Saudi Arabia pleading for an increase in Nigeria's OPEC oil production quota. This was granted as a personal favor to Buhari.

The economic situation remained serious. Countertrade (bartering of oil for food and other commodities) with countries in Latin America and Europe began to develop, but this could not make up for the lack of oil revenues. Nor was that outcome intended. What the government sought was to acquire hard goods, raw materials, and basic equipment for key ministries focused on economic development strategies.

General Buhari's economic objectives during this period included returning the National Electric Power Authority to power production and distribution; nationalizing universities, equipping secondary schools, and paying teachers' salaries; and resuming the construction of Ajaokuta steel, resuming work on phosphate and pharmaceutical industries, resuscitating Savannah and Bachita sugar companies, and strengthening various industrial projects such as Ashaka, Benue Cement, and Sokoto Cement.

A key initiative for Buhari was to strengthen Nigeria's river basin development authorities (RBDAs) to help improve irrigation of crops such as grain, tomatoes, onions, and potatoes. (For details, see Mahmud Tukur, *Leadership and Governance in Nigeria* [Zaira, Nigeria: Huda Huda; and London: Houghton and Stoughton, 1999], p. 490 ff.)

Yet splits in the Buhari government were beginning to show. Some cabinet members felt the administration was not as clean as it pretended to be. Later, General Aliyu Gusau, who had been director of Military Intelligence under Shagari and had been brought back in that same position by the Buhari team, would argue that Buhari's coup had been funded by practices such as the sale of import licenses by senior military officers—although this was unknown to Buhari himself at the time.

With normal government business, Buhari ran his cabinet meetings in a collegial manner. He would suggest steps to take, but if outvoted by his colleagues, he was quick to accept the collective decision. With the exception of the decision to change the currency, Buhari's time as head of state clearly qualified as "military rule," but it was not "one-man rule."

Chapter 4

Countercoup and Detention in Benin

This chapter sketches the events surrounding and following the ouster of Buhari, looking in turn at (1) the countercoup of August 27, 1985; (2) Buhari's life in detention; (3) lessons learned and his release from detention in December 1988.

The Countercoup of August 27, 1985

By late spring of 1985, the number of "big men" going to jail had increased. The tribunals were open and transparent. Buhari was insistent that the courts do their duty without fear or favor. Two-thirds of those arrested and charged came from the north, that is, from the NPN base.

As noted above, by the summer of 1985, splits were beginning to appear within the top military circle. Babangida had been part of every coup in Nigeria since 1967 and began to consider his options. He was very close to General Aliyu Gusau, who was in charge of security. As the summer unfolded, Buhari became aware that Gusau was trading in import licenses on the side. Gusau was retired by Buhari, a move that apparently upset Babangida.

Buhari confronted Babangida and asked what he would have done in the matter of Gusau's retirement. Babangida agreed that Gusau had to have been retired. A few days later, however, there was a knock on Buhari's bedroom door. He opened the door and was met by two soldiers, who told him, "General Buhari, sir, you are under arrest." Buhari would spend the next three years in detention in Benin. But at least he was alive.

The question has arisen subsequently as to whether Buhari knew about the countercoup in advance. Given his "appreciation" of complex situations, it is argued by some, how could he *not* have known? Some of those closest to Buhari at the time have subsequently argued that he did know a countercoup was coming. They insist that Buhari calculated that to preempt this plan would have meant executing six or eight senior officers. This he was unwilling to do.

Whatever the truth of these assertions, Babangida was now in charge, and Aliyu Gusau continued to be in charge of security. The person Buhari was closest to in his administration was his chief of staff, Tunde Idiagbon; at the time of the countercoup, Idiagbon was on pilgrimage in Mecca, as a guest of King Fahd. After learning of the countercoup, the king offered him protection, but Idiagbon insisted on returning to Nigeria, where he was put under arrest.

Most of those former politicians who had been jailed during the Buhari administration were released. The new administration of Babangida criticized Buhari for failing to turn around the economy. Two specific economic policies of Babangida were to devalue the currency and to discontinue the RBDAs. The devaluation wiped out about one-eighth of the wealth at the grassroots level. The closing of the RBDAs slowed the use of irrigation for key crops. (Buhari has subsequently noted that once devaluation begins, it tends to require further devaluation and that it is not an appropriate tool for a petro-state with dollar-denominated exports.)

Babangida also tried to look for ways to indict Buhari personally, but his integrity and grassroots popularity helped protect him. After the Babangida countercoup, three of the ministers were retained. Babangida also set up the Aboyade probe into the finances of Buhari and some key ministers, but the investigators could find no evidence of any personal aggrandizement on his part during his term as head of state. Significantly, the three ministers retained from the previous administration by Babangida—Lukman, Bali, and David-West—strongly defended the integrity of Buhari and his close associates, and no charges were ever brought against Buhari.

Meanwhile, Buhari had been taken from Lagos by plane to Akure in Ondo State. After a few months in Akure, he was taken to Benin City in the south of the country, where he would stay under house arrest until his release in December 1988. How he handled this next period in relative isolation would shape his perspective on future political events. It would also drastically affect his family life.

Life in Detention

Buhari was housed in a well-guarded small bungalow in Benin City. He was not harassed by soldiers or cut off from all communication. He was given a small television set that could pick up one or two channels, plus daily newspapers, and he was provided three meals a day. He was allowed visitors, but only on the specific authorization of Babangida. In most cases, his visitors were members of his family, although because they lived in the north of the country, and Benin was in Edo State in the south, travel was a problem.

Buhari's daily routine was much the same every day. He would get up around 5 a.m. for Muslim prayers, and then go back to bed; get up again around 8 or 9 a.m. and have breakfast; read; have lunch; rest; exercise; pray; eat dinner; read; and sleep. The only exercise he could get was to jog around outside the house.

He read not only newspapers, but also novels, history books, and the Qur'an. His chief uncertainty in detention was when he would be released. If Babangida had wanted to kill him, he realized, he would be dead by now. Hence, he had to endure not so much anxiety as a continual sense of boredom. He was used to a spartan lifestyle, and so he did not miss material comforts. But he did miss his family, and he felt acutely the loss of his freedom. He had absolutely no intention of ever reentering Nigerian political life.

Lessons Learned

Buhari had always known that his unrelenting fight against corruption would provoke a response; he realized that "corruption fights back," to quote a common Nigerian saying. Even in his early days in military administration, he had told one of his close confidants that he guessed they only had eighteen months to make the reforms before being thrown out of office. But that, he had stressed, should not slow them down. Rather, it should speed them up.

In retrospect, this can be seen as Buhari's "Baba go fast" period. Later, during his civilian presidency, he would be known as "Baba go slow." This shift to a slower pace was not just a matter of his getting older; it was a deliberate tactic to achieve his strategic goals.

These goals involved getting Nigeria back on track as a political culture based on discipline and ethical principles. At the time of his detention, however, Buhari was more concerned about getting back to a normal civilian life, after his years in military and national service.

In the end, after more than three years in detention, it was the death of Buhari's mother in December 1988 that led to his release. News of her death generated public pressure on Babangida to let Buhari return to Daura. Babangida acceded to the pressure, allowing Buhari to go back to Daura, where he would have to start his new life as a *retired* major general.

HOME AGAIN

Chapter 5

Return to Daura

This chapter picks up the Buhari story after his return to Daura in December 1988. This includes (1) a fresh start; (2) a new family; and (3) extended family and friends.

A Fresh Start

Buhari had married Safinatu Yusuf in 1971, and they had five children, a son and four daughters. In the end, Buhari and Safinatu would be divorced in 1988. He would marry Aisha Halilu in 1989, after his release from detention. They would also have five children.

After the death of his mother in December 1988, Buhari was released and traveled to Daura for the mourning. When he arrived in Daura, he found his farm much as he had left it. His senior brother (the father of Mamman Daura), along with the Barden Daura, had managed the cattle, sheep, and horses in his absence, although a number of cattle had been sold off to pay for feed during the drought.

Buhari was still in debt to the bank for building his home. Yet now he had no income. At that time there was no program to provide retirement funds for former heads of state. Babangida agreed to a policy to pay Buhari his military pension, a modest 1,643 naira per month for ten years.

Babangida had originally sent Buhari "a bag of money," but Buhari refused it and had it distributed to the poor. Buhari had negotiated his pension funds with Air Vice Marshal (rtd) Hamza Abdullahi, a military governor of Kano, who acted on behalf of Babangida. Buhari's argument with Hamza was that incentives were needed because heads of state were less likely to loot the treasury if they knew they had a retirement pension.

Meanwhile, Buhari spent his time growing vegetables, tending his orchard, and looking after his livestock. It was not clear what he would do next. He was forty-seven years old, and all he had was his family, his farm, and his reputation for integrity.

A New Family

Buhari had married his first wife, Safinatu (née Yusuf), in 1971. As noted previously, they had five children, four girls—Zulaihat, Fatima, Hadiza, and Safinatu—and one boy, Musa, who died in infancy from sickle cell anemia. In 1988, Buhari and Safinatu were divorced. In January 2006, Safinatu died from complications of diabetes.

(Note: In November 2012, Buhari's first daughter, Zulaihat Junaid, died of sickle cell anemia after giving birth. Buhari has become passionate and well informed about sickle cell anemia, having lost two children from his first marriage to the disease. According to Buhari, sickle cell is so serious in the north that many Muslim clerics now insist that a couple get a blood test before marriage to check for blood type compatibility.)

On December 2, 1989, Buhari married his current wife, Aisha (née Halilu). She was born in Adamawa on February 17, 1971, to a well-known Fulani family. Her grandfather was from the family of Muhammadu Ribadu, Nigeria's first minister of defence, and one of the most powerful figures in the First Republic. Her father was a civil engineer. On her mother's side, Aisha is related to the Ankali family, well known in farming and textile manufacturing.

Aisha went to primary and secondary school in Adamawa, and is fluent in English and Arabic. After her marriage, she earned a BA degree from Ahmadu Bello University in public administration, and a master's degree from the Nigerian Defence Academy, Kaduna, in international affairs and strategic studies.

Aisha also has advanced degrees in cosmetology and set up small enterprises in Kaduna and Abuja: Hanzy Spa and Hanzy Beauty Institute. She served as a resource person for the National Board for Technical Education (NBTE) and worked in curriculum development for small and medium businesses for NBTE. (She gave up her business interests when her husband became president.)

Aisha later became a women's rights and children's rights advocate. Today, she urges young girls to go to primary and secondary school before getting married. She also became an international advocate on issues of forced early marriage and sex trafficking, and has called for changes in Nigerian laws on these matters.

Aisha has been described by contemporary Nigerian journalists as calm, patient, soft-spoken, and unassuming. After her husband became president, Aisha insisted on being known as the wife of Buhari, rather than as "first lady."

Buhari and Aisha have five children, again a boy, Yusuf, and four girls: Aisha, Halima, Zahra, and Amina. Thus, while he was setting up his new blended family in Daura, Buhari was father to a boy and eight girls.

All of the Buhari children have had extensive educations. Several have studied at university and postgraduate levels, including abroad.

Buhari insisted that all of his girls continue their education through the tertiary level. This they did, although one continued in higher education after she was married. He told them explicitly that education would give them self-reliance, and that he would not have much in the way of an inheritance to leave to his family. Today, Buhari's entire family are not only well educated (see table 5.1) but also speak English, and are comfortable within the broader Nigerian and international social context.

Table 5.1. The education of Buhari's living children

- **Fatima.** Born March 7, 1975. Education: Airforce Primary School, Victoria Island, Lagos; Federal Government College, Kaduna; Ahmadu Bello University, Zaria; postgraduate degree, Business Academy, Stratford, United Kingdom
- **Nana-Hadiza.** Born June 23, 1981. Education: Essence International School; Cobham Hall, Kent, United Kingdom; University of Buckingham; National Youth Service Corps (NYSC); postgraduate degree, National Teachers Institute, Kaduna; master's in international affairs and strategic studies, Polytechnic, Kaduna
- **Safinatu.** Born October 13, 1983. Education: Essence International School; Cobham Hall, Kent, United Kingdom; University of Plymouth, United Kingdom; NYSC; presently, Arden University, United Kingdom
- **Halima.** Born October 8, 1990. education: International School, Kaduna; British School of Lome; Bellerby's College, Brighton, United Kingdom; University of Leicester, United Kingdom; NYSC; Law School, Lagos
- **Yusuf.** Born April 23, 1993. Education: Kaduna International School; British School

of Lome; Bellerby's College, Brighton, United Kingdom; University of Surrey, United Kingdom

- **Zahra.** Born December 18, 1994. Education: Kaduna International School; British School of Lome; Bellerby's College, Brighton, United Kingdom; University of Surrey, United Kingdom
- **Aisha (Hanan).** Born August 30, 1998. Education: Kaduna International School.
- **Noor (Amina).** Born September 14, 2004. Education: Kaduna International School

---

Buhari's passion for education has not been confined to his family. He has also brought that passion to the broader society in the north and nationally.

Extended Family and Friends

In addition to his wife and children, Buhari had an extended family in Daura and in the north. This included his own brothers and his nephew, Mamman Daura. Plus, he had an extensive network of friends throughout Nigeria.

The friendship of Buhari with Mahmud Tukur and Shehu Musa Yar'Adua has been mentioned previously. Buhari also continued to have close ties with other former colleagues from the military, including Theophilus Y. Danjuma, (late) Mamman Vatsa, Muhammad Magoro, and others. He had hundreds of civilian schoolmates and friends, and would attend numerous weddings and naming ceremonies during his "return to Daura period."

Chapter 6

Civic Contributions

This chapter focuses on Buhari's reengagement with civic life, including (1) his involvement with the Katsina Foundation, and (2) his work for the Petroleum Trust Fund.

When he returned to Daura, Buhari not only was determined to stay out of the country's political life but also had no plans to venture into public service at the state or national levels. But his natural leadership inclinations pulled him back into the public domain. His colleagues and others recognized his talents and reputation for honesty, and his sense of civic duty was deep seated. Plus, he was never willing to give up on the Nigeria Project.

The Katsina Foundation

According to an old adage, a good reputation is more valuable than gold. Buhari was certainly rich in terms of reputation, which had survived his ouster and detention intact. That reputation would only grow stronger during his years living in Daura, and among his grassroots supporters he would be known by the nicknames "Mr. Integrity" (*Mai Mutunchi*), "Mr. Truth" (*Mai Gaskiya*), and "Mr. Goodness" (*Mutumin Kirki*).

In the 1990s, private philanthropy was beginning to develop throughout Nigeria, especially at state levels. In the north—for example, in Kano—the Qur'anic injunction to give back to those in need had long inspired charitable activity. More recently, the Kano Foundation had been set up to engage in civic good works, as a complement to government efforts to help the poor and promote development.

In line with this trend, in 1991, the Katsina Foundation was established to encourage the development of education, health services, and small businesses. Contributors were not allowed to sit on the foundation's board of directors, which consisted of high-ranking public figures who would not risk their reputations by involving themselves in corrupt practices. The directors were well known in Katsina, and included former military officers Hassan Usman Katsina and Shehu Musa Yar'Adua, plus Justice Muhammad Bello and senior political figures Isa Kaita and Mamman Nasir.

Buhari was asked to become founding chairman of the board, a position he would hold for seventeen years. After its launch in 1991, the foundation raised around N50 million (about $10 million at the time). Five priorities were established: providing drinking water in rural areas; supporting health and education projects; setting up viable industries; fighting desertification with tree planting; and encouraging moral and cultural development.

Almost immediately, the foundation found itself facing a crisis, when the military governor requested funds from the foundation for his development projects. When the board refused, the governor dissolved the board and appointed a sole administrator. This action was challenged in court between 1991 and January 1992, when a new civilian governor was appointed. The dissolution was withdrawn, and thereafter the foundation encountered no further interference.

The Petroleum Trust Fund

The presidential election of June 12, 1993, was organized by Babangida after he authorized the founding of two political parties: the National Republican Convention (NRC) and the Social Democrat Party (SDP). The SDP presidential ticket included M. K. O. Abiola, a wealthy Yoruba businessman from the southwest, and Babagana Kingibe from Borno. The NRC ticket consisted of Bashir Tofa (from Kano State) and Sylvester Ugoh (from the southeast). Abiola was seen to be close to Babangida, and had financed some of his military efforts, including the coup to remove Buhari.

From all indications, both domestic and international, Abiola won the election, which Babangida then annulled. It appeared that a rift had developed between Abiola and Babangida, for reasons that were never quite clear to Buhari at the time. Subsequent speculations suggest that the reasons were deeply personal on thc part of Babangida.

Both the NRC and SDP candidates were close associates of Babangida. They had at various times canvassed for Babangida to continue in power as president. Their emergence as candidates of the two parties (SDP and NRC) created by Babangida to succeed him in office was clearly with his blessing.

According to one associate of Babangida, General Danjuma "doubted that Babangida was leaving because if indeed he intended to leave . . . he would have 'begun to say good-bye to the states' [before the election]. The former Chief of Army Staff appeared to have said much less than he knew or suspected" (Dan Agbese, *Ibrahim Babangida* [Abuja: Adonis and Abbey, 2012], p. 385).

Due in part to international pressure, there was a brief hiatus of temporary civilian leadership. Then in fall 1993, General Sani Abacha took control of the government, and a new era of military rule ensued. Abacha was from Kano and trained in NMDC (Kaduna), and Aldershot in Britain. In 1984–85, he was promoted to general officer commanding, Second Mechanised Division, and major general in 1984. He was promoted to lieutenant general in October 1987.

Abacha made several attempts to design a new constitution and began the process of returning the country to civilian rule. To most observers, however, he was seen as planning to run for president himself. He was also seen as increasingly paranoid, having jailed Abiola (who later died in detention). In 1995, Abubakar, who was Abacha's chief of defence staff, announced that seven people had been arrested for planning a coup. One of the alleged plotters was Shehu Musa Yar'Adua, a close colleague of Buhari's and a charismatic figure in his own right.

Shehu had met with Obasanjo in Kano, just before Obasanjo had planned to leave the country. Both were arrested and sentenced to death. Buhari himself intervened and saw Abacha, cautioning against extreme measures in an effort to save Obasanjo and Yar'Adua. Other domestic and international figures also intervened, including former US president Jimmy Carter, and the death sentences were commuted. Shehu, however, died in prison under mysterious circumstances. Abacha was becoming a despised figure domestically and internationally.

This brief background is necessary to understand the next phase of Buhari's career. Abacha had raised the price of fuel from 3.25 naira per liter to 11 naira per liter, which was extremely unpopular at the grassroots level. In part to assuage antigovernment sentiment, a Petroleum Trust Fund (PTF) was set up by Abacha in 1994 with the purported intent of using excess crude funds for public development projects. What the new body needed was a public face that inspired confidence.

Given Buhari's reputation for probity, in 1996 Abacha asked Buhari to serve as chairman of the PTF. Buhari had no brief for Abacha, but was convinced that the PTF could serve the welfare of ordinary Nigerians, if managed well. As Buhari has said many times subsequently, he agreed to take the position "not for the sake of Abacha, but for the sake of Nigeria." It was a position he would hold until 1999.

Serving as chairman of the PTF bolstered Buhari's reputation for integrity, which would serve him well when he later entered partisan politics. Buhari had insisted, as part of his agreement to serve, that he would have veto power over the makeup of his board of directors. Plus, he insisted that only three persons would have authority to sign checks: himself, the PTF director of finance, and the PTF secretary. For any check to be valid, it would require the signatures of two of these three people. Any check for more than N15 million would require approval by the board of directors.

The development projects funded by the PTF are part of Buhari's legacy, and also a prime indicator that he did not favor the north over any other region of the country. Indeed, a majority of the development projects went to the south. It is beyond the scope of this study to review all the projects undertaken by the PTF, which ranged from road construction to improvements in health, education, security, and water and food supplies. But a few examples of PTF projects indicate the kinds of work it supported.

The first major project was to build a 43-kilometer road in Lagos connecting the port, and to install drainage systems, mainly on Victoria Island. Overall, more than 12,000 kilometers of roads were constructed or rehabilitated by the PTF, including stretches from Abuja to Port Harcourt and from Port Harcourt to Enugu. Other projects were education related, including constructing schools, equipping laboratories, and purchasing fleets of school buses. The health agenda included building up stocks of drugs; providing inoculations, hospital blankets, and bedsheets; and clamping down on fake (and often toxic) medicines imported from abroad.

In short, PTF investment projects were not "ghost projects," existing on paper only; they were both concrete and valuable. Unfortunately, the whole system of government was broken in Nigeria. The PTF, at best, could serve only as a stopgap measure.

General Buhari led the PTF and showcased his capacity to give the country practical and widely spread development projects that could be useful to very many Nigerians. It was generally agreed that this was done effectively, honestly, and without fuss.

Yet although the PTF was a parastatal and legally independent, ultimate control over its funds lay in the hands of the president. As the PTF Enabling Act stated, "The Presidency exercises exclusive directory and supervisory control over the fund." As Buhari subsequently, sadly realized, Abacha had found ways to divert billions of petro-state dollars of government funds (albeit not PTF funds) to his own offshore accounts. After his death in June 1998, enormous efforts were made to try to recover such funds.

There has never been any evidence to suggest that Buhari was involved in Abacha's looting of the country's revenue. When Obasanjo came back to power in 1999 (see chapter 7), he tried to rationalize his intentions and determination to shut down the PTF, and launched a review of its practices, looking for signs of corruption by Buhari. Yet Buhari was cleared of any collusion in suspect contracts during the period he was chairman of the PTF. He challenged Obasanjo, and anyone else, to find even five cents that had stuck to his hands. No one could do this. It was clear to most Nigerians that Buhari had done his best to be an honest steward of the country's oil wealth, at a time of rapacious looting at the highest levels.

Eventually, about $1.25 billion of the Abacha stolen money was returned from bank accounts in Switzerland to the Obasanjo government. But exactly what happened to those repatriated funds was never clear. During the Jonathan administration, the situation became even murkier when Nigeria's attorney general was involved in negotiations with offshore banking authorities.

Because of perceived irregularities, the World Bank has kept some of these funds in escrow.

The Buhari stewardship of the PTF has remained part of his positive legacy, even in states of the south that would challenge his presidential ambitions.

FOURTH REPUBLIC ELECTORAL POLITICS, 1999–2015

Chapter 7

Buhari's Persistence and Vision, 1999–2011

This chapter examines the elections held under the Fourth Republic in 1999, 2003, 2007, and 2011. Buhari declared his intention to join partisan politics in April 2002. He was the major opposition candidate for president for the first time in 2003, and then again in 2007 and 2011. His persistence in the face of the incumbent's advantage was part of his legacy and mystique in the north and beyond.

Among the key questions addressed in this chapter are what motivated him to join partisan politics; what was his base of support; how did he manage his campaign and strategy; how did he respond to electoral losses; and to what extent did international observers and others regard the elections as fair?

Transition to Civilian Rule

The death of Abacha "from natural causes" in June 1998 is still shrouded in mystery. Muslim tradition requires burial within twenty-four hours of death, which did not allow enough time for an autopsy to be performed on the head of state. Urban legends have sprung up about how Abacha died, with poisoning featuring in some of those myths. Many Nigerians, with gallows humor, have termed the death "a coup from heaven."

When General Abdussalami Abubakar took over after Abacha's death, it was clear that most Nigerians were fed up with military rule. Abubakar set up an Independent National Electoral Commission and began the process of preparing for elections in February 1999. Party formation began in full view in fall 1998. The major power brokers throughout the country established the People's Democratic Party (PDP). Smaller regional parties formed in the southwest and far north. The Alliance for Democracy (AD) was based in the southwest, and the All People's Party (APP) took root in the northwest and northeast.

It was clear to leaders in the north that, for the sake of national unity, it was the turn of the southwest to claim the presidency. As noted in chapter 6, the June 1993 elections appeared to have been won by M. K. O Abiola, a prominent Muslim businessman from the southwest who was well regarded in the north. These elections were annulled by General Babangida, and later, under General Abacha's rule, Abiola was put in detention, where he died.

In spring 1999, the military wanted someone they could trust to lead the country during the transition. General Obasanjo was controversial among military officers, but overall seemed the best candidate: he had managed the transition from military to civilian rule in 1979; he had suffered in jail under General Abacha; and identity politics required that the choice be a Yoruba Christian, which Obasanjo was.

Behind the scenes, however, Obasanjo's election as president in 1999 was the project of General Aliyu Gusau. More than anyone, Aliyu had helped draft Obasanjo into party politics when he was released from jail in 1998. Aliyu had already played a key role in the rise to head of state of a number of his colleagues in the Army, among them Buhari, Babangida, Abacha, and Abdussalami Abubakar. Aliyu now wanted to set the stage for his own assumption of the presidency, and he calculated that he could follow in Obasanjo's footsteps, with the incumbent's full support, once Obasanjo had served one or two terms.

Aware that Babangida was still hoping for power, Aliyu persuaded him that because of the annulment of the June 12 election, it was necessary for a southwest candidate to serve as interim president, paving the way for Babangida to return to power after a first term by Obasanjo. As just noted, the real intention may have been for Aliyu himself to succeed Obasanjo.

The Babangida-Aliyu relationship had been salient to Buhari in the past and might be so again. Meanwhile, members of the northern political elite (like many in the military hierarchy at the time) were intimidated by the power of incumbency of the military, and grudgingly fell in line with the Obasanjo project. A few, such as General Ishaya Bamayi, the COAS under Abacha, were alleged by some to be the arrowheads of the opposition to Obasanjo's return. But the general consensus was that Obasanjo should get the job.

Thus, although the northern political elite felt that they were not responsible for the annulment of the June 12 election that denied a Yoruba from becoming president, the military were divided on Obasanjo, whom they had jailed in an alleged coup plot. Despite all of the above complex reasons, Obasanjo emerged as presidential candidate for the PDP. The AD/APP coalition chose another well-known Yoruba Christian from the southwest, Samuel Oluyemi Falae. Obasanjo's vice presidential running mate was Atiku Abubakar from Adamawa. Falae chose Umaru Shinkafi, a security professional from Sokoto. The north-south balance was correct in both cases.

The Election of 1999 and Its Aftermath

The February presidential election resulted in Obasanjo winning with an official tally of 18,738,154 votes, or just under 63 percent of the vote. Officially, Falae drew 11,110,287 votes, or 37 percent. Voter turnout was said to be 52.3 percent. Significantly, Falae drew 1,542,969 votes (88 percent of all votes cast) in Lagos State in the southwest of the country. Obasanjo won 1,294,679 votes (77 percent of the total) in Kaduna State in the northwest. These figures, however, were regarded skeptically by many people, in light of widespread allegations of fraud and rigging. This lack of faith in the integrity of the electoral process would be important in the later decision by Buhari to enter partisan politics, with his emphasis on anticorruption.

One of the major consequences of the return to civilian rule was the decision by the governors of the twelve far northern states to revive Shari'a as part of the formal criminal justice system in each state. Thus, state assemblies set up parallel systems of law in the criminal domain for Muslims who preferred a Shari'a system. Indeed, the Nigerian Constitution required that the Supreme Court include jurists well versed in Shari'a.

Yet, years of military rule and endless "decrees" had undermined confidence in a more Western-oriented "rule of law." There was a wide range of meanings and interpretations of "Shari'a," ranging from "effort to do the right thing" to a formalized legal code. It was the latter sense that was applied in each far northern state.

Riots broke out in some northern states with mixed Muslim and Christian populations, due to the mistaken perception in Christian quarters that Shari'a would apply to them. (The one circumstance in which Christians might be subject to Shari'a was in judicial decisions concerning a Muslim-Christian marriage, but litigation in such marriages was rare, and such decisions would be made in the civil domain, not the criminal domain.) Tensions were running high. Buhari was not yet involved in partisan politics but was well aware that every Nigerian Muslim believed that Shari'a should govern at least some aspects of their lives. Most thought it applied to an inner sense of right and wrong based on a holistic reading of the Qur'an and the traditions of the Prophet.

Not until the election of 2003, when national party coalitions precluded northern politicians of both major parties from raising the issue, would the Shari'a tensions die down. But in later election contests, many politicians in the South-South and South East would raise fears that a Buhari administration would force Shari'a on the whole country.

The overarching political reality in the north, however, and elsewhere in the country, was that the rich were getting richer and the poor were getting poorer. The realities of a petro-state were clear: resources came in at the top levels and tended to stay there. While those with access to oil wealth engaged in conspicuous consumption, those lower down in society could only hope for scanty trickle-down benefits.

The one national figure who epitomized a commitment to anticorruption was Buhari, despite efforts by the new president to discredit him.

Obasanjo, however, had grown increasingly suspicious of his northern former military colleagues—notably, Babangida and Buhari—and even of midranking officers from the north. By 2001, the mood in the north had swung against Obasanjo, in part because of his early retirement of northern officers. The question was who might challenge him in the 2003 elections. By 2002, there was a major crisis of confidence in the president in both the north and parts of the south.

Meanwhile, in Daura, Buhari had still not paid off his home mortgage. After Abacha died, Buhari had chosen to step down as PTF chairman and return to his hometown, where he continued working with the Katsina Foundation and managing his farm. He belonged to no political party. He was not looking for "contracts." He was not active in the military. He was fifty-nine years old and focused on his growing family. Yet, ordinary people kept looking to him for leadership.

Motivated by this grassroots support, Buhari considered rejoining the political fray. He was encouraged by political and military colleagues and by family and friends. He knew he could not join the PDP of Obasanjo. He opted instead, in April 2002, to join the strongest of the opposition parties, the APP, which later morphed into the All Nigeria People's Party (ANPP). Because of his leadership qualities and national reputation, he was selected to be the APP's presidential candidate. His running mate was Chuba Okadigbo, from the southeast.

By August, it was clear that Obasanjo was going back on his perceived "promise" of serving only one term. (Plus, there was speculation about the political ambitions of Babangida and Aliyu.) But with elections scheduled for early 2003, Buhari would need help if he were to take on the incumbents. His basic concern was "social justice." The income inequality that characterized the new elites of Nigeria called out for an antidote. Buhari believed that antidote involved clean government and robust development. Given the lack of resources of the new party, and its initial northern base, the APP's main asset was Buhari's reputation as incorruptible. Meanwhile, the PDP had formidable access to resources and political experience. It was the national party. But Buhari's recurrent theme of social justice could be valuable if ordinary people were registered to vote and if elections were free and fair.

The Election of 2003 and Its Aftermath

Buhari's campaign manager was Sule Hamma, a well-educated Kano man who had served as secretary to the Kano State government under Abubakar Rimi. The two men, and others, decided that Buhari's campaign would focus on the economy, on social justice, and on the problem of physical security, because armed criminals were creating havoc in the cities and along the roads connecting them. Buhari made a point of visiting as many states as possible, traveling to cities in no fewer than thirty-four states, where he interacted with community and religious leaders, as well as ordinary people. In the south, his PDP opponents tried to paint him as a Muslim fanatic, even though, while he had been in the military, almost three-quarters of his colleagues and his staff were Christian. He continued to meet with Catholic and Anglican religious leaders as he campaigned in the south, but the negative campaign of his opponents was hard to overcome.

The presidential election of April 19, 2003, was a victory for Obasanjo, again with Atiku Abubakar as vice president. The official figures gave Obasanjo a total of 24,456,140 votes (61.9 percent), and Buhari a total of 12,710,022 (32.2 percent). A small party in the southeast, led by Chukwuemeka Ojukwu, was given 1,297,445 (3.3 percent) of the votes.

The larger story, however, was the increase in election fraud. The police in Lagos found 5 million fake ballots. International observers reported serious flaws in eleven of the thirty-six states. Votes were reported from polling stations that were not open. Credible allegations pointed the finger at the supposedly neutral Independent National Electoral Commission (INEC), which was accused of favoring the incumbents.

The results of the presidential election of 2003 presented several lessons for Buhari. Campaigns require money, and the PDP incumbents had access to institutional and personal resources. Governors were the main financiers of the elections on all sides. A few wealthy ANPP supporters, such as Governor Attahiru Bafarawa of Sokoto, helped with ANPP finances, but the ANPP was no match for the PDP financially. Perhaps the main weakness in the ANPP's campaign was the lack of time and resources to put together a national coalition.

In the aftermath of the 2003 election, Buhari tried to challenge the flagrant vote rigging through the courts. This process would drag on until July 2005, before the Supreme Court finally rejected the ANPP's appeal. The role of the courts would continue to haunt the emergence of multiparty democracy in Nigeria. But in the process of the appeal, a major precedent was set: electoral challenges should be taken to the courts, not the streets.

Buhari became a voice for moderation as well as for integrity, urging his followers to show restraint. At a conference at Arewa House, Kaduna, he addressed student supporters:

> As the elections have come and gone, we have chosen the path of tolerance and pragmatism to protest the usurpation of your right to determine your leadership. It is not as if we did not know of faster and more effective methods for resisting the imposition of dictatorship, but as always uppermost in our minds is the fate and progress of our country. ("We Will Never Lose Heart in the Struggle for Democracy—Buhari," *Kano Triumph*, September 25, 2003)

The Election of 2007 and Its Aftermath

The presidential election of April 21, 2007, was preceded by an attempt by Obasanjo to stage-manage a constitutional change to allow him to serve a third term. This move was thwarted by the Senate—plus considerable international pressure—but he was able to influence the selection of his successors. Respecting the PDP's commitment to power-share/power-shift (i.e., the rotation of presidential leadership between north and south), the PDP picked a northern Muslim as PDP presidential candidate, Katsina State governor Umaru Yar'Adua, with the governor of Bayelsa State, Goodluck Jonathan, as running mate. The ANPP ticket was Buhari, with Edwin Ume-Ezeoke from the southeast as running mate.

On April 23, INEC announced that Yar'Adua had won with 24,638,063 votes (70 percent), while Buhari had gained only 6,605,299 votes (18 percent). Atiku Abubakar, who was also running, was given 2,637,848 votes (7 percent).

The international observers were shocked by the conduct of the election, although they were careful to be diplomatic in their written reports. Even so, Madeleine Albright, the leader of the US National Democratic Institute, told Obasanjo privately that it was the worst election she had ever seen, a charge she repeated on Nigerian TV. Both Buhari and Abubakar rejected the results.

The ANPP challenged the results of the election. Yet on June 27, 2010, a major faction of the ANPP agreed to join the Yar'Adua government. Buhari disowned the idea, denouncing the faction that joined the government as "looking for jobs for themselves." Buhari was still the public face of the opposition to the PDP.

In September 2010, new leadership emerged for the ANPP. At a convention in Abuja led by the governor of Yobe State, Ibrahim Gaidam, the former governor of Abia State, Chris Ogbonnaya Onu, was selected to be national chairman. Many of the new officers were from the southeast or far north. The party was leaving behind its conservative roots and becoming a much more progressive party, a shift confirmed in February 2013, when the ANPP merged with the Action Congress and Congress for Progressive Change to form the All Progressives Congress.

A few months earlier, in November 2012, personal tragedy had struck Buhari. His eldest daughter, Zulaihat, died in childbirth in Kaduna. Buhari had a special bond with Zulaihat, who had been named after his mother. Despite the condolences that came in from every quarter, Buhari was deeply shaken. Politics took second place to family concerns, and many observers felt that Buhari would retire from partisan politics and serve as an elder statesman from his home in Kaduna.

The Election of 2011 and Its Aftermath

Buhari's appetite for politics proved stronger than many people predicted. He not only prepared to contest the presidential election in 2011 but also set up a new political party, the Congress for Progressive Change (CPC).

President Yar'Adua had died in office in May 2010, and had been succeeded by his vice president, Goodluck Jonathan, who had selected the governor of Kaduna State, Namadi Sambo, as vice president. Initially, it was not clear whether Jonathan would run again, given that the power-shift principle in the PDP required a northern candidate. But on September 18, 2010, Jonathan declared that he would run in the elections to be held in April 2011.

In 2011, there were sixty-three political parties in Nigeria, but only twenty-three were listed on the presidential ballot. (Most parties reflected state-level politics and could not meet the stricter requirements for national tickets.) The PDP and CPC were the main parties. The PDP fielded Jonathan and Sambo, while Buhari selected Tunde Bakare from the southwest as his running mate. A smaller party in the southwest, Action Congress of Nigeria, ran Nuhu Ribadu—from Adamawa State—as its presidential contender.

The official results gave Jonathan 22,495,187 votes (58.9 percent). Buhari was given 12,214,853 votes (32 percent). Basically, Jonathan won the south, while Buhari won the far north. (Ribadu won only Osun State in the southwest.) The voting pattern was ominous. A stark north-south divide was now evident, and it was wider than it had been at any time in the Fourth Republic. This trend was especially noticeable in the South-South and South East zones, as shown in table 7.1.

Table 7.1. Percentage of votes for Jonathan in the South-South and South East zones, 2011

South-South		South East	
1. Akwa Ibom	95%	1. Abia	99%
2. Bayelsa	99%	2. Anambra	99%
3. Cross River	98%	3. Ebonyi	97%
4. Delta	99%	4. Enugu	99%
5. Edo	95%	5. Imo	99%
6. Rivers	98%		
Average: 97.3%		Average: 98.6%	

These percentages in the South-South and South East were clearly nonsensical. In addition to allegations of vote rigging—and most observers felt the official figures were false—the campaign was marred by attempts by politicians in the predominantly Christian areas of the south and Middle Belt to portray Buhari as a Muslim fanatic. One result was to inflame ethnoreligious tensions, which spilled over into violence after the election in Kaduna State, with its Muslim north and Christian south.

PRESIDENTIAL ELECTION RESULTS, 2011

Buhari termed the postelection violence "sad and unwarranted" but urged his followers not to burn their voter cards in protest, because the gubernatorial elections were coming up the following week. In early May, Buhari made the following media statement through his spokesman:

> General Muhammadu Buhari yesterday said he would not congratulate President Goodluck Jonathan until his demands of subjecting results of 11 states to forensic analysis is done. The states are: Abia, Imo, Ebonyi, Enugu and Anambra in the South-East and Akwa Ibom, Rivers, Cross River, Delta, Edo and Bayelsa in the South-South.
>
> Buhari, who spoke through his spokesman, Yinka Odumakin, also said that their demand for re-computation of the results using the Excel application has to be met by the electoral body. He said the results of the presidential election can only be

> adjudged to be credible if the issues he raised are tackled. ("Buhari: Why I Didn't Congratulate Jonathan," *Daily Trust*, May 2, 2011)

Several months later, Buhari was focused on the election tribunal process. The judicial process was necessary for a free and fair election. In early September, while in Abuja accepting the award for "Politician of the Year" bestowed by Leadership Newspapers, he was reported to have

> charged the political class to be serious on issues concerning the independence of the judiciary. He underscored the need to stabilize the nation's democratic system in order to revitalize and make Nigeria great again, stating that "We have got the riches. We have to stop being potential. We have to realize our potentialities."
>
> He said, "You know what happened to us in 2003; you know what happened up to December 12, 2008. For fifty months, we were in court. And do you know what is happening to us now? When the Presidential Tribunal started under Salami, he was kicked out and new composition was put in place." ("Buhari: If Judiciary Is Compromised, Nigeria Is Finished," *Daily Trust*, September 30, 2011)

On November 1, the court rendered its verdict on the 2011 elections, upholding Jonathan's election. The CPC challenged this decision to the Supreme Court, but it, too, upheld the election of President Jonathan.

By now, Boko Haram, the violent extremist group, was causing havoc in the northeast. Jonathan declared a state of emergency in the affected states. He also started the new year by announcing an end to fuel subsidies. (He later adjusted this to a 50 percent reduction in the subsidy.) Street protests exploded in most major cities, with Lagos being particularly hard hit.

Even PDP elders were openly wondering if Jonathan was up to the task of serving as commander in chief while also managing the economy. Opposition parties were sounding the alarm on corruption, as "moneybag" politics became ever more blatant.

In the far north, PDP governors were getting the message from constituents that Jonathan was deeply unpopular. The question was whether opposition parties could patch together a united front to challenge the PDP, and even lure away PDP sympathizers. Much of this would have to be done outside the scrutiny of public view, because PDP governors still needed to give the appearance of party unity.

The additional question was who could serve as a standard-bearer for such an opposition party. There was widespread speculation that Buhari was too old. Or that he was sick. Or that—as a "three-time loser"—he had lost his political touch. Or that he was too uncompromising to make the deals necessary to put together and keep together a coalition party composed of political rivals. Younger potential candidates were quietly testing the waters, seeing if they might replace Buhari on the ballot.

It was a time of uncertainty. It was not clear that Jonathan would seek the PDP nomination. Within the PDP, there were many, especially in the north, who had the political instincts to realize that Jonathan was not popular outside of his home base. Yet everyone knew that incumbents had enormous access to resources. Moreover, it was not clear whether a national opposition party was even feasible.

Chapter 8

The Challenges of Electing a New President

On December 31, 2011, President Jonathan declared a state of emergency (SOE) for selected local government areas in four states (Borno, Yobe, Niger, and Plateau) hit by Boko Haram violence. Heavy military equipment was moved to these areas. In reply, Boko Haram staged a series of attacks, killing more than 120 people. On January 20, 2012, a series of bomb blasts in Kano targeted police stations and an immigration office, killing at least 180. A splinter group from Boko Haram called Ansaru (its full name is Ansaru Muslimina Fi Biladis Sudan), probably based in Kano, objected to the killing of Muslims, but engaged in kidnapping Europeans.

Between May 2012 and April 2013, the north experienced 414 attacks. Of these, the highest number (179 incidents) occurred in Borno, and the next-highest number (64) took place in Kano. Top targets were the police and security forces, but civilians were also targeted. Clearly, security had broken down in key areas of the north. In May 2013, President Jonathan declared an SOE across the whole of three states: Borno, Yobe, and Adamawa.

Meanwhile, on the political front, Buhari encouraged his followers to prepare for the election of 2015. At his home in Kaduna, he considered both the fate of the country and his own future. He also started writing his life story through 2011, and soon had three hundred pages of a manuscript that was intended to form the basis of a future autobiography. This draft included notes on his activities during the Civil War, his military work in the early postwar period, his work in government in 1975–80, and how he spent the period from January 1984 to August 1985. It also included his activities in PTF and engagement in politics.

Buhari's popularity at the grassroots level in the north increased to almost messianic proportions. As terrorism increased, resulting in a lack of investment in the north, poverty also increased. Yet the beneficiaries of the petro-state were flush with wealth, both earned legally and obtained through corruption. Official figures showed that at least $6 billion in petroleum resources was being stolen each year. The gap between rich and poor was dangerously wide, which helped to fuel support for violent extremists. As law and order deteriorated, even the wealthy felt increasingly insecure.

From his home in Kaduna, Buhari met with northern political leaders, including Atiku Abubakar and Attahiru Bafarawa, to consider forming a national coalition to challenge the PDP, which at the time held fifteen of the nineteen northern state governorships. The lack of a national coalition had condemned the CPC to defeat in the 2011 election. Determined to avoid a similar fate in 2015, the CPC sought to build links with the ANPP in the north and the ACN in the southwest, plus the All Progressives Grand Alliance (APGA) in the southeast, to form a progressive new national opposition party.

Forming the All Progressives Congress

As the 2015 election approached, the opposition held only four northern opposition governorships: the ANPP governors of Yobe (Ibrahim Gaidam), Borno (Kashim Shettima), and Zamfara (Abdulaziz Yari), and the CPC governor of Nasarawa (Umaru Tanko al-Makura). The challenge for Buhari was to link this group with the five ACN governors in the southwest states of Osun (Rauf Aregbesola), Ogun (Ibikunle Amuson), Lagos (Babatunde Fashola), Ekiti (Kayode Fayemi), and Oyo (Abiola Ajimobi). The remaining southwest governor in Ondo State (Olusegun Mimiko) was a member of the Labour Party.

In the South East zone, the APGA governor of Imo (Rochas Okorocha), and in the South-South zone, the governor of Edo (Adams Oshiomole) also indicated an interest in joining the new national opposition.

The efforts to build a coalition—a "team of rivals," so to speak—came to fruition in February 2013, when eleven governors and their four political parties (the CPC, ACN, ANPP, plus a faction of the APGA) from all six geocultural zones committed to forming a national opposition party, the All Progressives Congress (APC). The new party was recognized by INEC on July 31, 2013.

Later that year, the new party was significantly strengthened by divisions within and defections from the PDP. President Jonathan had signed a pledge in 2011 to run for only one term, but he was widely believed to be reconsidering that decision, which was causing concern among northern PDP governors who were themselves interested in running for the presidency. These governors were from key states, including Niger, Jigawa, Bauchi, Adamawa, Katsina, Sokoto, and Kano.

By November 2013, five sitting PDP governors had defected to the APC. These included the governors of Rivers (Rotimi Amaechi), Kwara (Abdulfatah Ahmed), Adamawa (Murtala Nyako), Sokoto (Aliyu Wammako), and Kano (Rabiu Kwankwaso). They were called the "New-PDP governors." In addition, forty-nine legislators from the PDP had joined the APC, giving the APC a slight edge in the National Assembly.

Sokoto is the seat of the Sultan of Sokoto, and Kano is the major metropolitan area in the north. When those two governors defected to the APC, it set off a political chain reaction wherein their state-level rivals—former governor Bafarawa in Sokoto and former governor Ibrahim Shekarau in Kano—decamped to the PDP. The stage was set for a truly national political competition.

This APC "team of rivals" was united mainly by a concern that President Jonathan was too weak to address the basic issues of insecurity and corruption. Plus, there was apprehension that economic development favored the southern part of the country, and that the growing income gap was destabilizing the country. Jonathan's supporters began using a variety of carrots and sticks to try to get key governors to leave the APC, and to look for weak links in the coalition. The incumbent government had many carrots at its disposal: it controlled budgets, the military, campaign permits, and many elements of the media. In addition, no one knew how leadership struggles within the APC would play out. After all,

Buhari had lost the last three elections. Would he really have the energy and the support to launch a fourth attempt?

Contending for the APC Nomination

As 2014 unfolded, with the three North East zone states continuing in a state of emergency, the APC sought to decide who would be its presidential candidate. This required calculations as to regional balance and generational balance. The far north had voted overwhelmingly for Buhari in the 2011 election. Yet former vice president Atiku Abubakar (from Adamawa), only four years younger than Buhari, had an impressive political network, fueled by his wealth and long experience.

In addition, a crop of midcareer northern governors were eyeing the prize, although they did not have regional or national networks in place. The southwest was the key to a national coalition, and was likely to claim either the presidency or vice presidency. In 2011, the former governor of Lagos State, Bola Ahmed Tinubu, had flirted with the CPC, but in the end had kept his ACN block apart from a national coalition. In addition, religious and ethnic identity politics had to be calibrated.

During the spring of 2014, many of the midcareer northern governors traveled abroad to gauge the mood of the international community, which was growing increasingly frustrated by the Jonathan administration's inability to curb the Boko Haram insurgency and the blatant theft of oil and oil revenues. Given the number of billboards in Abuja celebrating Jonathan's leadership, it was clear that he was running for an additional term. He had even hired a top-level US lobbying firm to advise his campaign.

Key PDP advisers, such as Oronto Douglas, went to Washington, DC, to assure Nigeria specialists and others that another Jonathan term was needed to complete Nigeria's "transformation." The Nigerian GNP growth rate of 7 percent per annum was impressive, although much of that growth was due to investment funneled through Lagos and the southwest. Indeed, Lagos State was becoming the center of growth for the entire country.

In July 2014, while Buhari was traveling on the Kaduna-Kano road, an attempt was made on his life. A roadside bomb exploded as he was passing. Fortunately, Governor Kwankwaso had insisted on giving Buhari an armored-reinforced vehicle for his intercity travels, despite Buhari's protests that his life was in the hands of God. The cars in front of and behind Buhari's vehicle were destroyed, with considerable loss of life. The impact on Buhari was to inspire him to rededicate himself to the task of getting Nigeria back on track, although this close call was a reminder of the violence close to the surface in "democratic" politics. It was now clear that he would be a contender in the 2015 presidential election.

Meanwhile, the two-term limit on governors meant that those with further political ambitions needed to explore their options. Within the APC, many eyes were on the dynamic governor of Kano State, Rabiu Kwankwaso, who would challenge Buhari for the presidential nomination. What growth there was in the north tended to be in Kano, although the terrorists were limiting the prospects for Kano's further development. Kano, like other parts of the north, was also suffering economically from the competition to its infant industries from China's light manufacturing sector and Chinese exports to Nigeria.

Kwankwaso was born in 1956, the son of a district administrator in rural Kano. He trained as a civil engineer at Kaduna Polytechnic and then at Nottingham University in England (1987–91), where he was involved in student politics. In 1999, he was elected governor of Kano State on a PDP ticket. Four years later, he was appointed minister of defence (2003–6), and later served on a number of high-level federal commissions, including the Niger Delta Development Commission. In 2011, he was again elected governor of Kano State on a PDP ticket. In 2014, however, he switched to the APC and became a vocal critic of President Jonathan.

In October 2014, after Atiku Abubakar and Muhammadu Buhari had announced that they would contend for the APC presidential nomination, Kwankwaso also announced his candidacy. He argued that the time had come for a shift in political generations, and he emphasized that his experience in the PDP meant that he knew the weaknesses within the Jonathan administration.

Atiku Abubakar was a dozen years older than Kwankwaso, but Abubakar had also been a PDP insider, having served as vice president for eight years, from 1999 through 2007. He had been in the customs service until he resigned in 1989 to pursue business. He had amassed great wealth prior to government service in the Fourth Republic. Born in Adamawa, he had married into the various political factions in Yola (and elsewhere). He used his wealth to nurture his political ambitions, as well as to establish an American-style university in Yola that focused on technical training and entrepreneurship.

Another far northern potential candidate was Aminu Waziri Tambuwal, from Sokoto. Born in January 1966, he was trained as a lawyer and had been admitted to the bar in 1992. He had been Speaker of the House in Abuja since 2011 as a member of the PDP, but he had become increasingly disaffected with the Jonathan administration. While he quietly explored a presidential bid with the APC, in late October he announced his switch to the APC and registered to contest for the governorship of Sokoto, which he won in April 2015.

Two additional announced candidates for the APC presidential nomination were Sam Nda-Isaiah, a Christian from Niger State, who was the proprietor of the Leadership Media Group; and Governor Rochas Okorocha of Imo State, a Christian and an Igbo leader. But these were clearly long shots compared with Buhari, Abubakar, or Kwankwaso.

On December 3, 2014, former president Olusegun Obasanjo wrote an eighteen-page open letter to President Jonathan, available online, highlighting the failures of the Jonathan administration. Much of the criticism focused on the weakness of Jonathan himself. Obasanjo was widely regarded as the original "godfather" of Jonathan, having selected him as vice president in 2007, and the letter was interpreted as Obasanjo withdrawing his support for a Jonathan reelection bid in 2015.

The APC nominating convention was held in Lagos later in December, in a stadium that could hold the eight thousand local-level delegates. Buhari was overwhelmingly nominated—by nearly 90 percent of the delegates—in large part because delegates saw him as their best hope for change. Kwankwaso was a distant second, followed by Abubakar. The next decision for the convention was who to select as the party's vice presidential nominee. With Buhari coming from the North West zone, the vice presidency had been ceded to the South West zone.

Tinubu, former governor of Lagos State and political "godfather" of the South West zone, felt he should be the vice presidential candidate. His protégé and the popular governor of Lagos State, Babatunde Fashola, was also a possible candidate. Both Tinubu and Fashola were Muslims, which complicated the national balance.

A third candidate, Yemi Osinbajo, had been attorney general of Lagos State and was a senior law professor and a Christian pastor. When these three names were forwarded to Buhari, he chose Osinbajo, despite enormous pressure from Tinubu. The stage was now set for party elders to design an APC manifesto and begin the campaign.

APC Manifesto and Campaigning

The symbol of the ACP is the broom, implying a clean sweep of the problems of government. At many campaign stops around the country, Buhari would stand on the podium and hold up a broom to the thunderous applause of the tens of thousands of those (primarily youth) in the audience. Chants of "Change!" would resonate throughout the crowds. On some occasions, the crowds clamoring to see him or touch his car would grow so large that they would block roads and airports. Many other politicians—of all parties—might have to pay organizers to produce crowds for the television cameras. But Buhari clearly had a charismatic presence.

Charisma, however, did not preclude the need for a detailed platform. The party's manifesto, which was made available both in print and online (http://www.allprogressivescongress.org/manifesto/), reflected the ability of the Lagos component of the party to articulate a strong economic growth message and the north's deep concern with development and political countermeasures to Boko Haram. Some of the key elements of the message were concerned with countering the recruitment of youth by Boko Haram:

> JOB CREATION AND THE ECONOMY: Embark on vocational training, entrepreneurial skills acquisition scheme for graduates along with the creation of Small Business Loan Guarantee Scheme to create at least 1 million new jobs every year, for the foreseeable future. . . . Amend the Constitution and Land Use Act to create freehold/leasehold interests in land along with matching grants for states to create a nationwide electronic land title register on a state by state basis.

EDUCATION: Fully implement and enforce the provisions of the Universal Basic Education Act with emphasis on gender equality in primary and secondary school enrollment whilst improving the quality and substance of our schools. Targeting up to 15% of our annual budget for this critical sector whilst making substantial investment in training quality teachers at all levels of the educational system. . . . Provide more conducive environment for private sector participation in all levels of education.

AGRICULTURE AND FOOD SECURITY: Modernize the sector and change Nigeria from being a country of self-subsistence farmers to that of a medium/commercial-scale farming nation/producer. Inject an extra N30 bn into the Agricultural sector to create more agro-allied jobs by way of loans at nominal interest rates for capital investment in medium and commercial-scale cash crops. Guarantee a minimum price for selected crops and facilitate storage of agricultural products as and when necessary.

CONFLICT RESOLUTION, NATIONAL UNITY, AND SOCIAL HARMONY: Establish a Conflict Resolution Commission to help prevent, mitigate and resolve civil conflicts within the polity. Bring permanent peace and resolution to the Niger Delta, and other conflict prone areas such as Plateau, Taraba, Bauchi, Borno and Abia in order to engender national unity and social harmony. Initiate policies to ensure that Nigerians are free to live and work in any part of the country by removing state of origin, tribe, ethnic and religious affiliations and replacing those with state of residence.

HEALTHCARE: Increase the number of physicians from 19/1000 to 50/1000. . . . Increase the quality of all federal owned hospitals. . . . Provide free ante-natal care for pregnant women.

ENVIRONMENT: Create shelter belts in states bordering the Sahara Desert to mitigate and reverse the effects of the expanding desert. . . . Create teams of volunteers to plant and nurture economically viable trees in arid regions. . . . Ensure full compliance with town-planning and environmental laws and edicts.

INFRASTRUCTURE: Generate, transmit and distribute from the current 5,000-6,000 MW to at least 20,000 MW of electricity within four years and increase to 50,000 MW with a view to achieving 24/7 uninterrupted power supply within ten years, whilst simultaneously ensuring development of sustainable/renewable energy.

> NATIONAL SECURITY: Establish a well-trained, adequately equipped and goals-driven Serious Crime Squad to combat terrorism, kidnapping, armed robbery, militants, ethno-religious and communal clashes nationwide. Begin widespread consultations to amend the Constitution to enable States and Local Governments to employ State and Community Police to address the peculiar needs of each community. This would mean setting boundaries for Federal, State and Community Police through new Criminal Justice legislation to replace the Criminal Code, the Penal Code and the Police Act.

The manifesto saw that the longer-term solution to the insurgency in the north, as well as effective responses to other challenges in the country, would require efforts to create jobs, reform education, develop agriculture, enhance conflict resolution mechanisms, increase health care, reverse desert encroachment, build an electric power grid to enable economic growth, and revamp approaches to national security. Also needed were the political will and leadership to deal with more immediate challenges in the northeast, because the Boko Haram insurgency appeared to be gaining ground.

The international community was becoming increasingly alarmed as the insurgency spread to the neighboring states of Cameroon, Chad, and Niger. The Nigerian military seemed unable to stem the terrorism. President Jonathan seemed more focused on hanging onto power by looting the public treasury. Could Buhari meet this existential challenge to the future of Nigeria?

In a speech he gave at Chatham House (otherwise known as the Royal Institute of International Affairs) in London on February 26, 2015, he gave a clue as to his focus and determination. Although Chatham House discussions are normally off the record, Buhari insisted that his remarks be made public and be available online and on video:

> On security, there is a genuine cause for worry, both within and outside Nigeria. Apart from the Civil War era, at no other time in our history has Nigeria been this insecure. Boko Haram has sadly put Nigeria on the terrorism map, killing more than 13,000 of our nationals, displacing millions internally and externally, and at the same time holding on to portions of our territory the size of Belgium. What has been consistently lacking is the required leadership in our battle against insurgency. I, as a retired general and former head of state, have always known about our soldiers: they are capable, well trained, patriotic, brave, and al-

> ways ready to do their duty in the service of our country. . . . In the matter of this insurgency, our soldiers have neither received the necessary support nor the required incentives to tackle this problem. The government has also failed in any effort towards a multi-dimensional response to this problem, leading to a situation in which we have now become dependent on our neighbors to come to our rescue. Let me assure you that if I am elected president, the world will have no cause to worry about Nigeria as it has had to recently; that Nigeria will return to its stabilizing role in West Africa; and that no inch will be lost to the enemy because we will pay special attention to the welfare of our soldiers in and out of service; we will give them adequate and modern arms and ammunition to work with; we will improve intelligence gathering and border controls to choke Boko Haram's financial and equipment channels; we will be tough on terrorism and its root causes by initiating an economic development plan promoting infrastructural development, job creation, agriculture and industry in the affected areas. We will always act on time and not allow problems to irresponsibly fester, and I, Muhammadu Buhari, will always lead from the front and return Nigeria to its leadership role in regional and international affairs to combat terrorism.

Was this just rhetoric? Or could Buhari provide the leadership and political will to turn the tide of terrorism and insurgency in Nigeria? More to the point, could he win an election against an incumbent regime? This was something that had never been done in Nigeria's history.

Electing a President

An adage too often heard in some democracies declares, "It's not who casts the votes; it's who counts the votes." The relevance of this saying to Nigeria as the 2015 elections approached helped turn the spotlight on INEC, which was led by Professor Attahiru Jega.

Originally, the national elections for president and members of the National Assembly were scheduled for February 14, 2015, with the state gubernatorial and assembly elections due to take place two weeks later, on February 28. A February election date would give time—it was hoped—for any appeals against the election results to be lodged and heard before the presidential inauguration on May 29. At the last minute, however, the Nigerian security and military services insisted that the elections be postponed for six weeks, to allow time for an all-out attack on Boko Haram.

Jega had no choice but to accept this postponement, and he thus announced that the presidential election would be pushed back to March 28, 2015.

The task for INEC was daunting. There were more than 150,000 polling locations around the country, including in the northeastern SOE zones, often in schools or public places. Boko Haram had threatened to attack these places during the voting process. Poll watchers included many young people from the National Youth Service Corps (NYSC), in which all university graduates are required to serve for one year. Understandably, the parents of these young people were concerned about their safety, especially if they were serving out of state. Also, where would the millions of internally displaced persons (IDPs) vote? If they were to be effectively disenfranchised, Buhari's support base in the northeast would be dented.

Moreover, Professor Jega did not have control over the state-level regional electoral commissioners (RECs), most of whom were appointed by the Jonathan administration and who were suspected of helping to produce lopsided victories in the past for the incumbent party, especially in the South East and South-South. Jega himself was regarded as honest and effective. He would be required to announce the final results, and the political pressures on him were enormous, including physical threats.

The threat of postelection violence was palpable. There would be winners and losers, quite likely with a regional or ethnoreligious profile. The international community was deeply concerned. Was Nigeria on the brink? High-level diplomatic démarches were made to both candidates. A highly publicized "Peace Accord" was signed by Jonathan and Buhari. But would they be able to control grassroots supporters? As March 28 approached, enormous sums of money were withdrawn from the treasury by the incumbents. At the same time, enormous crowds of a size unprecedented in Nigeria's history thronged to Buhari's rallies.

As the voting results started coming in to INEC in Abuja, often delayed because of logistical challenges from the rural areas, it became clear that Buhari was winning a landslide victory. Despite some last-minute interruptions by Jonathan supporters at INEC headquarters, plus rumors of a takeover by military and security forces to prevent violence, Jega announced that Buhari had won

15,424,921 votes to Jonathan's 12,853,162. Buhari had won by almost 2.6 million votes, and had met the regional distribution requirement of 25 percent of the votes in two-thirds of the states.

Nonetheless, there was a clear regional pattern. Jonathan won the five South East and six South-South states, plus Plateau and Nasarawa in the North Central zone, along with Taraba in the North East. He also won the Federal Capital Territory and Ekiti and Ondo in the South West, making a total of sixteen states. Buhari had won the seven North West states and five of the six North East zones, plus four of the six South West states, and Benue, Kogi, Niger, and Kwara in the North Central zone, for a total of twenty states.

Faced with these results, would Jonathan concede, or would he challenge the results in the courts, where his influence was strong? Several former African heads of state, who had monitored the election for the African Union, held private meetings with Jonathan. They insisted, for the sake of democracy in Africa, that he accept the results. In addition, there was considerable international pressure on Jonathan, including by the archbishop of Canterbury and Western diplomats.

In a widely publicized phone call on March 31 from Jonathan to Buhari, Jonathan offered his congratulations and conceded the election. There was relief in the international community and among the thousands of Nigerians who had worked to broker peace efforts.

A new chapter in Nigerian history had just been written. For the first time, an incumbent had been defeated in an election by an opposition party. Two weeks later, on April 11, the elections for governors were held, along with elections for members of the thirty-six state houses of assembly. The election result patterns, for the most part, mirrored those in the presidential race. Overall, the APC had won 225 out of 360 seats in the House; 60 out of 109 seats in the Senate; and 22 out of 36 governorships.

The task for Buhari, however, was just beginning. He set up a transition team, headed by the venerable Ahmed Joda from Adamawa, to advise on the state of the economy, government restructuring, policy options, and candidates for positions in the new administration. He also tried to reassure the international community that he would tackle the Boko Haram challenge as a top priority. In an opinion piece in the *New York Times* published on April 14, he wrote the following:

> When Boko Haram attacked a school in the town of Chibok, in northeastern Nigeria, kidnapping more than 200 girls on the night of April 14, 2014, the people of my country were aghast. Across the world, millions of people joined them in asking: How was it possible for this terrorist group to act with such impunity? It took nearly two weeks before the government even commented on the crime. This lack of reaction was symptomatic of why the administration of President Goodluck Jonathan was swept aside last month, the first time an incumbent president has been successfully voted out of office in the history of our nation. . . .
>
> My administration, which will take office on May 29th, will act differently—indeed, it is the very reason we have been elected. . . . What I can pledge, with absolute certainty, is that the first day of my administration, Boko Haram will know the strength of our collective will and commitment to rid this nation of terror and bring back peace and normalcy to all the affected areas. Until now, Nigeria has been wanting in its response to their threat. With our neighbors fighting hard to push terrorists south and out of their countries, our military was not sufficiently supported or equipped to push north. As a consequence, the outgoing government's lack of determination was an accidental enabler of the group, allowing them to operate with impunity in Nigerian territory. . . .

President-elect Buhari also addressed the drivers of insurgency, and explained that education was his major counterstrategy:

> But as our military pushes Boko Haram back, as it will, we must be ready to focus on what else must be done to counter the terrorists. We must address why it is that young people join Boko Haram. There are many reasons why vulnerable young people join militant groups, but among them are poverty and ignorance. Indeed, Boko Haram—which translates into English roughly as "Western Education Is Forbidden"—preys on the perverted belief that the opportunities education brings are sinful. If you are starving and young, and in search of answers as to why your life is so difficult, fundamentalism can be alluring. We know this for a fact because former members of Boko Haram have admitted it. They offer impressionable young people money and promise of food, while the group's mentors twist their minds with fanaticism.
>
> So we must be ready to offer the parts of the country affected by this group an alternative. Boosting education will be

PRESIDENTIAL ELECTION RESULTS, 2015

> a direct counterbalance to Boko Haram's appeal. In particular, we must educate more young girls, ensuring that they will grow up to be empowered through learning to play their full part as citizens of Nigeria and pull themselves up and out of poverty. . . . My government will first act to defeat it militarily and then ensure that we provide the very education it despises to help our people help themselves. Boko Haram will soon learn that, as Nelson Mandela said, "Education is the most powerful weapon you can use to change the world."

Buhari then turned his attention to the need for international cooperation in the fight against Boko Haram:

> That is why the answer to defeating Boko Haram begins and ends with Nigeria. That is not to say that allies cannot help. My administration would welcome the resumption of military training agreements with the United States, which were halted

PRESIDENTIAL ELECTION RESULTS, 2015

> during the previous administration. We must, of course, have better coordination with the military campaigns our African allies, like Chad and Niger, are waging in the struggle with Boko Haram. But in the end, the answer to this threat must come from within Nigeria.

With the inauguration on May 29 approaching, the challenges of transitioning were enormous. The existing administration, including ministers and permanent secretaries, as well as the military service chiefs and security officials, were unsure about their own futures. Most were asked to write letters of resignation, which could be effected in due course. Jonathan's key planners were, however, responsible for making arrangements for the inauguration, including extending invitations to domestic and international dignitaries, and for forwarding letters of congratulations to the incoming team.

The Joda transition draft report ran to almost three thousand pages. The expectations of Buhari's grassroots supporters were sky-high. The international community was standing by to help as needed. The major challenges of leadership lay ahead. Would Buhari be able to manage expectations and also set a course that would take Nigeria in new directions?

PART II

CHALLENGES OF PRESIDENTIAL LEADERSHIP, MAY 29—DECEMBER 31, 2015

Part II focuses on the areas that were President Buhari's priorities during this initial period in office. There were four main policy priorities:

- ***Counterinsurgency***
    - *Appoint new service chiefs and a new national security adviser*
    - *Establish a coordination center in northern Cameroon*
    - *Crack down on military corruption*
    - *Retake local government areas in the northeast*
    - *Develop closer ties with regional and international partners*
- ***Anticorruption***
    - *Reform the Economic and Financial Crimes Commission*
    - *Set up special tribunals*
    - *Cultivate a hands-off judicial process*
    - *Arrest corrupt senior military officers and members of the office of the National Security Adviser*
    - *Arrest corrupt senior politicians*
    - *Work with international partners*
- ***Economic Recovery***
    - *Begin reforms in the petroleum industry*
    - *Tackle electric power issues*
    - *Work on access to education*
    - *Plan reconstruction in the Northeast*
    - *Facilitate help for internally displaced persons*
- ***Political Change***
    - *Rediscover constitutionalism*
    - *Learn electoral lessons*
    - *Strengthen judicial independence*
    - *Downsize bloated number of cabinet positions*
    - *Respect the two-party system*

CHALLENGES OF SECURITY AND UNITY

Chapter 9

Security

On Friday, May 29, 2015, in Eagle Square, Abuja, President Buhari was sworn into office. The Presidential Inaugural Committee, cochaired by Senator Anyim Pius Anyim and Timipre Sylva, had sent out invitations far and wide. Heads of state and foreign ministers were in attendance, along with senior diplomats from major countries and numerous domestic dignitaries.

Buhari used the occasion of his inaugural speech to articulate the priorities and commitments of his administration. This is an important document in its own right and will be used by the Nigerian public to gauge his accomplishments over time.

This chapter examines not only Buhari's speech but also his strategy in engaging the international community in his struggle with Boko Haram. In addition, a major challenge was the expectations of a population that had voted for "change." Bringing about change, especially swift change, was not going to be easy, however. First, Buhari would have to review the entire structure of government, which bore the imprint of many years of PDP rule. He would need to select service chiefs and ministers who were politically and zonally balanced and competent, and who were regarded by a skeptical public as ethically upright.

This would not be an easy task, but Buhari intended to move with all deliberate speed. By midsummer, he had acquired the nickname of "Baba go slow." Everyone was impatient for change and a new beginning. Buhari promised to announce the names of most of his ministers by the end of September. Others were pressing him to make major announcements during his first 100 days in office.

Inaugural Vision, May 29

Buhari's inaugural speech on May 29 was intended to underscore the challenges facing Nigeria and his proposed solutions. It was also intended to heal the rift with Jonathan and his supporters, including voters in the South East and South-South zones, who had overwhelmingly supported Jonathan.

It was meant to assure the international community that the new Nigerian government would focus on combating Boko Haram and widespread corruption. At the same time, an electoral change of government in Nigeria was unprecedented, and no one knew quite what to expect. Also, given the attempt on Buhari's life in July 2014, and the rumors of intervention by military and security forces after the March 28 election, security was at an all-time high.

Analysts and others would examine closely the words Buhari chose to bind up Nigeria's political wounds. There would be serious "content analysis" of his remarks, which were made widely available on social media and elsewhere. Given the importance of this inaugural address and the occasion, the speech is quoted here in full (the italics have been added for emphasis):

> I am immensely grateful to God, who has preserved us to witness this day and this occasion. Today marks a triumph for Nigeria and an occasion to celebrate her freedom and cherish her democracy. Nigerians have shown their commitment to democracy and are determined to entrench its culture. Our journey has not been easy, but thanks to the determination of our people and strong support from our friends abroad we have today a truly democratically elected government in place.
>
> I would like to *thank President Goodluck Jonathan* for his display of statesmanship in setting a precedent for us that has made our people proud to be Nigerians wherever they are. With the support and cooperation he has given to the transition process, he has made it possible for us to show the world that, despite the perceived tension in the land, we can be a united people capable of doing what is right for our nation. Together we cooperated to surprise the world that had come to expect only the worst from Nigeria. I hope this act of graciously accept-

ing defeat by the outgoing president will become the standard of political conduct in the country.

I would like to thank the millions of our supporters who believed in us even though the cause seemed hopeless. I salute their resolve in waiting long hours in rain and hot sunshine to register and cast their votes and stay all night if necessary to ensure their votes count and were counted. I thank those who tirelessly carried the campaign on the social media. At the same time, *I thank other countrymen and women who did not vote for us but contributed to make our democratic culture truly competitive, strong, and definitive.*

I thank all of you.

Having just a few minutes ago sworn on the Holy Book, I intend to keep my oath and *serve as President to all Nigerians.*

I belong to everybody and I belong to nobody.

A few people have privately voiced fears that on coming back into office I should go after them. These fears are groundless. *There will be no paying off old scores*. The past is prologue.

Our neighbors in the Sub-region and our African brethren should rest assured that Nigeria under our administration will be ready to play any leadership role that Africa expects of it. Here I would like to *thank the governments and people of Cameroon, Chad and Niger for committing their armed forces to fight Boko Haram in Nigeria.*

I also wish to *assure the international community of our readiness to cooperate and help combat threats of cross-border terrorism,* sea piracy, refugees and boat people, financial crime, cybercrime, climate change, the spread of communicable diseases and other challenges of the twenty-first century.

At home *we face enormous challenges. Insecurity, pervasive corruption, and the hitherto unending and seemingly impossible fuel and power shortages are immediate concerns.* We are going to tackle them head on. We must not succumb to hopelessness and defeatism. We can fix our problems.

In recent times Nigerian leaders have misread our mission. *Our founding fathers,* Mr. Herbert Macauley, Dr. Nnamdi Azikiwe, Chief Obafemi Awolowo, Alhaji Ahmadu Bello the Sardauna of Sokoto, Alhaji Abubakar Tafawa Balewa, Malam Aminu Kano, Chief J. S. Tarka, Mr. Eyo Ita, Chief Denis Osadeby, Chief Ladoke Akintola, and their colleagues worked to establish certain standards of governance. They might have differed in their methods or tactics or details, but they were united in establishing a viable and progressive country. Some of their successors behaved like spoilt children, breaking everything and bringing disorder to the house.

Furthermore, we as Nigerians must remind ourselves that *we are heirs to great civilizations*: Shehu Uthman Dan Fodio's caliphate, the Kanem-Borno Empire, the Oyo Empire, the Benin Empire and King Jaja's formidable domain. The blood of these great ancestors flows in our veins. What is required now is to build on these legacies, to modernize and uplift Nigeria.

Daunting as the task may be, it is by no means insurmountable. There is now a national consensus that our chosen route to national development is democracy. To achieve our objectives, we must consciously work the democratic system. *The federal executive under my watch will not seek to encroach on the duties and functions of the legislature and judicial arms of government.* The law-enforcing authorities will be charged to operate within the Constitution. We shall rebuild and reform the public service to become more effective and more serviceable. We shall charge them to apply themselves with integrity to stabilize the system.

For their part, the *legislative arm* must keep to their brief of making laws, carrying out oversight functions and doing so expeditiously. The *judicial system needs reform* to cleanse itself from its immediate past. The country now expects the judiciary to act with dispatch on all cases, especially on corruption, serious financial crimes or abuse of office. It is only when the three arms act constitutionally that governance will be enabled to serve the country optimally and avoid the confusion all too often bedeviling governance today.

Elsewhere, *relations between Abuja and the States have to be clarified* if we are to serve the country better. Constitutionally, there are limits to powers of each of the three tiers of government, but that should not mean the Federal Government should fold its arms and close its eyes to what is going on in the states and local governments. Not least the operations of the Local Government Joint Account. While the Federal Government cannot interfere in the details of those operations, it will ensure that gross corruption at the local level is checked. As far as the Constitution allows me, I will try to ensure that there is reasonable and accountable government at all levels of government in the country. For I will not have kept my own trust with the Nigerian people if I allow others to abuse theirs under my watch.

However, no matter how well organized the governments of the federation are, they cannot succeed without the support, understanding and cooperation of *labour unions, organized private sector, the press and civil society organizations.* I appeal to *employers and workers* to unite in raising productivity so that everybody will have the opportunity to share in increased productivity. The *Nigerian press* is the most vibrant in Africa. My appeal to the media today—and this includes *social media*—is to use its considerable powers with responsibility and patriotism.

My appeal today is based on the seriousness of the legacy we are getting into. With *depleted foreign reserves, falling oil prices, leakages and debts,* the Nigerian economy is in deep trouble and will require careful management to bring it round and to tackle the immediate challenges confronting us, namely: *Boko Haram, the Niger Delta situation, the power shortages and unemployment* especially among young people. For the longer term, we have to improve the *standards of our education.* We have to look at the whole field of *medicare.* We have to upgrade our dilapidated physical *infrastructure.*

The *most immediate challenge is the Boko Haram insurgency.* Progress has been made in recent weeks by our security forces, but *victory cannot be achieved by basing the Command and Control Centre in Abuja.* The command centre will be *relocated to Maiduguri* and remain until Boko Haram is completely subdued. But we cannot claim to have defeated Boko Haram without rescuing the *Chibok girls* and all other innocent persons held hostage by insurgents.

The government will do all it can to *rescue them alive.* Boko Haram is a typical example of small fires causing large fires. An eccentric and unorthodox preacher with a tiny following was given posthumous fame and following by his *extrajudicial murder at the hands of the police.* Since then, through *official bungling, negligence, complacency or collusion,* Boko Haram has become a terrifying force, taking tens of thousands of lives and capturing several towns and villages covering swathes of Nigerian sovereign territory.

Boko Haram is a mindless, godless group who are as far away from Islam as one can think of. At the end of the hostilities, when the group is subdued, the *Government intends to commission a sociological study to determine its origins, remote and immediate causes of the movement, its sponsors, and the international connections to ensure that measures are taken to prevent a recurrence of this evil.* For now, the *Armed Forces will be fully charged with prosecuting the fight against Boko Haram.* We shall *overhaul the rules of engagement to avoid human rights violations in operations.* We shall improve operational and legal mechanisms so that *disciplinary steps are taken against proven human rights violations by the Armed Forces.*

Boko Haram is not the only security issue bedeviling our country. The spate of *kidnappings, armed robberies, herdsmen-farmers clashes, cattle rustlings all help to add to the general air of insecurity in the land.* We are going to erect and maintain *efficient, disciplined, people-friendly and well-compensated security forces within an overall security architecture.*

The *amnesty programme in the Niger Delta* is due to end in December, but the Government intends to invest heavily in the projects and programmes currently in place. I call on the leadership and people in these areas to cooperate with the State and Federal Government in the *rehabilitation programmes,* which will

> be streamlined and made more effective. As ever, I am ready to listen to grievances of my fellow Nigerians. I extend my hand of fellowship to them so we can bring peace and build prosperity for our people.
>
> No single cause can be identified to explain Nigeria's poor economic performance over the years other than the *power situation.* It is a *national shame that an economy of 180 million people* generates only 4,000 megawatts and distributes even less. Continuous tinkering with the structures of power supply and distribution and close on $20 billion expended since 1999 have only brought darkness, frustration, misery, and resignation among Nigerians. We will not allow this to go on. *Careful studies are under way* during this transition to identify the quickest, safest, and most cost-effective way to bring light and relief to Nigerians.
>
> *Unemployment, notably youth unemployment, features strongly in our Party's Manifesto.* We intend to attack the problem frontally, including *the revival of agriculture, solid minerals mining, as well as credits to small and medium-size businesses to kick-start these enterprises.* We shall quickly examine the best way to *revive major industries and accelerate the revival and development of our railways, roads and general infrastructure.*
>
> Your Excellencies, my fellow Nigerians, I cannot recall when Nigeria enjoyed so much *goodwill abroad* as now. The messages I received from East and West, from powerful and small countries are indicative of international expectations on us. *At home,* the newly elected government is basking in a reservoir of goodwill and high expectations. Nigeria therefore has a *window of opportunity* to fulfill our long-standing potential of *pulling ourselves together and realizing our mission as a great nation.*
>
> "There is a tide in the affairs of men, / Which, taken at the flood, leads on to fortune; / Omitted, all the voyage of their life / Is bound in shallows and miseries."
>
> We have an opportunity. Let us take it.
>
> Thank you.

In short, Buhari would go after Boko Haram, tackle corruption, and facilitate economic development, and the three were clearly intertwined. But there would be no witch hunt for corrupt officials. Vice President Yemi Osinbajo had been attorney general in Lagos for eight years, and the Buhari administration promised it would be based on rule of law. The key to jobs and development would be education.

Tackling Boko Haram would be his top priority. To do that, Buhari would need the help of the regional and international communities. Even before his vetting of new ministers, he would need to change the leadership of the service chiefs, stop the corruption in the officer corps, and provide the political will required to thwart the insurrection.

Tackling Boko Haram

The first step in tackling the insurgency was to continue to set a personal example of probity and political will. Before he became president, Buhari was one of the few politicians who did not have a personal home in Abuja. During the transition periods, he had been given temporary residence in a guest house attached to the Presidential Villa.

With the treasury bare, Buhari knew he had to make deep cuts in the bureaucracy. He would have to cut the number of federal ministers down from seventy-two. In addition, one of his first acts was to abolish the office of "First Lady," which had come to be associated with the lavish lifestyle of "Dame" Patience Goodluck Jonathan.

He required that anyone serving in his administration declare their personal assets before and after leaving office. He had no problem with doing this himself, but he knew others might be reluctant to make public what they owned. He was also well aware that Abuja was filled with politicians who had taken advantage of their time in office and were looking for every opportunity to come back to power. Many had access to billions of dollars in hidden accounts, and they feared that Buhari might expose their ill-gotten wealth; they were waiting for Buhari to make political missteps, or would try to fabricate those missteps. Many defeated politicians had close ties to the military and retired senior officers. Some thirty years previously, as he remembered all too clearly, he had been put in detention for three years in Benin by fellow officers, who took a more relaxed view of "corruption" than he did. Many current officers were equally tolerant.

Meanwhile, Boko Haram was increasing its deadly attacks on mosques, civilians, and government facilities. It had declared its affiliation with Islamic State in Iraq and Syria. Three things were needed in a strategy to thwart this existential challenge to Nigeria: a change in military and security leadership; a robust regional and international coalition; and both a renewal of morale within

Nigeria's Armed Forces and real support for their sacrifices on the battlefield.

On July 13, Buhari retired the incumbent military service chiefs and national security adviser. He appointed the following: as chief of defence staff, Major General Abayomi Gabriel Olonisakin; as chief of army staff, Major General T. Y. Buratai; as chief of naval staff, Rear Admiral Ibok-Ete Ekwe Ibas; as chief of air staff, Air Vice Marshal Sadique Abubakar; as chief of defence intelligence, Air Vice Marshal Monday Riku Morgan; and as national security adviser (NSA), Major General Babagana Monguno (rtd).

Buhari did not have previous relations with any of these men, so there was no hint of favoritism. The team was zonally balanced and the appointees had reputations for competence and probity. Both Major General Buratai and NSA Monguno were from Borno and knew the area very well.

Buhari had promised to make regional cooperation his top international priority. Hence, his first external visits were to Cameroon, Niger, and Chad. This last was especially important, because Chadian president Idriss Deby had what many observers regarded as the finest and most experienced fighting force in Sahelian West Africa. The capital in N'Djamena had close working relations with France and hence had equipment and intelligence that would be crucial in the fight against Boko Haram insurgents, who increasingly moved back and forth across borders in the Lake Chad area.

The United States was part of the "fusion center" in N'Djamena, which coordinated intelligence regarding Boko Haram. This center became part of a Multinational Joint Task Force (MJTF) set up by the regional countries to coordinate intelligence gathering and facilitate military equipment procurement.

Buhari also consolidated ties with the African Union, which had become increasingly concerned with violent extremism on the continent. Buhari attended conferences in South Africa and at the AU headquarters in Addis Ababa, Ethiopia. But apart from moral support, the African Union did not have its own military, and often had to depend on the United Nations for support.

The major sources of support for Nigeria's war with Boko Haram would come from Europe and the United States, and more broadly the G-7 and the United Nations. Buhari traveled to Europe and held private meetings with David Cameron, Angela Merkel, and François Hollande. According to insider reports, all offered whatever help Buhari would need to stem violent extremism in Nigeria and the Lake Chad region.

During the third week of July, Buhari spent four days in Washington, DC, and stayed in historic Blair House, across from the White House. He held talks with President Obama. Again, according to insider reports, Obama offered to help in any way possible, including by providing military training, which former president Jonathan had canceled because the United States refused to sell Nigeria attack helicopters, given the dismal human rights record of the Nigerian military.

In addition, Buhari met with the US Joint Chiefs of Staff, the secretary of the treasury, the secretary of state, and other senior administration officials. These included USAID officials, with whom Buhari discussed development assistance in northern Nigeria to counter the Boko Haram message and allure for jobless youth. In what must have given him great pleasure, Buhari met with classmates from his 1980 year at the United States War college in Carlisle, Pennsylvania.

On July 22, on the morning of his last day in Washington, Buhari gave a major public address at the United States Institute of Peace. The auditorium was packed, with thousands of Nigerians and others outside the building watching on huge video screens. The speech was meant to summarize Nigeria's new policy of forward-looking, multipronged cooperation with the United States.

The speech had been written in advance by a senior adviser in Abuja, with longtime loyalty to Buhari. (The text of the speech can be found online at https://facebook.com/APCGovernment/posts/683534555080753.) The speech was going well until Buhari was about halfway through, and read sections 16 and 17:

> 16. In our efforts at combatting the activities of Boko Haram, the new Government has sought and obtained the support of our neighbours and other international friends and partners. Regrettably, the blanket application of the Leahy Law by the United States on the grounds of unproven allegations of human rights violations levelled against our forces has denied us access to appropriate strategic weapons to prosecute the war against the insurgents. In the face of the abduction of innocent school-girls from their hostels, indiscriminate bombings of civilians

> in markets and places of worship, our forces have remained largely impotent because they do not possess the appropriate weapons and technology, which they could have had, had the so-called human rights violations not been an obstacle.
>
> 17. Unwittingly, and I daresay unintentionally, the application of the Leahy Law amendment by the U.S. Government has aided and abetted the Boko Haram group in the prosecution of its extremist ideology and hate, the indiscriminate killings and maiming of civilians, in raping of women and girls, and in their other heinous crimes. I believe this is not the spirit of the Leahy Laws. I know the American people cannot support any group engaged in these crimes.

There was a shocked reaction in the auditorium. After a successful week in Washington, was Buhari really suggesting that the US government was aiding and abetting Boko Haram? This could undo all the goodwill the visit had so far generated. Moreover, it sounded like President Buhari was repeating the arguments of President Jonathan, not staking out a new position.

In subsequent, private discussions with the author of the original speech, it was clear that sections 16 and 17 had not been part of the original speech and were inserted by officials who had served under President Jonathan. Evidently, members of the old guard were intent on undermining Buhari's efforts to reengage with the international community.

Buhari needed a chief of staff who could monitor such matters, and also help manage Buhari's time so he was not so rushed as to make such missteps. On his return to Abuja, Buhari announced the appointment of Abba Kyari as chief of staff. Kyari is from Borno, with family ties in Bama (Borno State), and is a longtime friend and confidant of Buhari's. Most observers agreed that Kyari was an excellent choice.

Buhari and Kyari wanted to make sure that there would be no mishaps when Buhari came to New York in late September to address the United Nations. He would be focusing mainly on Boko Haram, and would also be participating in the subsequent UN conference on combating terrorism. But the Nigerian foreign service was still largely in the hands of the previous incumbents. Buhari would need to move quickly to fill key ministerial posts such as defence, foreign affairs, and petroleum, which he had promised to nominate in late September.

Meanwhile, the Nigerian military, under new leadership and in cooperation with regional neighbors and international partners, was pushing Boko Haram from its safe havens, despite continuing attacks by suicide bombers. Buhari's example of discipline and concern for the troops seemed to have an impact on the rank-and-file soldiers. He was seen by many as supporting their efforts and honoring their sacrifices.

Tackling Corruption

Most observers would agree that there has been a culture of moneybag politics in Nigeria since the early 1980s, when petroleum revenues began pouring in. A "cash-only" pattern emerged in all sectors, as banking and financial institutions had not yet been fully developed and legal institutions were lax. This facilitated the rapid development of high-level cultures of corruption, which in turn fueled resentment at the grassroots levels. And such resentment was exploited by insurgent groups—thus creating a link between corruption and security issues.

The sudden influx of wealth in the 1980s was especially noticeable among state governors, who could shape budget (and "off-budget") expenditures to their liking. They also found that they could gain access to international financial loans with little accountability. Indeed, this was one of the reasons that senior military officers, including Buhari, intervened in December 1983. Shortly thereafter, governors with stashes of cash in their homes found themselves rounded up and sentenced to twenty-one years in prison. This crackdown was popular at the grassroots levels, but it created a political backlash, and Buhari found himself deposed after twenty months. He would not make this mistake again, even though the looting of the treasury was even more egregious in many cases during the Fourth Republic than it had been in the 1980s.

In the run-up to the election of 2015, Buhari had promised to leave it to the courts to deal with allegations of fraud—and Buhari's commitment to the rule of law was underscored by the fact that his nominee for vice president was a distinguished law professor, legal practitioner, and former attorney general of Lagos State. Buhari's main concern was to try to retrieve looted assets, and to do so through persuasion and pressure, rather than force.

In Buhari's declaration to the Code of Conduct Bureau in summer 2015, it was clear he was one of the poorest presidents in Africa, despite having served previously as petroleum minister and head of state. He had less than $150,000 (N30 million) in the bank. His money was held in a single bank—Union Bank—and he had no foreign accounts or holdings. He had no registered companies or oil wells. He declared he had shares in Berger Paints, Union Bank, and Skye Bank.

Buhari had his modern home, where he lived, and two mud homes in Daura inherited from an older sister and his mother. He had borrowed money from Barclays Bank to build his home in Kaduna. He had two homes in Abuja, under contract. He had three undeveloped plots of land: one in Kano, one in Zaria, and one in Port Harcourt. On his Daura farm, he had 270 head of cattle, 25 sheep, 5 horses, and a number of orchard trees.

Buhari's vice president, Yemi Osinbajo, was much wealthier, based on his successful legal career in Lagos with his law firm, SimmonsCooper. He had assets of N94 million, plus an additional $900,000 in banks. He owned a four-bedroom home in Lagos and a three-bedroom flat in the Ikoyi neighborhood of Lagos, plus a two-bedroom flat at the evangelical "Redemption Camp" on the Lagos-Ibadan Expressway. He also had a mortgaged two-bedroom flat in Bedford, England. He had shares in five Lagos-based companies: Octogenerium Ltd, Windsor Grant Ltd, Taraposa Vistorion Ltd, Aviva Ltd, and MTN Nigeria.

After taking office, Buhari was confronted with the lengthy Transition Committee report by Ahmed Joda, which bluntly declared, "We found corruption everywhere" (http://saharareporters.com/2015/06/21/we-found-corruption-everywhere-says-buhari-transition-committee-chairman-ahmed-joda). The international community followed these revelations closely. On June 23, for instance, Voice of America reported that "Nigerian President Muhammadu Buhari Monday accused the former administration of Goodluck Jonathan of virtually emptying the treasury and leaving the country in debt" (http://www.voanews.com/articleprintview/2833535.html?displayOptions=1). Buhari knew that he would need the help of the international community in tracing stolen monies, which was part of his agenda in Europe and the United States in the early days of his administration.

Buhari also knew that he needed to remove one of the most visible symbols of government corruption: the military checkpoints on most roads leading into and out of towns and cities. On June 22, he ordered the immediate removal of all such checkpoints nationwide. Later, he would order probes of all weapons procurements since 2007. The message was getting out that even the military was not exempt from financial discipline. At the end of summer, the Navy clamped down on bunkering, arresting eleven sailors with 6,000 tons of stolen crude oil in Bayelsa State.

Yet these were small fry compared with the big fish associated with Jonathan's minister of petroleum resources since 2010, Mrs. Diezani Alison-Madueke. The big fish, however, were also being targeted. At the end of September, it was reported that "the National Crime Agency of the United Kingdom has confirmed the arrest of four persons, including Nigeria's former Minister of Petroleum Resources Alison-Madueke, for international bribery and corruption. A statement on NCA's website revealed that the arrests were made by its newly formed International Corruption Unit" (http://saharareporters.com/2015/06/21/we-found-corruption-everywhere-says-buhari-transition-committee-chairman-ahmed-joda). It was also reported that the United Kingdom had asked "Switzerland to arrest Kola Aluko for Alison-Madueke proceedings. . . . Mr. Aluko is the alleged money launderer for the former Minister of Petroleum Resources, Diezani Alison-Madueke, and ex-President Goodluck Jonathan" (http://saharareporters.com/2015/10/07/uk-asks-switzerland-arrest-kola-aluko-alison-madueke-proceedings). Aluko was holed up in Switzerland, where he had purchased a mansion, paying in cash.

The British connection had always been central to Nigerian fraud and money laundering cases, since the days when the London Metropolitan Police had arrested and successfully prosecuted Governor James Ibori. (He was later transferred to a Nigerian prison, and then released.)

In early October 2015, the Nigerian media were full of news of suspicious oil-related cases based in London. For example, "A senior executive of the Nigerian National Petroleum Corporation (NNPC), Kess Omiogbemi, is likely to face theft and money laundering charges over assets he owns in Nigeria and abroad, specifically the United Kingdom. . . . Mr. Omiogbemi, who is the NNPC's head of oil movement, owns two expensive cars and a house in the United Kingdom paid for in cash" (http://saharareporters.com/2015/10/07/nigerian-state-oil-executive-owns-unexplained-foreign-assets-including-uk-home).

Until the court cases in the United Kingdom produced firm evidence of wrongdoing and delivered judgments, no one could be sure who was guilty of what, if anything. But two things were clear: First, there was a deliberate strategy by Buhari to engage the international community in tackling Nigerian corruption. Second, the epicenter of such corruption was the oil industry under President Jonathan's watch.

Hence, it came as no surprise at the end of September that Buhari announced he would take over personally as minister of petroleum resources. He would appoint a minister of state to handle the technical and day-to-day details. But if Nigeria was to make headway in tackling corruption, Buhari would need to be directly involved.

Within Nigeria, the main federal agency in the war against corruption was the Economic and Financial Crimes Commission (EFCC). Ibrahim Lamorde had become executive chairman of the EFCC in 2011. On October 7, 2015, the "Concerned Staff" of EFCC wrote an open letter to Buhari, alleging that Lamorde and many of the senior officials (including police) were engaged in corrupt practices themselves (http://saharareporters.com/2015/10/20/efcc-staff-petition-buhari-alleging-impunity-and-screening-against-ibrahim-lamorde). The lengthy letter was published in the media and was filled with specific details and cases. While its publication spotlighted the need to do something about Nigeria's main anti-corruption watchdog, the letter also demonstrated that the EFCC whistle-blowers felt they could take their concerns directly to the president—the one figure in Nigeria with the stature and, since his inauguration, the power, to lead the anticorruption campaign.

Partnering Abroad

September would be an extremely busy month for President Buhari, with trips planned to Ghana, France, and UN Headquarters in New York to discuss security matters. Plus, the president had promised to issue an initial list of his ministers by the end of September, and there was considerable interest in the identities of the defence minister and minister of interior.

Also, in August, the president had announced that Nigeria would recruit an additional ten thousand police officers equally from each of the thirty-six states so as to encourage states to integrate police with members of the local communities, especially youth. This plan needed to be implemented, but nothing could be done until Buhari introduced his budget for 2016. Meanwhile, the corruption probes were going on quietly in the background.

On September 6, Buhari flew to Accra for security talks with President John Mahama. He was accompanied by his NSA, Major General Monguno, plus permanent secretaries from the defence, foreign affairs, and other ministries. He also met with the large Nigerian community in Ghana.

One week later, on September 13, Buhari flew to Paris for a three-day meeting with President Hollande and others on regional security. Again, he was accompanied by his NSA and key permanent secretaries. He also met with several African ambassadors to France. Hollande pledged more assistance to the MJTF to combat terrorism in Nigeria and West Africa.

On September 24, Buhari flew to New York for the seventy-ninth session of the UN General Assembly. He was accompanied by the governors of Sokoto, Kaduna, and Niger, plus his NSA and key permanent secretaries. He was scheduled to give a major address on global security on September 28.

In addition, according to one account:

> On the agenda of President Buhari's talks, [are] deliberations and interactions with the United Nations Secretary-General, Mr. Ban Ki-moon, President Barack Obama of the United States, President Francois Hollande of France, Prime Minister David Cameron of Britain, Chancellor Angela Merkel of Germany, President Vladimir Putin of Russia, President Xi Jinping of China, and Prime Minister Narenda Modi of India.
>
> President Buhari is also scheduled to address the World Leader Summit on Violent Extremism to which he was personally invited by Mr. Ban Ki-moon during the Secretary-General's recent visit to Nigeria. Also on the President's busy schedule in New York are a meeting of the African Union's Peace and Security Council [and] a High-Level Roundtable on South-South Cooperation organized by President Xi Jinping of China. (http://saharareporters.com/2015/09/22/

details-buhari%E2%80%99s-trip-un-revealed-he-speak-global-security)

In addition, Buhari held meetings with Bill Clinton, Gordon Brown, and Bill Gates. Other meetings were scheduled, but some were missed and, it was reported, "Members of President Buhari's delegation to the United Nations General Assembly have accused Prof. Joy Ogwu, Nigeria's Permanent Representative to the UN, of sabotaging President Muhammadu Buhari's participation, citing missteps that have embarrassed the delegation and undermined Nigeria's work" (http://saharareporters.com/2015/09/28/un-general-assembly-fiasco-buhari-team-accuse-ambassador-joy-ogwu-sabotage). Again, tensions seem to have emerged between the new administration and the holdovers from the previous one.

Meanwhile, Buhari had to prepare his October 1 National Day speech. In addition to discussing security issues, he would use the speech to reiterate that he was not engaged in a witch hunt, and that only the guilty had anything to fear: "I bear no ill will against anyone on past events. Nobody should fear anything from me. We are not after anyone. People should only fear the consequences of their own actions. I hereby invite everyone, whatever his or her political views, to join me in working for the nation" (http://www.pmnewsnigeria.com/2015/10/01/full-text-buhari-delivers-moving-speech-to-nigerians-at-55/).

The big news at the end of September was the announcement that the names of twenty-one ministers had been submitted to the Senate for confirmation. At last, Buhari was unveiling the team of ministers he had chosen to move the APC agenda forward. Although specific ministries were not attached to the names, the list of nominees did provide a clearer picture of what to expect from a Buhari administration. Prominent figures on the list included Lai Mohammed, spokesman for the APC; Rotimi Amaechi, former governor of Rivers State; Babatunde Fashola, former governor of Lagos State; Chris Ngige, former governor of Anambra State; Kayode Fayemi, former governor of Ekiti State; Ogbonnaya Onu, former governor of Abia State; Emmanuel Kachikwu, managing director of NNPC; Abdulrahman Dambazau, former chief of army staff; Abubakar Malami, former legal adviser to the CPC; Aisha Alhassan, former governor candidate of the APC in Taraba State;

Amina Mohammed, special adviser to UN secretary-general Ban Ki-moon; and Kemi Adeosun, former finance commissioner of Ogun State.

Other nominations were submitted for key administrative agencies. The number of initial nominees from northern and southern Nigeria had evidently been carefully balanced, signaling that Buhari was not trying to favor the north. The Senate would have many more names to consider throughout October. The larger question was how ministerial appointments could be used to promote security and national unity.

As September unfolded, a major development occurred with further international involvement in the war against Boko Haram, perhaps a dividend from Buhari's summer trips abroad. On September 24, the White House announced it would increase assistance to Benin, Cameroon, Chad, Niger, and Nigeria to fight Boko Haram. The $45 million package included military training, equipment, and intelligence.

Then, on October 14, President Obama announced that he was sending 300 troops, plus Predator drones, to West Africa to aid in the fight against "ISIS-affiliated militants." The troops, Obama, said, will "conduct airborne intelligence, surveillance and reconnaissance operations in the region. The troops will be equipped with weapons for the purpose of providing their own protection and security, and they will remain in Cameroon until their support is no longer needed" (http://saharareporters.com/2015/10/14/boko-haram-obama-sends-us-troops-drones-cameroon). The US force would be set up in Garoua in northern Cameroon, near the Nigerian border. The force would also provide intelligence to the MJTF, which consisted of troops from Nigeria, Niger, Cameroon, Chad, and Benin. To further consolidate this cooperation with the MJTF, the commander of the US African Command, General David Rodriguez, met with Buhari in Abuja.

"Structured attacks by the insurgents have reduced," Buhari said in a speech, "and by the end of the year we should see the final routing of Boko Haram as an organized fighting force." According to media reports, Buhari "restated his appreciation of the United States government's support to Nigeria's efforts towards defeating terrorism and insurgency. . . . Rodriguez told Buhari that his visit was aimed at strengthening the Nigeria–United States military relations. He said he also visited to explore further options for assisting the Multinational Joint Task Force (MJTF) established by Nigeria and her neighbours to fight Boko Haram."

> Later while speaking to State House correspondents, Rodriguez said the United States was working with Nigerian security forces on the things they needed to contain the insurgency. American Ambassador to Nigeria, James Entwistle, said no country was doing more to assist Nigeria in the fight against the insurgency than his country. (http://www.dailytrust.com.ng/news/general/boko-haram-won-t-last-beyond-dec-fg/115132.html)

Meanwhile, Boko Haram militants were striking ever deeper into Nigeria, beyond their strongholds in the northeast, although Borno was still their main target. On September 20, for instance, Boko Haram attacked a mosque and a soccer-viewing stadium in Maiduguri, killing fifty-four people. Subsequently, Abuja was hit by suicide bombers, and Nigerian troops were battling the militants in Kogi State. Whether Buhari's international partners could be helpful in the fight against Boko Haram remained to be seen.

Campaigning for the APC in spring 2015.

Candidate Buhari thanking the people of Daura at the end of a rally in 2015.

Greeting young Fulani girls in Niamey, Niger Republic, shortly after his election.

Signing the register and the oath of office after his inauguration. Seated opposite the new president is Chief Justice Mahmud. Standing next to the president is his wife, Aisha.

A winning team. At Eagle Square, after the inauguration (left to right): Hajiya Fatimatu Mai Talle Tara; Asiwaju Ahmed Bola Tinubu; President Buhari; former vice president Atiku Abubakar; and with his customary broad smile, Chief Bisi Akande. Hajiya Fatimatu was a market vendor who donated almost all her life's savings to President Buhari's campaign.

Congratulations from former president Alhaji Shehu Shagari after the ceremony. Former military president Ibrahim Babangida awaits his turn.

General Yakubu Gowon and Mrs. Victoria Gowon offer their compliments.

A firm handshake from a firm friend. President Buhari being greeted after the swearing-in ceremony by General Theophilus Yakubu Danjuma, a close friend since the Civil War. Just visible is another long-term friend of Buhari's, Dr. Ogbonnaya Onu, now minister of science and technology.

Former heads of state greet the new president. From left to right: an exuberant Abdussalami Abubakar, an expectant Ernest Shonekan, and a gung-ho Olusegun Obasanjo.

President Buhari with former president Goodluck Jonathan at the inauguration.

President Buhari greeted by his Chadian counterpart, President Idriss Deby.

Congratulatory handshake from the president of Gabon, Ali Bongo Ondimba. Looking on is Alhaji Muhammad Yusufu, president of Niger Republic.

US secretary of state John Kerry and British foreign secretary Phillip Hammond offer their good wishes.

Vice President Osinbajo and President Buhari get down to work on the day after swearing-in.

Chapter 10

National Unity

The central challenge of any Nigerian president is to ensure national unity. Since the trauma of the Civil War, during which Nigeria's political and military leadership worked to prevent the secession of Biafra, many mechanisms have been put in place to create horizontal links between the states throughout the country. The idea of "federal character"—namely, the idea that the composition of federal bodies should reflect the diversity of the country—has been expressed in numerous ways since the Civil War, but it is always especially salient in terms of the composition of the federal cabinet and the balance among other federal appointees. This chapter examines President Buhari's efforts to ensure zonal, political, and religious balance in his appointments; his calls for national unity; and his recognition of the key role that the military play in preserving that unity.

Zonal Balance: The Initial Round of Ministerial Nominees

The presidential election of 2015 revealed a clear divide between, on the one hand, the South East and South-South zones and, on the other hand, the rest of the country. As a consequence, close attention would be paid to Buhari's selections for cabinet positions and other federal appointments. In the event, as noted in the previous chapter, Buhari displayed a scrupulous concern for zonal balance: among the twenty-one initial ministerial nominees announced in September 2015, eleven were from the north and ten from the south. More detailed state balancing would go on at the next round of nominees.

Buhari also had a strong preference for technical and professional competence over political experience, but he would have to balance such competence against a full range of political realities. In addition, an age of globalization requires some assessment of the international experience of the initial nominees for the federal cabinet team.

A fuller sketch of the first round of cabinet nominees submitted for confirmation is shown in tables 10.1, 10.2, and 10.3.

Table 10.1. Zonal balance among initial federal ministerial nominees

North West zone (7 states; 4 nominees)

Abdulrahman Dambazau (Kano); Abubakar Malami (Kebbi); Suleiman Hussain Adamu (Jigawa); Hadi Sirika (Katsina)

North Central zone (6 states; 5 nominees)

Lai Mohammed (Kwara); Solomon Dalong (Plateau); Ahmed Isa Ibeto (nomination withdrawn, Niger); Audu Ogbeh (Benue); Ibrahim Usman Jibril (Nasarawa)

North East zone (6 states; 2 nominees)

Aisha Alhassan (Taraba); Amina Mohammed (Gombe)

South West zone (6 states; 4 nominees)

Babatunde Fashola (Lagos); Kayode Fayemi (Ekiti); Kemi Adeosun (Ogun); Adebayo Shittu (Oyo)

South-South zone (6 states; 4 nominees)

Rotimi Amaechi (Rivers); Udoma Udo Udoma (Akwa Ibom); Emmanuel Ibe Kachikwu (Delta); Osagie Ehanire (Edo)

South East zone (5 states; 2 nominees)

Chris Ngige (Anambra); Ogbonnaya Onu (Abia)

The principle of federal character was noticeable even at the state level. For example, Ahmed Isa Ibeto's name was withdrawn from the list and replaced with that of Abubakar Bwari Bawa because of political pressures from within the Niger State political establishment. The governor of Niger, Abubakar Sani Bello, met with Buhari to argue that the governor himself, the Speaker of the state assembly, and Ibeto were all from the same zone C within the state. Ibeto had to be replaced with someone from zone A or B, to respect the principle of rotation.

Overall, however, what was more noticeable than the regional balance was the high level of professional and educational achievement of the ministerial nominees. As table 10.2 shows, even by international standards, the number of law degrees, doctorates, and master's degrees held by the nominees was extraordinary, and their technical skills were no less impressive.

Table 10.2. Professional and educational training of initial federal ministerial nominees

Legal training and experience (9 out of 21 nominees)

Abubakar Malami (senior advocate Nigeria, national legal adviser to CPC); Aisha Alhassan (Taraba State attorney general and commissioner of Justice); Lai Mohammed (cofounded a legal firm); Adebayo Shittu; Babatunde Fashola (senior advocate Nigeria); Solomon Dalong; Udoma Udo Udoma (senior advocate Nigeria); Rotimi Amaechi; Emmanuel Ibe Kachikwu

Advanced professional training (8 out of 21 nominees)

Abdulrahman Dambazau (PhD in criminology, University of Keele, United Kingdom); Dr. Chris Ngige (MD); Kayode Fayemi (PhD in war studies, King's College, University of London); Ogbonnaya Onu (PhD in chemical engineering, University of California, Berkeley); Suleiman Hussain Adamu (MSc in project management, University of Reading, United Kingdom); Audu Ogbeh (University of Toulouse, France); Dr. Osagie Enahire (MD, Ludwig Maximillians University, Munich, Germany); Ibrahim Jibril (MSc in land resources, Bayero University, Kano)

Not surprisingly, most of the initial ministerial nominees had some recent political experience in the APC, and many had belonged to one or another of the parties that joined together to form the APC. Some nominees had not been politically active but had high-level administrative experience. These patterns are shown in table 10.3.

Table 10.3. Political experience of initial federal ministerial nominees

Governors and deputy governors

Babatunde Fashola (Lagos, AC, 2007–15); Kayode Fayemi (Ekiti, 2010–2014 on AC platform); Dr. Chris Ngige (Anambra, 2003–06; plus AC senator, 2011–15); Ogbonnaya Onu (Abia, 1992–93; national chair, ANPP); Ahmed Isa Ibeto (deputy governor, Niger; switched from PDP to APC; nomination withdrawn); Rotimi Amaechi (Rivers, 2007–15, defected from PDP to APC)

Other political experience

Abubakar Malami (chair, national legal team of CPC); Aisha Alhassan (senator, 2011–15; gubernatorial aspirant for APC, 2015); Lai Mohammed (national publicity secretary, APC); Adebayo Shittu (gubernatorial candidate for CPC in Oyo); Solomon Dalong (chair, Langtang South LGA); Udoma Udo Udoma (senator, PDP until resigned to join APC); Hadi Sirika (senator, CPC); Audu Ogbeh (former chair of PDP; former minister in Second Republic)

High-level administrative experience

Abdulrahman Dambazau (chief of army staff, 2008–10); Kemi Adeosun (CEO of her own accounting firm); Suleiman Hussain Adamu (cofounded Engineering Associates); Amina Mohammed (special to UN secretary-general); Emmanuel Ibe Kachikwu (legal adviser at Exxon Mobil); Osagie Ehanire (consulting surgeon, Shell Petroleum Development Company); Ibrahim Jibril (director of land administration, FCT)

The nonpolitical cluster was a combination of technocratic and senior administrators. It also includes two of the three women in the ministerial cohort: Kemi Adeosun and Amina Mohammed. The third woman, Aisha Alhassan, also known as "Mama Taraba," ran for governor for the APC in 2015, but lost. Some members of the third group had demonstrated a personal loyalty to Buhari; General Dambazau, for example, had served as chair of Buhari's Security Committee during the 2015 election cycle.

On October 12, a list of sixteen final ministerial nominees was delivered to Senate President Bukola Saraki by Chief of Staff Abba Kyari and Special Assistant for the National Assembly (House) Kawu Sumaila. In addition, it was hinted that Buhari might not be minister for petroleum resources but would closely supervise that sector.

The sixteen names exhibited a zonal/state balance, as indicated in table 10.4.

Table 10.4. Zonal balance among the second batch of federal ministerial nominees

North West zone

Brigadier General Muhammad Mansur Dan-Ali, rtd (Zamfara); Zainab Shamsuna Ahmed (Kaduna); Aisha Abubakar (Sokoto)

North Central zone

James E. Ocholi (Kogi); Abubakar Bawa (Niger)

North East zone

Khadijia Bukar Abba Ibrahim (Yobe); Mustapha Baba Shehuri (Borno); Muhammadu Bello (Adamawa); Adamu Adamu (Bauchi)

South West zone

Claudius Omoleye (Ondo); Prof. Isaac Adewole (Osun)

South-South zone

Heineken Lokpobiri (Bayelsa); Pastor Usani Usani Uguru (Cross River)

South East zone

Anthony Onwuka (Imo); Okechukwu Enelamah (Abia); Geoffrey Onyeama (Enugu)

As with most of the individuals in the initial round of nominees, most of those in the later list of sixteen were high-achieving professionals The list also featured an additional three women, who were no less technically qualified than their male counterparts. For example, the representative from Sokoto, Aisha Abubakar, had twenty years of experience in banking and investment, specializing in small and medium-size enterprise development, plus a master's degree in development studies from the University of Leeds in England.

Religious Balance

The religious identities of federal ministers do not tend to appear in the media. Since the Civil War, state identities have become informal sùrrogates for ethnoreligious identities. Thus, a minister from Kano is presumed to be Muslim (Hausa-Fulani), and one from Anambra is presumed to be Christian (Igbo). Furthermore, personal and family names tend to reflect such identities. Apart from distinctively Muslim names, it is clear to most people that Musa, Daoud, Ibrahim, and Yahaya are Muslim names, while their English equivalents, Moses, David, Abraham, and John are Christian names.

The one zone where is it not possible to use names as an indicator of religious identity is the South West, which is about half Muslim and half Christian. Yoruba Muslims in the southwest often kept their traditional Yoruba names, or even, if they went to European-style schools, adopted Western names. But in the world of politics, Yoruba religious identities tend to be well known—especially in the case of Christian pastors.

It is at the presidential level where Nigerian political culture has evolved to require a balance in religious identities. Sometimes this is expressed as a "north-south" balance, although it is clear to all that this means a Muslim president and a Christian vice president, or a Christian president and a Muslim vice president.

As noted previously, when Buhari was military head of state, his deputy was Brigadier Tunde Idiagbon, a Muslim Yoruba from Kwara State. Buhari was criticized at the time for having a "Muslim-Muslim" top leadership team, even though military officers at the time seldom thought in terms of religious identity, paying more attention to the need to balance regional or ethnic identities. The Buhari team was balanced ethnically (i.e., Hausa-Fulani and Yoruba) but not religiously at the top. His cabinet consisted of seven Muslims and thirteen Christians.

In 2011, Buhari chose Pastor Tunde Bakare as his vice presidential candidate. Bakare was a Pentecostal preacher from Abeokuta. He had been born into a Yoruba Muslim family, and grew up to be a successful attorney, practicing with the well-known human rights advocate Gani Fawehinmi.

In 1988, Bakare was called to the Christian ministry and founded the Latter Rain Assembly (End-Time Church). He became an extremely successful televangelist. His church even spread to the United States. More to the political point, Bakare was a vocal critic of the Obasanjo government and its growing corruption, and was put in jail for his views.

Since 2011, Buhari has remained friends with Bakare. Indeed, Bakare accompanied Buhari on his US trip in July 2015 to visit President Obama in the White House. Bakare's critique of corruption in Nigeria and his call to repent clearly resonated with Buhari's message, although voiced in different language.

Buhari's selection of Yemi Osinbajo as his vice presidential partner in December 2014 echoed his previous choice. Osinbajo was and remains a successful Yoruba lawyer, and has been a law professor and a state attorney general. But he is also a highly successful evangelical "pastor-in-charge" of the Lagos Province 48, Olive Tree provincial headquarters parish. He insists he is only "on loan" to the federal government.

In short, Buhari has evidently had no problem in working closely with deeply committed Christian leaders. This is in keeping with Nigeria's evolving political culture of "nonpreferentialism" in church-state relations. The culture does not demand a strict separation of religion and politics, but it does insist that both major religions be treated equally and with respect. In many situations, the principle is also extended to traditional indigenous ethnic leaders, who also serve as religious leaders in their communities.

In keeping with the spirit of the notion of the "People of the Book" (referred to by Muslims in Arabic as *Ahl al-Kitab*), the top leaders of major political parties have grown comfortable with interfaith cooperation. The military had set an earlier example, with the federal side in the Civil War including both Muslim and Christian officers and enlisted soldiers. In the Civil War, as has been the case in many other hot conflicts in different places and times, comrades tended to downplay religious identities in the fight for a common national cause. Today, the same emphasis on common interests (i.e., the unity of Nigeria) is widespread among Nigeria's elite and permeates interfaith relations. A similar attitude is also common at grassroots levels. It is the fringe elements in both faiths that have focused on sectarian differences rather than common national interests.

Some of Nigeria's national leaders are not always above deploying religious stereotypes and fueling sectarian animosities during election campaigns, but in the postelection calls for unity, these shrill voices tend to be muted.

Calls for Unity amid Regional Stress

Both major political parties and leaders have multifaith teams. But in the presidential election of 2015, the predominantly Christian South-South and South East zones strongly favored Goodluck Jonathan, while the far north, southwest, and most of the western portions of the Middle Belt supported Buhari. Consequently, the first and second rounds of ministerial selections by Buhari were seen as a litmus test as to whether a victorious opposition party would visit some form of retribution on the zones that did not support it. This did not happen.

Even so, tensions between the different parts of the country did not evaporate, and instead centered in many ways on the competing goals of cleaning up corruption versus keeping the peace between ethnoreligious segments of the country. Many of the close confidants of former president Jonathan were from the South-South and South East, and there was a perception among neutral observers that this group had abused its access to off-budget funds and might thus be a target of any anticorruption drive.

The National Peace Committee, which had been set up to ease ethnoreligious tensions in the lead-up to the general election of 2015, was headed by former military head of state General Abdussalami Abubakar, who had helped shepherd Nigeria through the transition from military rule to the Fourth Republic in 1999. The National Peace Committee had been instrumental in brokering the peace accord between Buhari and Jonathan before the election.

It was common knowledge that after the election Buhari was insistent on recovering the billions of dollars alleged to have been stolen under the Jonathan administration. It was also commonly recognized that efforts to retrieve the stolen funds would be seen to have ethnoregional implications and might exacerbate tensions. The National Peace Committee, including the highly respected bishop of Sokoto, Matthew Hassan Kukah, met with Buhari in August to express these concerns.

In mid-October, General Abubakar and his committee met again with Buhari to express fresh concerns. Although the results of this private meeting were not publicized, many observers suspected that the committee was worried about destabilizing Bayelsa State, whose prominent citizens had access to Nigeria's oil industry and which was the focus of some of the most egregious allegations of corruption, as will be explored in chapter 19.

The Military and Unity

The military governments that ruled Nigeria in the wake of the Civil War agreed that there would be equal intake from each state into the officer training program. Names and state affiliations of the trainees were—and still are—published each season for all to see. This was an extreme form of federal character, undertaken with the intention of promoting national unity. Once in the officer training program, however, young officers were then promoted on merit rather than state affiliation.

When President Obasanjo came to office in 1999, he gave early retirement to many of the northern officers, which caused stress in the north. When Jonathan became president, a clear pattern developed of using political or ethnic criteria in promoting senior officers. (The fear of coups in Nigeria has been perennial, and the loyalty of senior officers is always crucial to a government's survival.) One consequence was that the fight against the Boko Haram insurgency was led for many years by senior officers who lacked familiarity with the ethnolinguistic or religious cultures of the Borno.

Yet whatever the personal background of senior officers, and even junior officers, the military shared a strong sense of pride in having helped keep the country together. This sentiment was part of the DNA of military officers in Nigeria. In their personal lives and circles, officers seemed to relish the friendship of fellow officers from other parts of the country. Their lives depended on it. Their common uniforms gave them unity of purpose. The Civil War slogan remained meaningful: "To keep Nigeria one is a task which must be done."

But like the leaders of many institutions in Nigeria, the military hierarchy was subject to the temptations of an oil-rich economy. Even as the defence budget ballooned under Jonathan, allegations of corruption within the military proliferated. Equipment funds were being siphoned off. Enlisted soldiers often found themselves short of bullets, food rations, allowances and other equipment.

Some of this corruption was reported in the Nigerian media after Buhari took office. In mid-October, Brigadier General Enitan Ransome-Kuti was sentenced to six months in jail for failing to do his duty in the fight against Boko Haram, specifically in the battle of Baga, which the insurgents won. He had failed to account for weapons and ammunition under his supervision.

During his lengthy trial, General Ransome-Kuti's attorney, Femi Falana, argued that "the Nigerian army had simply failed to provide necessary equipment for the Brigadier General to perform his lawful duties. Falana also presented several statements from officers and soldiers who repeatedly stated that the Army was ill equipped to fight Boko Haram, an assertion that was later affirmed by a former chief of defence staff, Alex Badeh, after he was fired from that position earlier this year" (http://saharareporters.

com/2015/10/15/nigeria-army-court-martial-sentences-brigadier-general-ransome-kuti-six-months-jail).

For whatever reasons, the morale of enlisted military soldiers was extremely low in the final days of the Jonathan administration. Despite the military consuming nearly one-fifth of the Nigerian budget, ordinary soldiers could not get the equipment they needed, or medical supplies, or even funeral services. Clearly, the funds were being "chopped" long before they got to the level of the foot soldier.

After Buhari dismissed Jonathan's senior commanders—one of the new president's first acts after his inauguration—the challenge for the new team of military leaders was not only to introduce better management practices, but also to rebuild morale. Thus, in mid-October, the Chief of Army Staff Lieutenant General Tukur Buratai addressed his troops fighting the insurgents in the northeast:

> The next few days will be crucial to Operation Lafiya Dole. It is also crucial to our country, Nigeria. Our sovereignty as a nation is threatened. The Nigerian Army and indeed the military as the symbol of our nationhood is being challenged. Our ability to stand and defeat the Boko Haram terrorists in the next few weeks will determine the future of our country. . . .
>
> We cannot afford to lose the fight. We are better trained and better equipped. The whole nation is behind us. Mr. President is with us. Let us remain steadfast in this noble cause. Be courageous. We must degrade and defeat the terrorists. This job must be done. We must make our country proud. (http://www.dailytrust.com.ng/news/general/future-of-nigeria-depends-on-fighting-troops-buratai/115400.html)

Buhari's challenge to the troops and their officers was to degrade or defeat Boko Haram by the end of December. Although the Nigerian military could not stop every suicide bomber, it could try to retake the territories that had been previously lost. This they accomplished.

CHALLENGES OF ECONOMICS AND POLITICS

Chapter 11

Economic Development

As noted previously, the challenges of security and national unity are closely tied to the challenge of economic development. Nigerian strategic planners and the international community had long seen reconstruction in the north as a necessary (but not sufficient) condition to counter violent extremism. Buhari had urged heavy investment in education as the key to human resource development in general and to countering Boko Haram in particular. But education would need to be reformed to meet this goal.

Buhari had also charged that corruption was a curse that negatively impacted development. During the summer of 2015, vivid posters appeared in Abuja and other big cities with the slogan "Corruption Kills," coupled with pictures of desperate poverty. How the new president would handle the corruption issue could be a make-or-break issue for his administration.

One of the first policy decisions of the Buhari administration was to limit the amount of cash that could be moved overseas by converting naira into dollars (or pounds sterling) to $10,000. The purpose was to regulate the capital flight that followed the defeat of the PDP incumbents. But there were howls of protest, as many senior officials and others needed to move money in September to support their children's school fees in Britain and the United States.

The Buhari government was confronted with a formidable array of interrelated problems. The inflow of foreign currency was extremely meager owing to the low price of crude oil. Allegations were circulating that the treasury had been largely depleted by the outgoing administration. Debts were coming due that had not been reported previously. And fuel subsidies were eating a big piece of the national budget.

The funds needed to tackle the electric power crisis in Nigeria would need to come largely from outside investment. But international companies needed to be able to have a smooth two-way flow of hard currency. The apparent delay in vetting and nominating his ministerial finance team left many people wondering whether Buhari was up to the task of stemming corruption while also encouraging infrastructure investment and other development projects.

Some international bloggers were counseling that "the perfect is the enemy of the good." That is to say, the goal of putting together an executive cabinet with flawless ethical records, in a context in which the coalition components of the APC all asserted their rights to the spoils of victory, was not only elusive but was also creating a vacuum of leadership and implementation at the ministerial level.

When the first round of ministers was announced, PDP supporters protested that some APC governors who were on the list did not have clean hands. The one initial nomination that was delayed for Senate confirmation was former governor Rotimi Amaechi (Rivers), the first PDP governor to defect to APC. It was argued that the Senate Ad Hoc Committee on Ethics should be allowed to submit its report before Senate confirmation. By October 14, however, the first eighteen nominees were confirmed. Amaechi was finally confirmed in late October.

During the election campaign, it was widely assumed that the APC presidential ticket was balanced between Buhari, who would focus on terrorism and corruption, and his vice presidential partner, Osinbajo, who would focus on the economy. After all, during the Fourth Republic (i.e., since 1999) Lagos was booming economically and Osinbajo was part of that process. Foreign investment was robust, the stock market was effective, and the "local taxation" policy by Lagos State allowed for basic infrastructure to be built and maintained. Could that feat be duplicated on a national level?

This chapter will focus on Buhari's initial efforts in four main areas: (1) reconstruction and resettlement in the northeast; (2) reform of the petroleum industry; (3) electric power reforms; and (4) education and human capital development. While his ministerial team was being assembled and confirmed, attention was focused not only on the selections for ministers of defence, foreign affairs, justice, finance, and petroleum resources, but also on Buhari's choice for minister of education, because education was his signature issue, especially in the north. Educational reform would go to the core of the challenge of changing the hearts and minds of jobless youth in the north.

Violence was continuing in Borno, Yobe, Adamawa, and Cameroon. Although the revitalized Nigerian military had made progress in reclaiming territories from the insurgents, a continuing series of suicide bombers was causing havoc in the region, and even as far south as Abuja. Buhari often met with the families of the victims, both Christian and Muslim, to offer condolences.

Something had to be done to cut off the fresh supply of terrorist recruits and cash to Boko Haram. A new NSA committee was set up. Behind-the-scenes efforts were made on the "Bring Back Our Girls" issue—securing the return of the Chibok secondary school girls who had been abducted in 2014, much to the horror of the international community.

Reconstruction and Resettlement in the Northeast

A basic problem in the Lake Chad area was the shrinkage over time of the watershed. Desertification was drastically curtailing traditional means of farming and fishing, imperiling livelihoods, threatening jobs, and creating the potential for major out-migration from the area. Having served as a governor in the north-east region as a military officer in 1975, Buhari knew the challenges of desertification firsthand.

On October 12, Buhari requested from the auditor general the $5 million study commissioned by President Obasanjo. Climate change was causing Lake Chad to dry up, and the question was whether there were new ways of replenishing the lake. According to media coverage, Buhari made the following remarks:

> He [Obasanjo] gave $5m to the study, and the study's report was that unless some of the rivers from the Central African Republic are diverted to empty into Chad Basin, Lake Chad will dry up. . . . One of the recommendations was that at that time the report was submitted, the cost of diverting one of the rivers to empty into Lake Chad would be between $13bn and $15bn. . . . I think this government will like to see this report and see how we can ask our foreign friends how they can help us.
>
> This is because if that river is diverted to empty into Chad Basin, I think it will affect at least two million Nigerians and another two million from Cameroon, Chad and Niger to resettle, and perhaps that will help us to stop Boko Haram around that area. (http://saharareporters.com/2015/10/13/buhari-demands-report-obasanjo%E2%80%99s-5m-study)

A megaproject to revitalize Lake Chad would require the cooperation and combined efforts of the Lake Chad Basin Commission countries. It would also take massive investment from the international community. Such issues were on Buhari's agenda during his trips to Europe and the United States in summer 2015 as well as during his participation in the Climate Change Conference in Paris in December.

The longer-term solution in the Lake Chad area would be to move inhabitants beyond subsistence farming and fishing and into a range of more modern alternatives. For this, the imperative was education. Providing such education would be a direct challenge to the basic Boko Haram message, which was enshrined in the group's very name, which translates as "Western education is prohibited."

Until the Boko Haram challenge was quelled, the prospects for reconstruction and resettlement would have to wait. As the insurgency moved into a phase of suicide bombers, the government would have to focus on making defensive precautions in the urban areas and equipping the IDP camps with basic necessities. At the same time, the government could begin to plan for postconflict reforms and development, the costs of which would be enormous.

Reforming the Petroleum Industry

If any of the proposals by Buhari or the APC were to be funded, the country's petroleum industry had to be reformed. The petroleum industry was a sector that Buhari knew firsthand. He had been oil minister in the 1970s under General Obasanjo. He had been head of the Petroleum Trust Fund (PTF) in the 1990s. He had earned a reputation as an incorruptible leader in this highly corrupt domain.

The complexity of the Nigerian oil industry meant that only an experienced hand could reform or lead it. And given the petroleum industry's centrality to the Nigerian economy, observers speculated in summer 2015 that Buhari would serve as his own minister of petroleum resources—a prediction that seemed to come true when, in September, Buhari announced as much.

But then Buhari may have had second thoughts. Buhari appeared to have confidence in the group managing director of the Nigerian National Petroleum Corporation (NNPC), Ibe Kachikwu. In October, he was confirmed by the Senate to be a minister, and the widespread assumption was it would be in the Ministry of Petroleum Resources. (In the end, Kachikwu became minister of state for petroleum resources, under Buhari, who would serve as minister.)

One of the reasons Buhari was elected was to curb corruption in the oil sector, which in recent years has been plagued by scandals and whose tarnished reputation in the international arena as well as at home has tarnished the reputation of Nigeria as a whole. When Buhari was elected, many people hoped that some of the stolen oil money could be returned for development purposes. Some Nigerian scholars argued that because the temptation to use oil revenues for personal or party purposes would always be present, any returned monies should be kept in internationally safe escrow accounts.

The depth of feeling about corruption in the oil industry was indicated by a Nigerian media observer, who was assessing Buhari's first 100 days in office:

> As the "juiciest" fragment of the national economy, the Nigerian National Petroleum Corporation (NNPC) has, for decades, been the nexus of unchecked, gargantuan corruption. Administration after administration either abetted the wild corruption going on in this organization or simply failed to properly keep it in check. This, it seems, will no longer be the case as concerted efforts are now being made to declutter the cesspit. (http://saharareporter.com/2015/08/31/100-restless-days-buhari-chukwudi-enekwechi)

The international community was cooperating with the Buhari team. Yet Buhari's reputation in the 1980s in going after corruption had caused him to hold back on a full-scale assault on obvious targets. Indeed, in his first few months as president he frequently insisted that there would be no witch hunts and that any allegations of wrongdoing must be evaluated in a court of law.

Yet part of the legitimacy of any new Nigerian government—military or democratic—is to tackle not just corruption in general, but corruption in the petroleum industry specifically. The old adage "Sunlight is the best disinfectant" became part of the Buhari administration's policy for the petroleum industry, with the new government doing what it could to encourage transparency and accountability.

In August, for example, the NNPC canceled offshore processing agreement (OPA) contracts with three companies having close relations with the former minister of petroleum resources, Diezani Alison-Madueke, who was under investigation in London for bribery and fraud. The process of reopening contracts led to 101 applications by Nigerian and multinational companies. The vetting process was open to public and media scrutiny.

Diezani Alison-Madueke was undoubtedly the key figure in the petroleum drama. Born in 1960 in Port Harcourt, she was educated at Howard University in Washington, DC, (where she earned a degree in architecture in 1992) and later at Cambridge University (earning an MBA in 2002). In 2006, she was appointed executive director of Shell Petroleum in Nigeria. Subsequently, she was appointed minister of transportation (2007–8), and minister of mines and steel development (2008–2010). In April 2010, she was appointed minister of petroleum resources by Acting President Jonathan, replacing the highly regarded Dr. Rilwanu Lukman. She worked extremely closely with President Jonathan and was involved at the highest levels of international oil and finance.

On October 2, 2015, Reuters reported that she and several others had been arrested in London by the British National Crime Agency on charges of bribery and corruption. While she awaited trial in the British courts, the Nigerian media were full of speculation and allegations.

One example of such allegations was the opinion editorial in mid-October in *Sahara Reporters* by Hafsatu Ali, "Seven Questions on the Crimes of Former Petroleum Minister." The "questions" concerned (1) the petrol subsidy scam; (2) the private jet charter scam; (3) management instability in the NNPC; (4) the kerosene subsidy scam; (5) unremitted billions to the Federal Government Account; (6) last-minute "shenanigans"; and (7) an allegedly inappropriate "relationship with Mr. President" (http://saharareporters.com/2015/10/16/seven-questions-crimes-former-petroleum-minister-hafsatu-ali).

Meanwhile, the international community was weighing in on suggested reforms. The US-based Natural Resource Governance Institute published a detailed study in August 2015, *Inside the NNPC Oil Sales: A Case for Reform in Nigeria*. The report focused on five areas: domestic crude allocation; revenue retention by the NNPC and its subsidiaries; oil-for-product swap agreements; the abundance of middlemen; and corporate governance, oversight, and transparency.

In short, the petroleum industry was beset by a host of major challenges, ranging from a reputation for corruption, to pending trials for corruption, to a larger leadership issue of how to return potentially billions of dollars to the Nigerian treasury without appearing to be conducting a witch hunt against the inner circle of the Jonathan administration. Most important was how to rebuild confidence in the new team of petroleum industry managers led by Kachikwu to undertake reforms and to build a firewall between the industry and partisan politics.

Investment in Electric Power

The key to most sectors of economic development in Nigeria—from education to small business—is electric power. This has been the bane of Nigerian development, despite the investment of billions of dollars. The Lagos State solution was not to wait for the federal government, but to set up its own state-level electric grid. This was a major issue during the presidential election, especially because Yemi Osinbajo could recite all the details of the Lagos situation, and promised to try to scale up its experiment to a federal level.

Perhaps by coincidence, after Buhari took office on May 29 there was an upswing in electric power supplies in many parts of the country. As one media observer commented:

> According to the Transmission Company of Nigeria (TCN), power generation in the country reached an all-time high of 4,810.7MW on August 25, 2015. This represents a major departure from what was obtainable in the past, when it usually hovered around 2,000MW and sometimes dipped below that. However, it should be noted that the power supply is still far from stable and hardly is 4.8 thousand megawatts enough for a country of over 175 million people. (http://saharareporters.com/2015/09/05/100-days-office-8-key-achievements-president-muhammadu-buhari-chinedu-george-nnawetanma)

Buhari's choice for minister of power, Babatunde Fashola, the former governor of Lagos, would face the formidable task of building on this initial upswing and would have the successful Lagos example to draw on.

Education and Human Capital Development

Buhari had always been passionate about encouraging education. His preference for technocratic and professional ministers was a reflection of this passion. As mentioned previously, he came up through a military educational system, graduating from Nigerian Military Training College, Mons Officer Cadet School in the United Kingdom, and Defence Services Staff College in India, and receiving his master's degree in strategic studies at the US Army War College in Carlisle, Pennsylvania.

The post–Civil War era Nigeria witnessed efforts by the senior officers who had fought to keep the country together and who took over its government to emphasize national unity by creating a new federal capital in Abuja. They also kept a centralized, federal set of functions, such as police and education, which in most Western-style federations were located mainly in the subnational component states.

In the educational domain, whatever the formal constitutional guidelines or the funding streams, the idea of using education to foster national unity has long been part of the evolving political culture in Nigeria. This has meant that the federal government has sought to create some degree of educational uniformity throughout the country. Whether at the levels of primary, secondary, or tertiary education, the tendency has been to design (and in most cases fund) the curriculum in Abuja. Thus, a child in Sokoto in the far northwest of Nigeria would be taught in English in the same way as a child in Anambra in the south.

The obvious exceptions in the north were the basic Qur'anic schools and the higher-level *Ilm* schools, which were almost entirely private, and could reflect local preferences and perspectives. In the far north, most Qur'anic pupils would have been taught in the Hausa language, and would have learned basic tenets of Islam in Arabic. The Fourth Republic politicians have not known what to do about policies toward such schools, and in most cases whatever monitoring has taken place has been left to state governors.

At public primary schools throughout Nigeria, children may spend their first few years being taught in the local vernacular language, but in the higher grades they are taught in English. This did not mean, however, that English was the de facto lingua franca of the entire country. In the north, where Hausa was a widespread lingua franca, those children taught in Hausa in Qur'anic schools and those taught in English (known as "boko" in Hausa) in higher public school classes had significantly different chances of employment and career prospects. Of course, in some cases there was significant overlap between these parallel systems, because parents from wealthier families could send their children to primary school, and also make arrangements for Qur'anic education.

It is not surprising that a religious backlash developed during the Fourth Republic—a backlash that came to be known by the label "Boko Haram," meaning "Western education is prohibited." Boko Haram represented some of those left behind in the modern sector by education, the inequalities within which compounded the extreme income gap that characterizes many petro-states. As in the First Republic in the north, an educational "war on ignorance" (*Yaki da Jahilci*) is needed that will use both lingua francas (English and Hausa).

The lag in Western education in the north was compounded by the historical fact that literacy in that region was in Arabic or in Hausa language in Arabic script (*ajami*). If the 1963 Nigerian census was accurate, 30 percent of the country's population at that time was ethnically Hausa-Fulani. During the colonial era in the north, basic education was in Hausa, and colonial officers were expected to learn Hausa, and a great number of them did so.

In modern times, with Nigeria's overall population estimated at around 185 million, this would mean that the number of Nigerians who speak Hausa is approximately 55 million—approaching the number of people who live in the United Kingdom or in France. Furthermore, for millions more in the north, Hausa has become a second or third language. Indeed, Hausa had become the lingua franca of the Boko Haram insurgents.

The challenge for Buhari, with his passion for education, is how to restructure the educational system to make better use of all relevant language tools. At the same time, he cannot be seen as favoring "Islamic education." But leaving millions of children behind because they are not bilingual (or trilingual) has never been a good way to lay the groundwork for successful careers.

The challenge for Buhari's educational policy in a federal system, as with his police policy, is how to balance the local, state, and national interests. To do this, especially in the north, he would need professional help from colleagues who were familiar with constitutional issues of federalism and with best practices in education (including the use of modern technology), but who also had a keen sensitivity as to what was possible politically. In addition, Buhari would need to spend considerable political capital to foster his passion for the education of girls.

There would be keen interest in Buhari's appointment of minister of education, Adamu Adamu, a well-known journalist from Bauchi. One of the close associates of Adamu is Dr. Usman Bugaje, from Katsina State, who had been a lecturer in pharmacology at Ahmadu Bello University, and has a PhD in Islamic studies. He had run for governor of Katsina State in 2007, on an opposition ticket, but was beaten by a PDP candidate. He has been an associate of Buhari's for more than thirty years.

As mentioned in chapter 1, Barewa College was the premier educational institution for the first generation of northern leaders in independent Nigeria. The Barewa Old Boys Association (BOBA) has been the informal core of the northern elite, with BOBA's members including the 1950s northern teachers and professionals. On October 10, 2015, Dr. Bugaje gave the annual lecture to BOBA in Kaduna, entitled "Prudent Management of Nigeria's Natural Resources for the Development of the Nation." He discussed the "oil curse" and also the need for a knowledge-driven future:

> Unfortunately, we have spent so much time talking about oil. In the twenty-first century, knowledge, rather than oil, is the greatest capital. Oil is not only a fading resource; it is as we have seen, a problematic resource. The world is moving on into the knowledge industry. Many here will recall that in the seventies the face of wealth was an "oil shaykh." Today, the richest man on earth, Bill Gates, has nothing to do with oil; he sells software, a product of creativity and which is the essence of knowledge. The world has so changed that hard work, as we used to know it, does not work; it is smart work that works. The earlier we realize that oil is part of our past, and not a very glorious one at that, and that knowledge holds our future, the better for us. We have to make a total paradigm shift from oil to knowledge, from a dark past to a brighter future, from hard work to smart work. This entails a heavy investment in human capital development, especially education. . . . Today, we have no chance to survive and thrive except through knowledge. (Usman Bugaje, "Prudent Management of Nigeria's Natural Resources for Development of the Nation," typescript, October 10, 2015, pp. 9–10)

Dr. Bugaje was speaking for many of the elites in the north (and elsewhere), who were aware that the first generation of northern leaders were teachers, including Northern Premier Ahmadu Bello and Federal Prime Minister Abubakar Tafawa Balewa. How Buhari would tap into this reservoir of human capital, which had a moral as well as a knowledge component, might well determine the fate of his presidency.

Chapter 12

Political Change

Revealing the enduring influence of his military training, Buhari is a "by the rules" type of leader. The rules in 2015 were the 160 pages of the Fourth Republic's Constitution. The political change that Buhari was trying to achieve was getting the country back to the basics of Nigeria's democratic federalism—in short, getting Nigeria back on track politically.

Thus, if the rules required submitting names of ministerial nominees to the president of the Senate, Buhari would do so even if that person was under indictment for lying in his declaration of assets. It would be up to the courts, a coequal branch of government, to weigh evidence of wrongdoing. The executive branch would respect the legislative and the judicial branches, and not try to run roughshod over them.

The idea of a constitution-based framework for politics would run up against an evolved old-boy system in which "moneybags" could achieve almost anything the power brokers desired, including the outcome of elections. In a petro-state, most of the money came from the central government.

Thus, for example, in 2014 when the legislature of Adamawa State consisted mainly of APC followers, the PDP president could fly them to Abuja and make it financially worthwhile for them not only to switch their allegiance to the PDP, but also to return to Yola and impeach the vocal APC governor, who would be charged with crimes and have to go into exile.

The "do or die" Nigerian slogan representing Fourth Republic political culture did not refer solely to incumbents, although they held the levers of power. The APC was a coalition of four major parties or factions: the CPC, the AC, the ANPP, plus the "new PDP" (i.e., those who had decamped from the PDP to the APC), and components of the APGA. As such, even with Buhari as the standard-bearer, many of the APC governors were old hands at playing hardball politics in back rooms. Would Buhari's election turn out to be a case of "the more things change, the more they stay the same"?

The "do or die" politics also pertained to the election process of 2015. With the principled integrity of INEC chair Attahiru Jega making it harder for incumbents to rig outcomes, other incumbent strategies came into play to make sure that the opposition party would once again lose the election.

At a media summit in Lagos in mid-October, 2015, Buhari was represented by his senior special assistant on media and publicity, Garba Shehu, who commented on the 2014–15 electoral process from the perspective of the opposition at the time:

> Muhammadu Buhari's goodwill greetings to you are on account of the fact that he won an election many people thought he was not going to win. . . . Americans say that elections are won on the dollar. It's very improbable that anybody can win an election without money. We didn't have any advertising money on our campaign. Even when we had [a] little money to spend on advertising, the Nigerian Television Authority [NTA] was not making slots available to us. . . .
>
> I remember on a particular night I called NTA, they had 16 slots of one-minute adverts and I said I wanted to buy one minute for the Buhari campaign; they said all 16 had been sold. Some other instances that exposed the partisan nature of NTA was when money was returned to us. . . . They simply won't advertise for us.

Garba Shehu went on to talk about the role played by the security services during the campaign:

> The day there was a security siege at my home, I woke up to see that my house had been surrounded by armed policemen in the course of the campaign. . . . In fact it was the cocking of their guns that woke me and my family members from our sleep, only to discover that tens of policemen, police vehicles, and some other unidentified vehicles darkened our windows around my home. . . .
>
> Of course it was much later that we came to know why they had come. Even the APC Presidential Campaign was penetrated

> by fifth columnists. I will make this confession because a day before that siege we had a meeting with the security committee at which we agreed that we were going to run a story announcing that the National Security Adviser at that time, Mr. Sambo Dasuki, was staging a second coup d'état against Muhammadu Buhari. The former National Security Adviser was involved in a coup that threw out Muhammadu Buhari as military president in 1985.
>
> This time around, all the things that followed, the postponement of the election on account of this and that, and a lot of thinking of the campaign was that this was yet another coup being hatched by the National Security Adviser, and we eventually discovered that this siege on our homes was to pre-empt the story. (http://saharareporters.com/2015/10/16/how-nta-ait-maltreated-us-during-2015-presidential-campaigns-buhari)

Whatever the truth of these allegations, they reflect the high stakes of the 2015 election and the perception that incumbents controlled all the levers of power, from state-owned television to the security forces. The integrity of the process election itself would be the final test as to whether an opposition party had a chance to win. The postelection period would see soul-searching on all sides.

This chapter will sketch some of the political change challenges Buhari faced in his first year in office. These include (1) rediscovering constitutionalism; (2) stabilizing the political party system; (3) learning electoral lessons; and (4) dealing with the main opposition party.

Rediscovering Constitutionalism

The 36 states of Nigeria (plus the Federal Capital Territory) and the 774 local government authorities all have highly specified roles under the Constitution. Some of these roles are exclusive and some are concurrent. The challenge in a petro-state is that most funding comes in through the center and then "trickles down" (or not) to grassroots levels. Very few petro-states have managed to decentralize powers effectively to lower levels of government. But with a population as large as 185 million, the prospect of not decentralizing was ominous, because it would leave many parts of the country feeling left out of the process of government.

For example, as mentioned previously, policing was clearly a federal rather than a state or local matter. There were historical reasons for this centralization in the Fourth Republic. But the tensions that this produced, from the northeast insurgency to the violence in the Delta, indicated the need for a state and local police force to improve community relations and to interact more effectively with grassroots populations.

The vacuum at the community level was being filled by well-organized local vigilante groups. Some vigilantes functioned well in terms of cooperation with the police. Others less so. Despite their colorful clothing, glossy national magazines, and often well-regarded local status, they had no official standing or training. Indeed, because they were not allowed to carry arms, they often became targets of insurgents or other violent extremists.

The idea of creating state and local police forces was part of the APC's manifesto. But it also raised constitutional issues. Buhari would have to figure out a way either to change the Constitution or to work with senior legal advisers to interpret the Constitution in a way that was respectful but also filled the deadly vacuum at the state and local levels. Otherwise, the steady stream of states of emergency could continue, and an ill-prepared military would continue to be forced to intervene.

As with other key provisions of the Constitution, the role of the minister of justice, who also serves as attorney general, would need to be played by someone who was not beholden to partisan needs. It would have to be someone who could guide the country along in its quest for a constitutional order, without being held in ridicule for looking the other way on matters of corruption. If the courts were to serve their constitutional function, they would have to be seen to be independent from the executive branch and the dominant party.

The rediscovery of and respect for constitutionalism required a ministerial cohort familiar with the law. Gone were the days when a military team at the center could simply order change. The legal paradigm was crucial. Hence, the names and occupations of ministerial nominees (listed in chapter 10) were scrutinized for constitutional or legal experience.

This was the first time in Nigerian history that so many lawyers had been on the Federal Executive Council (i.e., the ministerial cabinet). Table 12.1 lists the nominees with legal experience, and it should be remembered that the vice president, Yemi Osinbajo , is a constitutional law professor and that Buhari's chief of staff, Abba Kyari, is a lawyer.

Table 12.1. Ministerial nominees with legal backgrounds

- Lai Mohammed: practiced in the field of human rights
- Abubakar Malami (senior advocate Nigeria); a constitutional lawyer
- Babatunde Fashola (senior advocate Nigeria); former notary public of the Supreme Court of Nigeria
- Adebayo Shittu: active in CPC and APC politics on legal matters
- James Ocholi: national deputy legal adviser to the APC
- Solomon Dalong: represented Plateau State in legal matters
- Aisha Alhassan: former Taraba State attorney general and commissioner of justice
- Dr. Ibe Kachikwu: has master's and doctorate degrees in law from Harvard
- Geoffrey Onyeama: a specialist in trade-related legal agreements
- Udo Udo Udoma: the chair of the Nigerian Securities and Exchange Commission

In addition, some of the key APC governors were constitutional lawyers, including the former PDP Speaker of the House of Assembly, governor of Sokoto State, Aminu Waziri Tambuwal.

Ultimately, the positions of minister of justice and attorney general were filled by Abubakar Malami, who had political as well as legal experience.

Stabilizing the Political Party System

The whole world noticed that Nigeria's election of 2015 produced, for the first time, an opposition party victory. In a historic moment of this magnitude, there were many pitfalls to be avoided. One of the most crucial moments for Nigeria, Africa, and the democratic world was the concession call from Jonathan to Buhari.

This could have gone in a different direction, if Jonathan had decided to contest the election in the courts, which he controlled. The pressures on Jonathan by the United States, the United Kingdom, Germany, and African former heads of state will be described in history books not yet written. But at the time, it was evident that Western diplomats, concerned that any delay in releasing the election results could result in widespread violence and perhaps even civil war, were leaning on Jonathan to remind him that the rules of the game of democratic politics required electoral losers to concede defeat. By the same token, Buhari had to perform the role of a gracious election winner, and declare his intention to serve all his constituents, not just his supporters. Both men fulfilled their roles, but the challenge then became how to incorporate such experiences into future expectations. The key to this would be to improve Nigeria's electoral systems to the point that they would be seen to be free and fair.

This meant having an electoral law that was clear and understandable. Such a law would make clear which parties met legal criteria. It would also set rules of campaigning and election processes that could be adjudicated quickly and fairly. It would mean that the National Assembly or president could not use budget cut threats to ensure incumbent advantage.

It also meant that impeachments of governors or the president could not be done capriciously, thwarting the will of the electorate. It also meant clarifying the immunity clauses of the Constitution so that incumbents could be held responsible for their actions.

In short, it meant that the election of 2015 would set a precedent for future party behavior, and not simply be an aberration from Nigeria's underlying political culture. The key to this shift in political culture would be the tone set at the top by President Buhari himself.

If the primary purpose of political parties in a democratic system is to win elections, then their subsequent purpose is to govern. Normally, in a parliamentary system, the leader of the dominant party becomes the prime minister, and he or she selects a cabinet best equipped to manage the various ministries and participate in the overall governance of the party.

In a presidential system, the various demographic and regional components of a winning coalition or single party make their claims on representation in the president's cabinet, which is usually confirmed by a portion of the legislative branch, such as a senate. In the Nigerian presidential model, the president is constitutionally constrained to have a cabinet in which each of the component states is represented.

This means that the cabinet should contain a minimum of thirty-six persons, and it often contains many more; in the Jonathan administration, for instance, the cabinet sometimes had no fewer than seventy-two persons. There are not seventy-two ministries in Nigeria, and so many cabinet ministers are "ministers of state" who can act as junior ministers. This large number also allows for a larger degree of political representation or patronage.

In a party such as the APC, which is a coalition of component parts, the natural tendency would be to have a large number of ministers. This situation is complicated by the fact that each state is served by three senators, each representing a distinct zone, often labeled A, B, and C. Depending on the state, there may be a rotation system so that each zone gets equal treatment in state and national government allotments of budget and political benefits.

Yet another complication is presented by the fact that many people move around, either for employment purposes or via marriage. Indeed, many of the most qualified personnel in any given state may recently have been living and working outside the country, and may not be well known in their original home state.

Finally, ministers are subject to constitutional requirements and prohibitions. Thus, certain kinds of criminal convictions or even formal indictments at the state level may delay or prevent a ministerial nominee from getting Senate confirmation. The scope for state-level partisan politics to be used to disrupt confirmation—especially of individuals who have decamped to the opposition party—is immense.

All of the preceding circumstances came into play in trying to put together a Buhari cabinet. Moreover, Buhari had pledged to cut the size of his cabinet as a way of maximizing scarce budget funds. The only way that gridlock could be prevented was for the presidential party to also control the Senate. Fortunately for Buhari, this was the case when he came to office, although the political complexities were endless, especially because he had promised to encourage the participation of women and to use competence, not politics, as his top criterion for selection.

Although this complexity was filled with frustration on many fronts, the fact that Buhari had made a career attacking corruption, promoting austerity, and encouraging competence allowed him to retain popular support throughout this process. Needless to say, many of the political forces in each state were quick to protest the nominees from their states, often taking their appeals directly to Buhari. The precedent of withdrawing the nominee from Niger

State—on the grounds that the state already had several high-ranking leaders from his zone—opened the floodgates for other states to make similar appeals.

Meanwhile, ordinary people, as well as the international community, were getting impatient. Where was the change they had been promised? But this was the Nigerian political system at work, and if there were to be changes, the Constitution would have to be amended or at least reinterpreted on such basic matters as to who was an "indigene" and who was a "settler" in each state.

Buhari would not be rushed on such matters. Certainly, a military regime could have made quick decisions. But in the Nigerian context, military rule was not a stable solution. Too often, coups led to countercoups or assassinations. In one case, it led to a civil war. Patience was now a virtue, even though the challenges facing Buhari were enormous, and many required urgent attention. Reforming Nigerian political culture would be a long-term project. One political system issue, however, could not wait, because there were a number of state elections the courts had mandated to be rerun. This was the ongoing challenge in a democratic system of running free and fair elections. What were the lessons of the remarkable elections of 2015?

Learning Electoral Lessons

The main lesson from the 2015 elections is that the system worked! The Independent National Electoral Commission was able to function independently, despite political pressures, personal threats, and an unstable environment in the northeast. The reasons that it worked had to do with leadership courage, personnel training, clear processes, transparency throughout, the use of technology (including social media and voting equipment), and police cooperation. Success also depended crucially on the active participation of thousands of Nigerians who were committed to democratic processes, and on the international community, which had allocated funds and used its diplomatic weight to encourage a fairer than usual election.

None of these factors could be taken for granted in the future. The Electoral Act, as amended in 2014, was clear. In the run-up to the elections, the INEC website was filled with practical advice for candidates and voters. Yet registering millions of potential voters with a permanent voter card that had biometric requirements, staffing more than 150,000 polling booths, arranging for collation centers, managing the INEC center in Abuja, and providing police security at every step were Herculean tasks.

The leadership qualities of the INEC chairman, Professor Attahiru Jega, cannot be overestimated. He finished his five-year term in late June as a hero to many in the country who had been yearning for a free and fair election. His immediate successor, acting chair Amina Bala Zakari from Jigawa State, is a pharmacist by profession. She also has a certificate in business management from Harvard Business School. Clearly, her appointment was a stopgap measure.

On October 21, Buhari appointed Professor Mahmud Yakubu as the new chairman of INEC for a five-year term. Professor Yakubu has extensive experience in university circles and in federal executive appointments. He is widely respected as brilliant, capable, and straightforward. Acting chair Amina Zakari was appointed commissioner representing the northwest.

The major political problems in Fourth Republic elections, however, reside in two areas: the appointment of the zonal and state-level regional electoral commissioners (RECs) and the inability to regulate money. In both cases, the incumbents have enormous advantages. RECs are appointed by the president. The cash-and-carry petro-economy meant that those with power have access to treasuries at all levels.

These practices had been the heart of the electoral fraud and rigging in the past. How Buhari would ensure the independence and integrity of the INEC process in the future would be a test of his commitment to changing the political culture of money politics, with its propensity for corruption.

Dealing with the Main Opposition Party

In a parliamentary democracy, as Nigeria was during the First Republic, there is a clear leader of the opposition party. In a presidential democracy, as Nigeria had become by the Fourth Republic, there is no clear leader of the opposition. With the defeat of the PDP at all levels in the 2015 elections, the question arose as to whether Nigeria would again slip into a dominant-party mode, with the APC controlling all the levers of power. Such a shift in power would have political consequences, because much of the support for the PDP had come from the South East and South-South zones, with their histories of instability.

After his defeat at the polls, former president Jonathan engaged in an extended holiday, and when he reappeared on the Nigerian scene, it was to announce that he was setting up a "Goodluck Jonathan Foundation" to enhance the general welfare. The national chairman of the PDP, Ahmed Adamu Mu'azu, and the chairman of the PDP Board of Trustees, Chief Tony Anenih, both resigned from the party. The acting national chairman of PDP was Prince Oche Secondus from Rivers State.

The highest-ranking PDP elected official was Senator Ike Ekweremadu from Enugu State, who was serving as deputy president of the Senate for the third consecutive term. He has a PhD in law from the University of Abuja. He has served in the Senate since May 2003.

The Senate president is Bukola Saraki, who had been a member of the PDP, but then decamped to the APC. He was the key person in getting Buhari's ministerial nominees confirmed by the Senate, but was facing trial by the Code of Conduct Tribunal on grounds of corruption (to be discussed in chapter 19). Saraki is a medical doctor—and the son of a medical doctor—from Kwara State, and he was governor of that state from 2003 to 2011. In April 2011, he was elected to the Senate. He was elected Senate president on June 9, 2015, succeeding David Mark of the PDP.

Saraki's situation mirrored that of many of the "new-PDP" members of the APC: he had been part of the old order, which many other factions of the APC regarded as corrupt. Would the courts seek to prosecute former PDP senior leaders, or would the tribunals focus on PDP politicians currently in office, along with former officials from the Jonathan administration?

At the national level, as noted above, the most senior PDP politician is Senator Ike Ekweremadu. The spokesman for the PDP was the acting national chair, Oche Secondus. In addition, the PDP governors who had been elected in 2015 remain an obvious power base within the party. The question is whether that power base was national or regional. Ekweremadu is from the South East (Enugu) and Secondus is from South-South (Rivers).

Table 12.2 shows the zonal distribution of nine PDP governors elected in 2015.

Table 12.2. The zonal distribution of the nine PDP governors elected in 2015

South East zone
- Abia State: Okekie Ikpeazu
- Enugu State: Ifeanyi Ugwuanyi
- Ebonyi State: Dave Umuahi

South-South zone
- Akwa Ibom State: Udom Emmanuel
- Cross River State: Benedict Ayade
- Delta State: Ifeanyi Okowa
- Rivers State: Nyesom Wike

North East zone
- Gombe State: Ibrahim Dankwambo
- Taraba State: Darius Ishaku

The ethnoreligious profiles of the new PDP governors, plus their national leaders, were clear to all: predominantly southern ethnic minorities, plus Igbo in the east, and predominantly Christian. The challenge for the PDP would be to try to regain its national scope, rather than becoming a regional party. Could the PDP regain its standing in the north? Or had all the major politicians in that area decamped to the APC? What about the two former opposition governors who had decamped to the PDP (Bafarawa and Shekarau)? Time would tell.

Thus, of the twenty-nine governors elected in 2015, nineteen are APC, including the governors elected in the North West and North Central zones, and most of the governors in the South West zone, plus the far northern portions of the North East zone. Most are Hausa-Fulani or Yoruba; some belong to other predominantly Muslim northern minorities. The challenge for Buhari would be to make good on his inaugural promise: "I belong to everybody and I belong to nobody." How would PDP politicians from Rivers State react to the ministerial nomination of Rotimi Amaechi, the former

PDP governor who was the first major politician to decamp to the APC?

Of major political importance to the future of Nigeria as a predominantly two-party democratic system is the PDP leadership's response to their party's role reversal. On October 15, the National Executive Committee (NEC) of the PDP issued a communiqué that stated, among other things, the following: "7. NEC assures that the PDP will continue to ensure credible issue-based opposition as well as strict adherence to democratic tenets and the supremacy of the constitution of the Federal Republic of Nigeria. 8. NEC reassures on the repositioning of the party to regain its preeminence in the polity and return to power at the center come 2019."

The full speech by Prince Uche Secondus to the NEC was positive in tone and forward-looking. He called for "training and mobilizing our legislators to excel in their new role as the leading opposition Party." He called for the party to reinvent itself and respect "the sanctity of the zoning principle." He called for "reconciliation." He claimed that "the PDP brand is still dear to the hearts of the majority of Nigerians because it is the only national party" (http://peoplesdemocraticparty.com.ng/?p=2515).

While the PDP elders were getting used to their role in opposition after sixteen years in power, trouble began brewing in the South East and South-South zones. In the South-South, many Ijaw militants—such as Dokubo Asari—are calling for independence from Nigeria. The amnesty program in that area—meant to provide education and training to militants who turned in their weapons—would run out in December, and tensions were mounting among militants. Meanwhile, in the South East and parts of the South-South, supporters of an independent Biafra were becoming more active. According to one media report:

> Biafran-flag-waving protestors stormed the streets of Port Harcourt, Rivers State, southern Nigeria, over the continuous detention of Mazi Nnamdi Kanu, the director of the pirate radio, Radio Biafra. The protest paralysed commercial activities in the oil rich city as the procession made its way towards the Government House. . . . The founder of the Indigenous People of Biafra is being held as he is yet to fulfil his bail term of N2million and a "surety" in the same sum, coming from a civil servant of Grade level 16. His arrest had provoked criticism from his group and the Movement for the Actualization of the Sovereign State of

> Biafra, MASSOB. . . . Kanu, leader of the Indigenous People of Biafra (IPOB) is selective to delicacies . . . he vowed never to eat food served by the Federal Government of Nigeria. (http://saharareporters.com/2015/10/20/biafrans-protest-port-harcourt)

Buhari was thus facing not only the challenge of insurrection by Boko Haram in the northeast, but also the increasing disaffection of grassroots political forces in the South East and South-South. Security forces would need to be active in areas. Would those forces also involve international components, as is the case in fighting Boko Haram?

Experienced statesmen would be required to handle these political challenges. Buhari would need to rely on APC political links in the southern zones, such as ties to Amaechi (of Rivers State) and Governor Okorocha (of Imo State). He would also need the cooperation of PDP stalwarts from the area. Fortunately, the entire senior cadre of the PDP was fully committed to the unity of Nigeria, and thus would be prepared to cooperate with him to defeat existential threats to the country.

Buhari had achieved several policy objectives during his first seven months in office, including phasing out amnesty for Delta militants and trying to engage militants. He also tried to consolidate links with both APC and PDP governors. But the key to assuaging anger and frustration in the South-South and South East was the selection of a team of disparate but competent cabinet ministers.

CHALLENGES OF IMPLEMENTATION AND CHANGE

Chapter 13

Continuing Challenges of Insurgency and Corruption

In the final quarter of 2015—October, November, and December—the challenges of insurgency and corruption continued. Yet in addition to fighting on the ground in the North East and the increased involvement of the international community in containing Boko Haram, Nigerian policy planners turned their attention to the longer-term issues of reconstruction.

The efforts against the insurgency in the North East, however, were complicated by the emerging "troubles" in the South East, with the symbols of "Biafra" growing more visible and grassroots pressures for greater autonomy growing. Some of these pressures were also evident in the South-South, as a proposed "million man march" organized by dissident youth across the Niger River called attention to discontent in the broader Niger Delta zone.

Driving both active and latent insurrection movements was the fact that Nigerian budget constraints were extreme, due to the low price of oil and the depletion of the treasury by the outgoing administration. In short, there was less money for amnesty programs and reconstruction efforts.

Finally, impacting both the passive support for insurgencies and the amount of budget funding available to counter these threats was the continuing battle against corruption at all levels. Unless corruption could be curbed—and could be seen to be curbed—and unless some of the looted funds could be returned to the treasury, little could be done to counter insurgencies. The international community would be forthcoming with counterinsurgency funds only if it was confident that the funds would be used appropriately.

This chapter will focus on four themes that were center stage in the final quarter of 2015: (1) the continuing challenge of Boko Haram; (2) the development of a national plan for reconstruction in the northeast; (3) the prospect of a politically resurgent Biafra; and (4) the continuing challenge of corruption. These were major issues that Buhari had been elected to tackle, and by the end of 2015, expectations for effective action were growing.

The Continuing Challenge of Boko Haram

President Buhari's first and foremost challenge was Boko Haram. This was not something that could be delegated to senior officers, no matter how capable they might be. Presidential action was required. And the president had already taken action: the service chiefs had been replaced and the center of the operations had been moved to Maiguduri. But what about strategy, professionally one of Buhari's strong points? What was Buhari doing to develop a more effective strategy to combat Boko Haram?

From outward appearances, the major elements of the Buhari strategy were as follows: strengthen credible military and political leadership at all levels; restore morale and logistical support to the troops, including improving the welfare of the troops and their families; regain and hold all lost territory; provide more effective countermeasures against lone-wolf suicide bombers by improving grassroots intelligence; partner with regional and international allies and secure international resources; and begin the process of policy planning for reconstruction in the devastated areas of the northeast. The first five of these strategic components are discussed in this section; the sixth, reconstruction, is discussed in the following section.

Toward the end of October, the governor of Borno State, Kashim Shettima, reported that Boko Haram was still in control of two local government areas (LGAs), Abbadam and Mobar, and in partial control of a third, Marte. The governor also reported that in 2014 Boko Haram had overrun twenty of the twenty-seven LGAs in Borno State. The insurgents had also overrun seven LGAs in Adamawa and two in Yobe.

Chief of Army Staff Lieutenant General Buratai disputed that any areas were still under Boko Haram control, although he acknowledged that it was a fluid situation. He personally visited his troops on the front lines in an effort to improve morale. He also promised to ensure that their salaries were paid.

But the number of suicide attacks was not decreasing, despite the increased efforts of the military (and local vigilantes). Nigerian fighter planes and ground troops were driving Boko Haram insurgents out of their strongholds in the towns and villages, but the borders with Cameroon and Chad were porous, and the insurgents were regrouping. The battle zone thus widened. Female suicide bombers were now attacking villages in Chad and Cameroon.

The need among Nigeria's neighbors for military surveillance planes was met by the United States at the end of October. The Niger Republic received not only two Cessna C-208 planes but also thirty military vehicles and ambulances. Similar efforts to ramp up surveillance in northern Cameroon were also under way.

Meanwhile, President Buhari visited New Delhi on October 27–30 for the Third India-Africa Forum Summit. Bilateral meetings were held between Buhari and Prime Minister Narendra Modi to strengthen ties on several fronts, including economic and military ones. The commandant of the Defence Services Staff College at Wellington, which Buhari had attended in 1972 and 1973, paid a social visit and reminded Buhari that his report at the time characterized him as "sober and balanced. Straightforward, simple and mature. . . . Buhari is a quiet, unassuming and honest individual" (http://saharareporters.com/2015/10/30/passage-india-femi-adesina).

Buhari's early training abroad was helping him to garner support for the struggle with Boko Haram insurgencies at home. To make an impact at home, however, he would need a hearts-and-minds approach as well as good intelligence, weapons, morale, and allies.

A National Plan for Reconstruction in the Northeast

While Buhari was in India, Vice President Osinbajo flew to Maiduguri to open the North-East Humanitarian Multi-Stakeholder

Engagement (NEHMSE) Conference. Participants included the National Emergency Management Agency (NEMA), the Presidential Initiative for the North East (PINE), the Victim Support Fund (VSF), and the Save the Schools Initiative (SSI). The meetings were also attended by the governors of Adamawa, Borno, and Yobe, and the deputy governors of Bauchi, Gombe, and Taraba, plus the shehus of Borno and Bama.

According to an editorial printed on November 1, 2015, in the *Daily Trust*:

> Vice President Professor Yemi Osinbajo was in Maiduguri last week where he attended a two-day Humanitarian Multi-Stakeholder engagement with the theme "Coordination, Communication and Cooperation." He seized the opportunity to unveil a five-year Marshall Plan for the reconstruction of the North East, which has been ravaged by six years of the Boko Haram insurgency. . . .
>
> He said: "The tasks before us are many and profound, to fix brick and mortar and to mend hearts and minds damaged by senseless, murderous violence. But we are called not just to mend the hearts and minds of the victims but also of their traducers and killers. The young men and women who have been brainwashed to kill, maim and destroy in the warped belief that by so doing they please God. ". . .
>
> At the launch, Chairman of the Presidential Committee on North East Intervention, General Theophilus Danjuma (rtd) said the Federal Government will spend N233 billion on post-insurgency reconstruction and rehabilitation of the affected communities. He said N97 billion is to be spent on short-term measures while another N116 billion is to be spent on a medium-term plan to assist victims of the insurgency to restart their businesses. . . .
>
> Similarly, in July, this year the World Bank had pledged during a meeting with President Buhari in Washington that it will spend $2.1 billion on rebuilding infrastructure in the northeast. The funds will be spent through the World Bank's International Development Agency in the form of low-interest loans, which will be interest-free for the first ten years and then accrue at a below market rate thereafter. (http://dailytrust.com.ng/news/editorial/as-rebuilding-north-east-begins/117330.html)

In short, the federal government of Nigeria and its agencies, state governors, civil society organizations, and the international community had begun to develop plans for the reconstruction of the northeast after the defeat of Boko Haram. Rebuilding the infrastructure of the area and giving start-up business grants will be critical components of reconstruction (and require that the pledges of financial assistance are in fact redeemed), but no less important will be efforts to heal the psychological and social wounds of violence.

The Prospect of a Politically Resurgent Biafra

The 2011 and 2015 presidential elections revealed overwhelming support in the South East zone for Goodluck Jonathan, and the campaigns in that area sought to raise suspicions of Buhari's "real" intentions and to vilify him personally. After the 2015 election, the leadership of the PDP resided largely in the hands of politicians from the South East and adjoining states in the South-South. They were now "the opposition." Although most of those leaders accepted this new reality, some of the youth in those parts of the country had a hard time adjusting to a Buhari presidency, the lack of national and local resources, and the status of now being in opposition.

By selecting some individuals from the South East and South-South for key appointments in his government, Buhari helped to reduce apprehensions among some South East and South-South politicians that the new president would punish those parts of the country for their support of Jonathan. Buhari's commitment to pursuing corruption cases through the courts also helped allay fears that his anticorruption drive might become politically motivated. Even so, suspicions and resentment remained, and helped to fuel potentially secessionist sentiments.

Discontent came to a head with the detention of Nnamdi Kanu of Radio Biafra when he returned from London to Lagos on October 19. Kanu, who has dual citizenship—British and Nigerian—was arrested for sedition and jailed in Abuja, sparking sympathy protests in Nigeria and abroad. In Bayelsa State, eighty-three members of the Biafra Movement were arrested.

This situation led the British High Commission to issue a statement clarifying its position on the whole Biafran affair, including the case of Kanu. As reported in the media:

> "The British government does not support the agitation for a separate nation of Biafra. . . . The UK Government's position, which reflected the Charter of the Organization of African Unity, was to recognize the borders laid down at independence. . . . The Biafran War caused great suffering and the UK sup-

> ported the reconciliation work that followed the conflict. The UK supports the territorial integrity of Nigeria and President Buhari's commitment to work for a secure and prosperous Nigeria for all Nigerians. "...
>
> The British High Commission also noted that in cases of dual citizens, "the British government only provides consular assistance to dual nationals in the country of their other nationality in exceptional circumstances." (http://saharareporters.com/2015/11/03/british-government-does-not-support-biafra-agitators-high-commission-says)

In France, Kanu's sympathizers posted videos showing themselves tearing up their Nigerian passports. Some of them claimed to have registered in France as "indigenous people of Biafra." The Nigerian Immigration Service, in turn, reminded such persons that the Immigration Act of 2015 provides for a prison term of three years and/or a two million naira fine for destroying Nigerian travel documents (http://saharareporters.com/2015/10/25/pro-biafra-activists-tear-nigerian-passports).

With scarce government resources being promised to reconstruct the northeast, some cynics in the southeast may have wondered if a "crisis" in the southeast could also bring additional budget disbursements. Others may have felt this was a moment of opportunity, given the government's preoccupation with Boko Haram, to create the political conditions for future separation. The mainstream Igbo leaders in the southeast, however, disowned Kanu, and claimed he was pursuing "a personal ambition."

The challenge for the Buhari administration was not to let the issue grow to a point that it might threaten to reignite a largely dormant conflict. The Biafran war had ended in 1970, and what remained of the Movement for the Actualization of the Sovereign State of Biafra (MASSOB) was largely associated with the southeastern diaspora communities in the United States and the United Kingdom. There had been little recent evidence of MASSOB being active inside Nigeria, and certainly the movement did not enjoy the public support of any governors or senior politicians from the southeast. Indeed, General Ojukwu, the leader of the Biafran revolt, had returned from exile and led a political movement to reintegrate the southeast into Nigeria before his death (of natural causes) in November 2011.

The Continuing Challenge of Corruption

In November, another development occurred in the unfolding saga of the former oil minister that was being played out in London and Switzerland. As noted previously, the former petroleum minister, Alison-Madueke, had been arrested in London but was out on bail. She had been working with Kola Aluko, who had Swiss citizenship, on a variety of oil deals. Now the Swiss authorities began to get involved.

Aluko's Atlantic Energy Company was at the center of a controversial $6 billion scheme, which was alleged to have defrauded the Nigerian treasury. He was paying the rent for Alison-Madueke's mother in London, and covering many of the mother's additional expenses. According to the media:

> The UK government has officially filed a Mutual Legal Assistance request seeking to interrogate Mr. Aluko in Switzerland. The *Sunday Times* reported that the request has now been sent to the Swiss Attorney General for implementation. Another Nigerian involved in the multibillion scam, Jide Omokore, has reportedly offered to refund $500 million to the Nigerian government, but his offer has not been accepted by President Muhammadu Buhari, according to a source in the Nigerian Presidency. "President Buhari wants him (Mr. Omokore) to increase the amount he is offering to refund to the country," the source said. (http://saharareporters.com/2015/11/01/fugitive-oil-tycoon-kola-aluko-admits-paying-uk-rent-alison-madueke%E2%80%99s-mother)

Also in November, the Nigerian media was filled with news of former high-ranking officials being investigated for fraud and corruption. For example, the Code of Conduct Bureau arraigned the former minister of Niger Delta, Godsday Orubebe, on counts of bribery and false declarations of assets.

The former minister of finance, Ngozi Okonjo-Iweala, was also subjected to press and civil society scrutiny. A coalition of NGOs called Civil Society Network Against Corruption (CSNAC) raised questions about the allocation of $2.2 million she authorized for the Global Alliance for Vaccine and Immunization (GAVI), given her subsequent appointment as chairperson of GAVI's board (http://www.dailytrust.com.ng/news/general/group-insists-on-okonjo-iweala-s-probe-over-2-2m-gavi-s-refund/117298.html).

Meanwhile, the controversy over the accusations of corruption within the EFCC continued, and seemed to implicate the chairman himself. Also, the issue of the EFCC's possible merger with the Independent Corrupt Practices Commission (ICPC) raised questions about the best means of pursuing overlapping types of corruption. In short, there needed to be some organizational delineation of responsibilities (http://www.dailytrust.com.ng/news/general/icpc-efcc-merger-ll-cripple-anti-graft-war-machine-nta/117315.html).

Even the issue of large-scale tax evasion by major companies came under scrutiny, especially by investigative reporters. Fake "shell companies" and offshore tax havens made front page copy, as in the case of the major telephone company MTN, which was using MTN Dubai and MTN International in Mauritius to facilitate "transfer pricing" to lower tax zones and hence apparently avoiding Nigerian tax liabilities. Whether this was legal would be up to the courts (http://saharareporters.com/2015/10/26/how-mtn-smuggles-billions-shell-companies-abroad-evade-tax-nigeria).

Another kind of fraud, electoral fraud, came under special scrutiny by President Buhari himself. At the swearing in of new members of INEC in November, Buhari is quoted as saying:

> Another area of concern is the justice administration of the electoral tribunals. It is long overdue that our justice system addresses these shortcomings. It is not enough for an election to be cancelled and a new one ordered. It would be much better if all whose actions or inactions led to the cancellation of such an election to be investigated and if culpable prosecuted whether they are individuals such as candidates or party agents, institutions such as political parties, electoral bodies, or public officers such as electoral staff or security agents. (http://www.dailytrust.com.ng/news/politics/buhari-wants-punishment-for-election-offenders/118544.html)

Buhari's anticorruption message was clearly having an impact. International actors were pursuing cases of alleged corruption by former Nigerian officials. At home, the media and civil society organizations were investigating and spotlighting various forms of corruption. Administratively, proposals to restructure the government's anticorruption bodies were being weighed. And at the heart of the new administration, Buhari's nominees for ministerial positions had been vetted and had declared their assets. The ministers were inaugurated on November 11. The question now was whether his team of ministers could be effective in implementing the kind of change and providing the kind of leadership that Buhari had promised.

Chapter 14

Team Building and Change

On November 5 and 6, Buhari held a two-day retreat for his ministers-designate. The theme of the retreat was "Delivering Change: From Precepts to Practice." The purpose was to familiarize everyone with the policies of the administration and to provide an update on the economic situation. It was also a team-building exercise.

A few days later, on November 11, Buhari officially inaugurated his Federal Executive Council (i.e., his cabinet). The allocation of portfolios followed immediately. After more than five months, the team had been vetted and was in place. This chapter will discuss the following topics: (1) the ministerial team and mandate; (2) the challenges of implementing change; (3) the realities of a petro-state; and (4) the Buhari leadership factor.

The Ministerial Team and Its Mandate

After the initial nominations for ministers were submitted in late September and early October, the vetting process commenced, along with strategic assessments of how best to deploy the team. As noted previously, the challenge was to balance experience and competence with zonal and state representation.

The inaugural ceremony for the ministers was held in Abuja and broadcast live on national television. Attendees included President Buhari, Vice President Yemi Osinbajo, Senate President Bukola Saraki, and Speaker Yakubu Dogara. Ministers swore their oaths of office on either a Qur'an or a Bible, depending on the person's faith.

Their ministerial assignments were also announced. The number of ministries had been reduced to twenty-three. In addition, eighteen permanent secretaries were retired and new ones announced. (The Joda Committee had gone even further. It had recommended reducing the number of ministries to nineteen, and scrapping all ministries, departments, and agencies not mandated by law.)

Table 14.1 shows the final picture of ministerial appointments by zone. Significantly, Buhari reserved the petroleum ministry for himself, with Ibe Kachikwu (from Delta State) as his state minister. Each of the six zones had at least one state minister. Each zone also had at least one "power" minister—that is, a minister in charge of a ministry with high international visibility or special significance (indicated with an asterisk in table 14.1).

The mandate for the new ministers and permanent secretaries was clear. They were to implement the APC agenda and manifesto. They were to run the ministries efficiently and effectively with no hint of scandal. They were to work in unison across ministries. Together, they would implement the changes promised during the election.

Table 14.1. Buhari's ministerial team by zone (November 2015)

Zone and State	Name	Minister/State Minister (S.M.)
South East		
Abia	Okechukwu Enelamah	Industry, Trade and Investment*
Anambra	Chris Ngige	Labour and Employment
Ebonyi	Ogbonnaya Onu	Science and Technology
Enugu	Geoffrey Onyeama	Foreign Affairs*
Imo	Anthony Onwuka	S.M. Education
South-South		
Akwa Ibom	Udo Udo Udoma	Budget and National Planning*
Bayelsa	Heineken Lokpobiri	S.M. Agriculture
Cross River	Usani Usani Uguru	Niger Delta
Delta	Ibe Kachikwu	S.M. Petroleum
Edo	Osagie Ehanire	S.M. Health
Rivers	Rotimi Amaechi	Transportation and Aviation*
South West		
Ekiti	Kayode Fayemi	Solid Minerals
Lagos	Babatunde Fashola	Power, Works and Housing*
Ogun	Kemi Adeosun	Finance*
Ondo	Claudius Daramola	S.M. Niger Delta
Osun	Isaac Adewole Folorunsho	Health
Oyo	Adebayo Shittu	Communication

North Central		
Benue	Audu Ogbeh	Agriculture*
Kogi	James Ocholi	S.M. Labour and Employment
Kwara	Lai Mohammed	Information
Nasarawa	Ibrahim Usman Jibril	S.M. Environment
Niger	Abubakar Bwari Bawa	S.M. Solid Minerals
Plateau	Solomon Dalong	Youth and Sport
North East		
Adamawa	Muhammadu Bello	Federal Capital Territory*
Bauchi	Adamu Adamu	Education*
Borno	Mustapha Shehuri	S.M. Power, Works and Housing
Gombe	Amina Mohammed	Environment
Taraba	Aisha Alhassan	Women Affairs
Yobe	Khadija Bukar Abba	S.M. Foreign Affairs
North West		
Jigawa	Suleiman Adamu	Water Resources
Kaduna	Zainab Ahmed	S.M. Budget and Planning
Kano	Abdulrahman Dambazau	Interior*
Katsina	Hadi Sirika	S.M. Transport (Aviation)
Kebbi	Abubakar Malami	Justice*
Sokoto	Aisha Abubakar	S.M. Industry, Trade and Investment
Zamfara	Mansur Dan Ali	Defence*

The Challenges of Implementing Change

The overarching challenge of implementing change, apart from the newness of the ministerial team, was the severely constrained budget. In late April, after the election but prior to the swearing-in of the new administration, the Senate passed a national 2015 budget.

This budget assumed a benchmark price for oil of $53 per barrel. (The benchmark for the 2014 budget had been $77.5 per barrel.) The Senate passed a N4.49 trillion ($23 billion) budget, which was 3.2 percent smaller than the 2014 budget. It assumed an exchange rate of 190 naira to the US dollar. The oil production estimate was 2.2782 million barrels per day.

The 2015 inherited budget deficit was N1.075 trillion. This was to be paid for by domestic borrowing of N750 billion, plus N255 billion from other sources, such as the sale of government properties and proceeds from the privatization of such properties.

By November 2015, the situation was even more dire. The price of light sweet crude was well below $50 per barrel. Inflation in Nigeria was increasing. The naira moved to a high of more than

300 naira per dollar. The world glut of oil meant that international oil and gas companies operating in Nigeria were cutting back on capital expenditures and even staffing. With oil revenues having dropped by 50 percent since 2014, there was little prospect of attracting new investment in the oil industry.

The managing director of Shell Petroleum Development Company called for a renegotiation of terms with the Nigerian government. The managing director of ExxonMobil criticized the government's tendering process. The chairperson of the Oil Producer Trade Section of the Lagos Chamber of Commerce and Industry called for the cancellation of infrastructure projects in the country.

Business interests in oil-related areas were pressing the Nigerian government to pass the Petroleum Industry Bill, restructure finances, remove subsidies on petroleum products, and explore Asian markets. In the final year of the Jonathan administration, a report from PricewatehouseCoopers, an internationally respected financial advisory firm, had issued "Fit for $50 Oil in Africa: Will the Boom Go Bust?" The document called for budget austerity measures. It also called attention to the murky world of the Nigerian oil industry. The report was ignored by Jonathan.

Meanwhile, the NNPC was calling for government investment in a number of capital projects that had been languishing. These included the Nigerian Liquefied Natural Gas project, which held the promise of securing a larger market share for Nigeria in the global natural gas market and the resuscitation and rehabilitation of domestic refineries, aging pipelines, and product depots.

The central role of petroleum revenues in the Nigerian budget, coupled with the projected long-term global drop in oil prices and the murkiness of the business practices of the Jonathan administration, meant that Buhari had to provide the kind of leadership that would quickly get Nigeria back on track economically. In part, this challenge required an assessment of Nigeria's condition as a petro-state and a consideration of diversification options.

The Realities of a Petro-State

Many of the challenges facing Nigeria in the oil sector reflect the realities of being a petro-state and thus depending, to an extreme degree, on a single product to sustain the economy. Coping with the inevitable boom and bust cycles of the oil industry, plus the structural changes in Nigeria's NNPC, requires a political and fiscal budget discipline that is all too uncommon. Petro-states are usually rated as "highest risk" (both politically and as investment prospects) by global risk management companies.

The essential nature of an oil economy is that it is global. Nigeria is a member of the Organization of the Petroleum Exporting Countries (OPEC). It is bound by the rules of this cartel, although in the past the quotas have been "bent" by barter practices between Nigeria and various Latin American countries that could supply foodstuffs, raw materials, equipment, and other products in exchange for crude oil.

A petro-state economy is by its nature "centralized," because oil royalties come in through the central government. Even in federal systems, revenues accrue to the center and then are disbursed to the various states within the larger system, creating a sort of federal trickle-down effect.

The oil industry is also technology intensive rather than labor intensive. Hence, it is not likely to generate a large number of jobs, except for "protection" arrangements by local militias, who often have their own agendas. If jobs are to be achieved, they may be in the upstream or downstream sectors, but even there, they may require high levels of technical training.

Also, by its nature oil is fungible (i.e., completely exchangeable for cash) and hence is susceptible to "bunkering," with stolen supplies being sold on international spot markets, such as Rotterdam. No foolproof method of "fingerprinting" oil has yet been discovered, so bunkered oil cannot be identified.

The corruption scandals in the Nigerian oil industry were complicated by the country's land tenure arrangements. According to the Nigerian Constitution, all land is "Crown land," in the British tradition. Rights of usage (the legal term is "usufruct") depend on land laws, and usually involve long-term use agreements. Also, all subsoil minerals (including oil) belong to the Nigerian federal state.

This constitutional reality has been a point of contention between the central government and local oil-producing areas, which feel that the oil under "their land" belongs to them. Hence, when locals choose to tap into the pipelines of oil companies, they feel they are really just reclaiming their rights. This issue been ongoing for decades, and the constitutional compromise has been to allocate extra federal budget funds to states producing the oil. The exact formula, however, has been contentious.

More broadly, some small OPEC countries, such as Kuwait and Qatar, have set up investment funds—on which they have drawn to finance the acquisition of overseas property—as a hedge against oil dependency. A country with a large population, such as Nigeria, is under pressure to use oil royalties to meet current revenue needs and does not have the luxury of setting funds aside to cushion it from the effects of future downturns in oil prices. The challenge for Nigeria has been to diversify so that it is not so dependent on a single resource. And diversification—into agriculture, solid minerals, infrastructure, and so forth—requires firm and clear-sighted political leadership

The low prices of oil at the time President Buhari inaugurated his cabinet were seen by some as both a danger and an opportunity. The danger was that Buhari had been elected to produce "change," which in the eyes of many voters meant providing economic opportunities for those at the grassroots levels and not just for those at the top. If these expectations were not met, Nigeria's political system might become perilously unstable.

The opportunity was that low oil prices made it more feasible to introduce austerity policies that could eliminate the kind of waste in the economy (such as a bloated civil service and exorbitant housing allowances) that might not be so objectionable in the good times. Low oil prices also meant that the diversification of the economy could be seen as a clear and urgent need.

Diversification required a restructuring of the educational system. The APC election manifesto had emphasized education. Buhari had spent his entire career encouraging education. The educational challenge was especially acute in the north. The good news was that the international community was willing to help Nigeria improve its educational system. The bad news, however, was that education reform would take time to implement and produce results; the immediate and complex realities of the global oil and gas industries had to be addressed without delay.

What were the specific global petroleum realities when Buhari announced his cabinet on November 11? According to projections by the *Wall Street Journal* published the day before:

> December crude oil settled up 34 cents, or .8%, to $44.21 a barrel on the New York Mercantile Exchange. Brent, the global benchmark, gained 25 cents, or .05%, to $47.44 a barrel on ICE Futures Europe. Both snapped a four-session losing streak. . . .
>
> World Energy Outlook said: "a lasting switch in OPEC production strategy in favor of around $50 a barrel [is expected] through the end of the decade" . . .
>
> Market watchers expect OPEC will stick to that strategy and keep its output target unchanged at the organization's next meeting on Dec. 4 in Vienna. . . .
>
> Meanwhile, there are signs that Saudi Arabia, OPEC's largest member, is taking the battle for market share to Europe. Riyadh has recently lowered its selling prices for Europe and started supplying crude to Sweden and Poland in a direct challenge to Russia, which sees Europe as one of its main markets. . . .
>
> The EIA on Monday said it expects U.S. shale oil production to fall by 118,000 to less than 4.95 million barrels a day in December. . . . Analysts at Commerzbank said in a report, "At present, the prices are too low for many shale oil producers." (http://www.wsj.com/articles/oil-prices-fluctuate-as-iea-warns-opec-over-strategy-1447152940)

With falling oil prices and the growing potential of shale gas and oil to reduce the demand for conventional oil imports, Nigerian leaders could afford to waste no time in considering their options within OPEC, and also their diversification strategies. Even Saudi Arabia was in the process of developing a diversification strategy, while removing an oil production freeze within OPEC to retain its market share.

Within this macro context, there was some irony to the fact that the presidency of OPEC for the year 2015 had rotated (it does so alphabetically) to Nigeria. But the president of OPEC, Alison-Madueke, was under arrest in London. Instead, it would be up to Buhari to sort out this complex drama. In 2015, Minister of State for Petroleum Resources Ibe Kachikwu was designated to represent Nigeria in OPEC.

(Note: In spring 2016, Buhari would nominate Dr. M. S. Barkindo a close associate of Dr. Rilwanu Lukman's in the pre-Jonathan era, to be OPEC secretary general in Vienna. Barkindo was elected unanimously by the OPEC members to that position on June 2, 2016. Nigeria was seen as neutral in the tensions between Saudi Arabia and Iran, which was just emerging from international sanctions. Thus, Nigeria would be represented within OPEC at the highest levels by two trusted associates of Buhari's. It would regain its status as a significant and trustworthy international energy producer.)

The Buhari Leadership Factor

From the perspective of many Buhari supporters, Buhari had always been a team player. Colleagues recall that Buhari exhibited these characteristics since his early days of military training. They also recall him as a "long-distance runner" with the persistence to never give up. But could he manage the challenges of a collapsing oil economy? Was there time to redirect the Nigerian economy and also manage the implementation of structural changes?

Buhari also prided himself on leading from the front, whether in battle or in politics. Conscious of the deep-seated problem in the petroleum sector, he took personal responsibility by taking on the portfolio of minister of petroleum resources. This leadership quality was recognized by those he had worked with in various political parties, and who continued to nominate him for president. It is also recognized by those at the grassroots level who have placed their trust in him.

In a broader perspective, the challenges of leading a complex democratic nation of more than 180 million people meant that Buhari had to focus on team building and unity of purpose. His military and governmental assignments over the years seemed to have prepared him for this task. The new ministerial team consisted of individuals who were not used to working together. They represented different elements of the APC coalition, and some as well who had professional careers outside of politics.

The "Baba go slow" nickname for Buhari reflected the care that went into the selection of his ministerial team. The zonal and state balance was impeccable. But could they work together? The November–December 2015 period would be a test of whether team leaders of the Nigerian Project could adjust to the new austerity and at the same time make the changes the electorate had demanded, including ensuring basic domestic security.

It is often said that *leadership* is about establishing a direction and then aligning people to move in that direction. In this endeavor, leadership by example is crucial. By contrast, *management* involves making things work, by aligning budgets and personnel. Often, management entails trying to create order out of chaos, especially in developing countries with fragile democracies.

Both leadership and management qualities were needed as President Buhari closed out the fateful year of 2015. Nigerian history had often been written in blood. The scars of civil war and insurrection were still raw. The demands of leadership would test not only President Buhari and his team but the entire nation.

Buhari's commitment to the unity of Nigeria would require getting the oil sector under control and responding to the need for economic diversification. It would also mean that military officers, the guarantors of national unity, had a duty to be honest and professional. Hence, the emerging military procurement scandal would hit at the heart of Buhari's concerns and challenges.

CHALLENGES OF LEGAL ACCOUNTABILITY

Chapter 15

Military Procurement Accountability

Most observers agree that money is the lifeblood of terrorism. Groups such as Islamic State are known to fund their activities by means of bank heists (or takeovers in conquered territories), illicit oil sales, the illegal sale of smuggled antiquities, kidnappings and ransoms, protection rackets, or donations from wealthy international supporters. Such funds are then used to purchase weapons and other equipment on the international black market, as well as pay the monthly wages and other costs of the terrorist group's operatives and fighters. Some of these patterns characterize the funding of Boko Haram in northeastern Nigeria and elsewhere in the country.

Yet money is also the lifeblood of governmental efforts to combat terrorism. To upgrade security and defence capacities, and to engage in robust counterterrorism training, often requires going beyond routine budget allocations. Of course, intelligence (and some security) allocations are off-budget (i.e., hidden in other defence expenditures), yet it is still essential for accountability that the highest political leaders in a country have full knowledge of such expenditures.

Hence, it was unwelcome news to many Nigerians in mid-November, when the thirteen-person committee set up on August 31, 2015, by President Buhari's national security adviser (NSA),

Babagana Monguno, to audit procurements by the Nigerian military from 2007 to date, issued its interim report. Basically, these procurements were funds allocated to fight the insurgency in the northeast and to tackle related security challenges.

The committee uncovered a number of illegal and fraudulent acts involving vast sums. The amounts unaccounted for in the report totaled billions of US dollars, and hundreds of billions of naira. The retrieval of such funds would not only send a serious warning about using military funds for political (or personal) purposes, but also could relieve some of the current budget stress in Nigeria.

Buhari ordered the arrest of all those implicated, including both civilians and members of the military, thus directly challenging the impunity of senior officials from the Goodluck Jonathan administration.

This chapter focuses on the following facets of the scandal that followed the public dissemination of the NSA report in November: (1) defence and security budget issues and alleged missing funds; (2) the political implications; and (3) preparations for the trial of the former NSA.

Defence and Security Budget Issues and Alleged Missing Funds

On November 17, the special adviser to the president, Femi Adesina, issued a press release that noted:

> So far the total extra budgetary interventions articulated by the committee is Six Hundred and Forty Three Billion, Eight Hundred and Seventeen Million, Nine Hundred and Fifty-Five Thousand, Eight Hundred and Eighty-five Hundred Naira and Eighteen Kobo (N643,817,955,885.18).
>
> The foreign currency component is to the tune of Two Billion, One Hundred and Ninety Three Million, Eight Hundred and Fifteen Thousand US dollars and Eighty-Three Cents ($2,193,815,000.83). . . .
>
> The committee also discovered that payments to the tune of Three Billion, Eight Hundred and Fifty Million Naira (N3,850,000,000.00) were made to a single company by the former NSA without documented evidence of contractual agreements or fulfilment of tax obligations to the FGN.

> Further findings revealed that between March 2012 and March 2015, the erstwhile NSA, Lt. Col. M. S. Dasuki (rtd) awarded fictitious and phantom contracts to the tune of N2,219,188,609.50, $1,671,742,613.58 and €9,905,477.00. The contracts, said to be for the purchase of 4 Alpha Jets, 12 helicopters, bombs and ammunition, were not executed and the equipment was never supplied to the Nigerian Air Force. . . .
>
> Even more disturbing was the discovery that out of these figures, 2 companies were awarded contracts to the tune of N350,000,000.00, $1,661,670,469.71, and €9,905,477.00 alone. This was without prejudice to the consistent non-performance of the companies in the previous contracts awarded.
>
> Additionally, it was discovered that the former NSA directed the Central Bank of Nigeria to transfer the sum of $132,050,486.97 and €9,905,473.55 to the accounts of Societe D'equipmente Internationaux in West Africa, United Kingdom and United States of America for un-ascertained purposes, without any contract documents to explain the transactions.
>
> The findings made so far are extremely worrying considering that the interventions were granted within the same period that our troops fighting the insurgency in the North-East were in desperate need of platforms, military equipment and ammunition. Had the funds siphoned off to these non-performing companies been used for the purpose they were meant, thousands of needless Nigerian deaths would have been avoided.
>
> Furthermore, the ridicule Nigeria has faced in the international community would have been avoided. It is worrisome and disappointing that those entrusted with the security of this great nation were busy using proxies to siphon the national treasury, while innocent lives were wasted daily.
>
> In light of these findings, President Muhammadu Buhari has directed that the relevant organizations arrest and bring to book, all individuals who have been found complicit in these illegal and fraudulent acts. (http://saharareporters.com/2015/11/17/state-house-press-release-president-buhari-receives-interim-report-investigative-0)

The former NSA Sambo Dasuki was not the only person charged, but he was the most prominent. He was placed under house arrest in Abuja, his passport was taken away, and he was prohibited from leaving the country. His response was to deny all charges while threatening "to open a can of worms"—but not until his trial. He insisted that all contracts had been approved by former president Jonathan.

When Jonathan, who was giving a lecture in Washington, DC, was asked about the alleged procurement fraud, he claimed to know nothing about a $2 billion arms contract. According to Nigerian media:

> Mr. Jonathan touched on the contract issue after he stated he was aware of allegations of huge sums of money that were said to be missing from the Nigerian treasury, but he claimed that some of the figures mentioned are not believable. "Sometimes I feel sad when people mention these figures," he said.
>
> Speaking pointedly about his successor, President Jonathan said, "When President (Buhari) paid official visit to the US, there were some figures that were mentioned that I don't believe." . . .
>
> The former President said he does not want to join issues with the new government. "I wanted to keep away from the public for at least twelve months." (http://saharareporters.com/2015/11/20/2b-arms-procurement-jonathan-finally-speaks)

The larger issue was how these allegations would play out in Nigeria, both in the courts and in the court of public opinion.

The Political Implications

The Nigerian press had a field day with the allegations against Dasuki. Some queried whether Dasuki was a proxy for Jonathan or others in the former administration:

> The interesting thing about these power plays is that everybody knows what is really going on. Dasuki knows he is NOT the real target of Buhari's investigations. Yes, he will pay for being complicit in the frauds, but he is not the biggest fish being sought by Buhari. There is no way any single person could steal so much all by himself in our system of government. And Dasuki almost admitted that much when he threatened to expose others. The way military procurement works, the end-user unit commander sends a request of what he needs to his higher command . . . the NSA is officially notified. . . . He reviews it and . . . bypasses the Minister of Defence altogether and takes it up with the President. Upon approval by the President, the Minister of Defence is directed to make the funds available to the NSA for the items. The Minister of Defence now, of course, has to know how much the items cost. Normally, contractors already registered by the government [will] bid for the supply and the one most favorable to the government will be awarded the contract. The Minister of Defence now raises funds for the purchase. But when things are not normal, you have the Minister of Defence in cahoots with the NSA and all those in the chain of approval,

selecting whatever company in which they have interests to supply the item. . . .

For Buhari who has said openly that he wants to be remembered for fighting corruption, it will be an unmitigated disaster for his legacy if such a gargantuan fleecing went on in his primary constituency—the military—and he failed to unearth it and punish the culprits.

Dasuki should therefore stop reveling in his delusion of grandeur—seeing himself as such an important guy against whom Buhari would be vindictive. Yes, he stabbed Buhari in the back by joining Babangida in the 1985 palace coup that ousted Buhari. Yes, Babangida made him his ADC [aide-de-camp] and accelerated his promotion. But he was just a pawn in these power games. Dasuki is right; it was not he alone . . . all by himself . . . who is culpable. And Buhari knows that. Buhari knows that Task Force and Division Commanders knew of and approved these arms purchases; Service Chiefs knew too; Ministers of Defence and Finance knew; Chiefs of Staff knew; civil servants in the Ministries of Defence and Finance knew; Chiefs of Staff to the President knew; the Vice President knew; and the President knew. It is why Buhari will keep his foot on Dasuki's throat until he fesses up. . . .

Didn't this guy get his NSA job only because he was a protégé of Babangida? Was this Babangida's way of getting even with Sanni Abacha who deposed and banished Dasuki's father, Ibrahim Dasuki, as Sultan of Sokoto in 1996? . . .

Who really was Sambo Dasuki fronting for in Jonathan's cabinet? That is the main question to which Buhari is also seeking answers. (http://saharareporters.com/2015/11/19/who-was-sambo-dasuki-fronting-goodluck-jonathan%E2%80%99s-government-abiodun-ladepo)

It is beyond the scope of this study to assess all the backstories of the relationship between Buhari and Dasuki. Suffice it to say that the so-called grudge between the two has never really existed. Dasuki is twelve years younger than Buhari, even though Dasuki did participate in the 1985 countercoup. The family of Ibrahim Dasuki and the Buhari extended family have been linked by marriage for more than four decades. In addition, in his inaugural address, Buhari had professed that although "the past is prologue," he had no time to pursue alleged "enemies."

Other personal relationships in play included Buhari's relationship with Jonathan's minister of defence, General Aliyu Gusau, which was discussed in chapter 4, and Buhari's relationship with

General Babangida, who has played such a ubiquitous role in Fourth Republic politics.

Yet the real story probably has little to do with personal or political relationships. As noted throughout this study, Buhari has a strong belief in right and wrong. He also has an abiding respect for the Nigerian military as an institution that can help hold Nigeria together. From Buhari's perspective, if corruption in military procurement undermines the integrity of the military, that corruption must be confronted. And if such procurement allegations weaken the military response to Boko Haram and put ordinary foot soldiers at risk, that corruption poses a double threat, endangering even the Nigeria Project itself.

Preparations for the Trial of the Former NSA

On July 17, 2015, well before the NSA committee looking into military procurement began its work, the Department of State Security (DSS) raided the home of Sambo Dasuki in Abuja and found a number of weapons "without requisite license" and charged him under the Firearms Act Cap F28 LFN 2004.

The DSS also found cash in several places—$40,000 plus $20,000 plus N5 million—and charged him under Section 15(3) of Money Laundering (Prohibition) Act 2011 (as amended). At the same time, the DSS raided Dasuki's home in Sokoto and found $150,000 plus N37.6 million, and again charged him with money laundering.

Thus began a legal process in which Dasuki was represented by Ahmed Raji and J. B. Daudu, both of whom have been awarded the title of "Senior Advocate of Nigeria" (SAN) for their distinguished legal work. The case also involved an appeal in Abuja to Hon. Justice A. F. A. Ademola for the release of Dasuki's passport so that he could go abroad for medical treatment for three weeks. Dasuki was being treated for possible colon cancer.

On November 3, Justice Ademola ruled that "an order is hereby made for an interim release of the Applicant's International Passport, in order to enable him to travel abroad for a three-week medical appointment, over a deteriorating medical condition."

Certain conditions were applied to the passport release, including a surety to guarantee Dasuki's return. The surety is a senior government official who agrees to take the place of the defendant and to be detained in prison unless the defendant submits himself for trial. The trial was set for just over three weeks later, on November 26 and 27.

The complication came when the DSS refused to release the passport, citing a flight risk. At that point, the November 17 interim report of the NSA Inquiry Committee was published. It was now clear that the firearms charge and money laundering charge were meant to hold Dasuki until more serious charges could be leveled against him regarding his role in the military procurement scandal. Dasuki remained under house arrest in Abuja.

Rumors were rife that the Dasuki trial would be held behind closed doors, rather than conducted in public. Dasuki insisted on a public trial and protested his innocence. How the judicial system handled such a high-profile case would be a major political test for Buhari. If the focus of the Dasuki case was on procurement corruption within the Jonathan military and political teams, the public exposure of the facts of the case would be in the public interest. But if national security issues that required confidentiality were involved, then a nonpublic trial might be warranted.

The stakes were high for the Buhari administration. Buhari had insisted that legal accountability be left to the courts. He also had insisted that he was not interested in settling scores. Whether the judicial system was capable of handling such cases without fear or favor remained to be seen. The key was to deliver equal treatment under the law, and to be seen by the wider public to be doing so. The last thing Buhari wanted was a show trial. His own administration would be on trial over how this matter was handled.

The most ominous consequence of what came to be called "Dasuki-gate" in fall 2015 was that evidence seemed to point to former president Jonathan's compliance in authorizing the $2.1 billion in funds. Furthermore, there were indications that such funds had been spent to boost Jonathan's chances of winning the 2015 presidential election. Although he did not in fact win, if the money had already been spent on buying votes, it might well be irretrievable.

The court case would spill over into 2016. Whatever the outcome, the moneybag politics of the Fourth Republic would be visible. Furthermore, Nigerians would get a much clearer idea of how the Jonathan administration had addressed, or had failed to address, the formidable security challenges facing the country during Jonathan's tenure.

Chapter 16

Government Austerity, Due Process, and End-of-Year Assessment

The necessity for government austerity gave even greater impetus to President Buhari's drive to tackle official fraud and corruption. It also meant that top officials could expect to see deep cuts in their salaries and benefits. Could such officials be persuaded to see government service as a privilege rather than an opportunity for personal enrichment? Buhari's abiding memory of the First Republic's senior leaders would be a benchmark of probity in his efforts to get Nigeria back on track.

The Buhari administration was making every effort to retrieve past stolen funds from previous officeholders. This had to be done not only publicly but also discretely so as not to produce a crisis in the political order. It also had to follow due process, which was inherently slow.

In addition, Buhari had to convince the international community that he was serious and capable of bending the trajectory of Nigerian political culture away from a petro-state get-rich-quick mentality. Fighting corruption would entail engaging the international community—both the business community and governments—to win its support. It would also be necessary to lure back international companies reluctant to invest in Nigeria because of corrupt practices.

The clearest example for both domestic and international communities in establishing rule of law in Nigeria would come from Buhari himself. But his entire cabinet would also have to set a high standard of probity.

This chapter focuses on the following issues: (1) terms of ministerial service; (2) due process and the retrieval of past stolen funds; (3) the need for international support; and (4) national accountability and end-of-year assessment.

Terms of Ministerial Service

During the last week of November, the secretary to the Government of the Federation, Babachir David Lawal, sent a letter to each of the new federal ministers detailing the terms of office, salaries, and benefits. The salaries were lower than expected, and the benefits severely curtailed from what ministers had enjoyed in previous administrations. The terms and conditions were taken from the Certain Political, Public and Judicial Office Holders (Salaries and Allowances) (Amendment) Act 2008, which seems to have been disregarded previously.

Essentially, substantive ministers would earn N2,026,400 ($8,514.28 at 2015 exchange rates) as their annual basic salary. Ministers of state would earn N1.8 million ($7,563.02) per annum. In addition, provisions were made for an overseas ("Estacode") allowance of ($900 per diem), a domestic allowance ("Duty Tour Allowance") of N35,000, plus allowances for domestic staff, medical treatment, a special assistant, security, and newspapers. Many would regard these salaries as unrealistic, given the high costs of living at home and abroad. The one perk that remained was business-class air travel.

The letter to ministers also explained:

> As a political Office Holder, you must obtain permission from Mr. President before you travel out of Abuja. If the trip is official, Ministers are entitled to a Duty Tour Allowance of N35,000 per diem. However, all private journeys will attract no Allowance. . . . 200% of Annual Basic Salary will be paid to you to enable you to acquire accommodation of your choice in line with monetization policy. . . . Motor vehicle fueling allowance of 75% of annual basic salary for the maintenance of your vehicle(s), as Government no longer provides chauffeur driven vehicles to Political Office Holders for house to office running. . . . Plus annual leave of 30 days. (http://thenationonlineng.net/buhari-shocks-ministers-with-austere-package/)

According to media reports, "some of the ministers were uncomfortable with the salary and allowance package because it might not be able to pick up their bills. The package caused rumbles in the cabinet because while Nigerian ministers earn $8,514.28, per annum (N2,026,640), their counterparts in Ghana are on $50,000 (N11,900,000) and those in South Africa (the highest paying in the continent) were said to be taking home about $302,521 per annum" (ibid.).

Buhari was trying to eliminate the allure of ministerial appointments as a means of accruing wealth either through receiving a generous salary or through exploiting power for corrupt personal gain. Of course, the effort to combat corruption also required creating disincentives for corrupt practices strong enough to dissuade ministers from "chopping" on the side. The penalty if caught would be dismissal and public shaming.

Due Process and the Retrieval of Past Stolen Funds

Buhari set a high bar for anticorruption efforts during a speech he gave in Tehran in mid-November; he spoke to Nigerians living in Iran, but his comments were aimed at a wider Nigerian audience. According to a media report of the speech:

> Government officials and their allies who have stolen from the public purse since 1999 must prepare to return what they took, President Muhammadu Buhari has said. The Nigerian leader made the ominous remark on Tuesday during an interaction with the Nigerian community in Tehran, Iran, as he spoke on issues of corruption, revealing that a number of past officials have voluntarily begun the return of stolen funds.
>
> He, however, stressed that his government will not accept tokenism. "We want to have everything back—all that they took by force in 16 years," he declared in a statement signed by presidential spokesman Garba Shehu.
>
> It had erroneously been thought that his anti-corruption focus would only cover the previous administration of Mr. Goodluck Jonathan. His statement means the drive will be broader and bigger. He told his audience that the necessity for compliance with due process is responsible for the delay in commencing prosecution of the looters of the country's economy, but that the "day of reckoning is gradually coming." (http://saharareporters.com/2015/11/24/all-who-have-looted-1999-must-return-everything-buhari-declares)

Even the return of the funds stolen by General Abacha during 1993–98 and held in escrow since 1999 by the World Bank came under increased scrutiny. A Nigerian NGO that does its best to monitor stolen public funds, the Socio-Economic Rights and Accountability Project (SERAP), made inquiries of the World Bank as to the status of the Abacha funds, and was sent a 700-page report suggesting that the funds had already been returned. In a January 9, 2005, letter to the World Bank, Ngozi Okonjo-Iweala, who was then minister of finance, explained that "funds were spent in 2004 and 2005 on roads, electricity, education, water and health across all 6 geo-political zones of Nigeria" (http://saharareporters.com/2015/11/29/abacha-loot-spent-roads-electricity-education-health-and-water-world-bank).

Unfortunately, SERAP could find no record of such expenditures. Consequently, SERAP, noting "Mrs. Okonjo-Iweala's involvement in the spending of the Abacha loot," called on Buhari "to urgently probe the role of the Ministry of Finance and relevant federal ministries at the time in the spending of Abacha loot particularly given the strong allegations of mismanagement that characterized the use of the funds" (ibid.).

The political question for Buhari was the extent to which he was willing to pursue disbursement of the Abacha monies with the World Bank. There seemed to be no end in sight in terms of possible probes. Meanwhile, civil society critics of the Buhari administration were insisting that he make public the details of all returned funds and prosecute the culprits who had stolen them. Doing so might create chaos in the political system, but such hardliners were persisting, perhaps as a way of embarrassing Buhari into moving even more forcefully against corrupt officials (http://thenationonlineng.net/buhari-and-the-returned-loot/).

The Need for International Support

The US Foreign Corrupt Practices Act (FCPA) of 1977 led many US companies to avoid investing in Nigeria because it might expose corporate executives to criminal liability in the United States. According to the FCPA, CEOs could not use the excuse that they did not know what was going on in the field in the bids for contracts, which often involved bribes or "facilitation fees," and would be

At the G7 Summit in June 2015 in Bavaria, Germany. Buhari is third from right in the front row, flanked by British prime minister David Cameron and French president Francois Hollande. President Barack Obama is fifth from right, front row, and Angela Merkel (in a red blouse) is in the middle.

Guards of Honor

In Daura, accompanied by the governor of Kano State, Alhaji Abdullahi Ganduje.

In Yaoundé, accompanied by President Paul Biya of Cameroon.

At Schloss Elmau, Krun, Bavaria, during the G7 Summit.

The US ambassador to Nigeria Mr. James F. Entwistle and US assistant secretary of state for Africa Ms. Linda Thomas-Greenfield, welcome President Buhari to the United States in July 2015.

President Buhari with Lawal Idris of Gusau (left), a longtime supporter, and the author Professor John Paden at Blair House in Washington, DC.

With President Barack Obama in the Oval Office.

Shaking hands with Secretary of State John Kerry amid a flutter of Nigerian and US flags.

With Vice President Joe Biden outside Blair House.

In apparent contemplation with Vice President Joe Biden in the garden of Blair House.

In the Oval Office with the governors of five Nigerian states. Left to right: Governor Umaru Tanko al-Makura (Nasarawa), Governor Rochas Okorocha (Imo), Vice President Biden, President Buhari, President Obama, Governor Adams Oshimole (Edo), Governor Abiola Ajimobi (Oyo), Governor Kashim Shettima (Borno), and Ambassador Bulus Lolo (Permanent Secretary, Ministry of Foreign Affairs).

With Secretary of the Treasury Jack Lew.

With His Majesty King Abdallah of Jordan at the United Nations in September 2015. Buhari found the king affable and knowledgeable about world and African affairs.

President Buhari (left) with His Majesty King Salman of Saudi Arabia (center left); Lawal Kazaure, Buhari's chief of protocol (center right); and Minister of State for Petroleum Resources Emmanuel Kachikwu (right).

President Buhari's wife, Hajiya Aisha Buhari, with her children. In the back row, left to right, are Yusuf, Halima, Aisha, and Zahra. In the front row, left to right, are Noor (Amina) and Aisha (Hannan).

President Buhari seated amid a riot of grandchildren.

held personally and criminally responsible. In many cases, rival companies seeking to do business with the Nigerian oil industry would lodge complaints, and the legal cases would be tried in Houston, Texas. It was a major disincentive for US companies to invest in Nigeria. Not surprisingly, therefore, many US companies, as well as the US government, welcomed the anticorruption efforts by Buhari.

British companies did not face similar legal constraints. Yet the close ties between Buhari and British prime minister David Cameron facilitated efforts to launch a coordinated effort to bring money launderers to book, as demonstrated in the role of the London Metropolitan Police in the case of Diezani Alison-Madueke.

In late November, the Commonwealth heads of government meeting in Malta focused on the corruption issue more broadly. According to a report in the Abuja-based *Daily Trust*:

> President Muhammadu Buhari says corruption in Nigeria's oil sector and outright theft of Nigeria's crude oil has been exacerbated by the culture of impunity which reigned under previous administrations.
>
> The president said this in Malta on Saturday during a group meeting of Commonwealth leaders on corruption, chaired by British Prime Minister David Cameron. The meeting was attended by leaders of Australia, Canada, Singapore, Malta, Sri Lanka, Botswana and Trinidad and Tobago. Buhari said corruption in the oil sector had also thrived because of the ease of transferring illicit funds abroad and the institutional protection given to corrupt officials in the past.
>
> President Buhari urged the international community to do more to support his administration's efforts towards curbing corruption in Nigeria's oil and gas industry. "Now that we have the political will to stop impunity, we need the cooperation and assistance of the international community. We must all work together to compel multinational oil companies, international financial institutions and international shipping lines to stop aiding and abetting corruption in the oil sector in Nigeria," he said. (http://www.dailytrust.com.ng/news/general/buhari-impunity-aided-oil-sector-corruption-under-my-predecessors/121754.html)

These remarks were seconded by David Cameron, who urged the Commonwealth and the international community as a whole to do more to fight corruption. "If we want fair economic growth, we need to reject corruption. If we want to see fair and sustainable development, we need to deal with corruption. I think this is an absolutely vital issue. It is an issue for all of us because so much of the money stolen from developing countries is hidden in developed countries" (ibid.).

National Accountability and End-of-Year Assessment

As the year 2015 drew to a close and Buhari marked his seventy-third birthday, only the most cynical of observers could question his commitment to strengthening legal accountability and due process in government. He had insisted that his own ministers serve with minimal remuneration and out of a sense of public service. He would hold them personally responsible for corrupt practices. Buhari had expressed his determination to pursue stolen government funds as far back as the beginning of the Fourth Republic. The president was working with international partners to secure financial and legal accountability and cooperation.

Would these reforms stand the test of time? Could the example of one leader begin to shift Nigeria's political culture? Did Buhari have his priorities in the right order? How would his efforts to clean up government affect the struggle with grassroots insurgents in the northeast?

Most important, would those who stood to lose by these reforms retaliate in some way? The memories of the countercoup of August 1985 were still fresh. The difference in 2015 was that Buhari had been overwhelmingly elected to deal precisely with a lack of accountability and an abundance of corruption. Plus, he had support from key members of the international community, who were well aware that Nigeria needed to tackle corruption if it was to live up to its economic potential as a responsible player in the global economy.

In his first seven months in office, Buhari had drawn on his popular and international support to launch a number of significant reforms. Other problems facing Nigeria—such as weaknesses in its power sector, educational system, and industrial sector—would require longer-term initiatives.

In Nigeria and elsewhere in the world, people were watching Buhari with great interest, trying to see if he could make a difference—or, indeed, if he was already making a difference. In December 2015, for instance, the Abuja-based Centre for Democracy and Development (CDD), an NGO that serves as a watchdog on government practices, issued a report entitled *7 Months After: Delivering on Campaign Promises.* The report rated the president's performance on the CDD's "Buharimeter":

> *Security*: Since the inauguration of PMB on May 29, 2015, the Nigerian military has made progress in curtailing the Boko Haram insurgency in North East Nigeria. President Buhari rejigged Nigeria's counterterrorism architecture, forged regional alliances, appointed new security chiefs and gave orders for the insurgency to be defeated by December 2015. The Nigerian army is making gradual gains in the war against terror: recovering territories and rescuing abducted citizens. Consequently, the administration has claimed a technical victory, arguing that Boko Haram is no longer capable of carrying out conventional attacks on security forces or population centres. According to President Buhari during an interview with the BBC: "I think, technically, we have won the war. . . . Boko Haram has reverted to using improvised explosives (IEDs). They have now been reduced to that. . . . Boko Haram is an organized fighting force, I assure you [but] we have dealt with them." (President Buhari, on BBC, 23rd December, 2015). . . .
>
> *Corruption*: Since the inauguration of the new administration, there have been visible efforts to combat corruption in the country. The administration has reached out to several foreign states to assist in the recovery of stolen funds. The United States has pledged to cooperate with the PMB administration in locating and retrieving stolen monies. The government has set up several "corruption probes," targeted at recovering looted funds and dismantling the setup that had previously engendered financial maladministration. . . . The anti-graft agencies are also pursuing cases of high level corruption among the political class. Notable amongst the investigations is the ongoing arms deal under former President Goodluck Ebele Jonathan. . . .
>
> *The Economy*: Following the crash in the price of crude oil from $115 per barrel in June 2014 to the current low of around $37 per barrel, the revenues of the country have been hugely impacted. This is because oil accounts for a huge proportion of the Nigerian economy, with the oil sector generating up to 80% of the government's revenue and 90% of foreign exchange earnings. The crash in the oil price has impacted the foreign exchange rate, leading to volatility. The Naira continues to depreciate against

> other foreign currencies, with, for example, the official exchange rate by the Central Bank of Nigeria (CBN) currently $1 to N197. [Yet] $1 is trading for N270 on the parallel market. Several policies have recently been introduced by the CBN in an attempt to reduce this pressure on the Naira. These include restricting the supply of foreign exchange to importers, and limiting products that can be bought using dollars to a list of 40 items. . . .
>
> The deplorable state of infrastructure in the country is also disturbing given its relevance to boosting investment, industrial growth and the economy. There is hardly any part of the country that has well-maintained roads. The railway system is dysfunctional and the air transport sector is largely inefficient, as well as being unaffordable for the vast majority of the population.
>
> The unreliable power supply has been a major challenge for the development of Nigeria's economy. For example, a recent study of power generation statistics between January and August 2015 conducted by the Power Advisory Group, revealed that only 25% of Nigeria's 112,522 MW of installed capacity reaches the end users. The shortfall is due to obsolete equipment and poor maintenance of existing power plants. To help address the unemployment rate—that currently stands at 9.9%—the government needs to formulate policies to address problems of power and transportation sectors and provide adequate social amenities. Mechanisms to ensure the effective implementation of the policies should be put in place, coupled with political will. (http://www.buharimeter.ng/assets/uploads/docs/file_mKkr8ynEBI.pdf)

* * *

The challenges of insurgency, corruption, and the economy would carry over into the new year. These are the focus in part III of the story of Buhari's leadership challenges. But 2016 would also spotlight another challenge—perhaps Buhari's biggest challenge—the need to change a political system and culture that was the direct cause of many of Nigeria's accumulated problems.

PART III

CHALLENGES OF PRESIDENTIAL LEADERSHIP, JANUARY 1—MAY 31, 2016

Part III focuses on the areas that were President Buhari's priorities during the first five months of 2016. There were four main policy priorities:

- **Counterinsurgency**
    - *Continue to work with international partners*
    - *Work with local civilian "vigilantes"*
    - *Set up a human rights department*
    - *Prepare vehicles and conduct training for Sambisa offensive*
    - *Recruit and "localize" police*
- **Anticorruption**
    - *Work with Swiss, British, US, and UAE law officials*
    - *Strengthen EFCC's capabilities*
    - *Go after high-value targets*
    - *Move systematically on military procurement scandals*
    - *Set personal example of probity*
- **Economic Recovery**
    - *Set budget priorities*
    - *Launch new initiatives to help women, the poor, and education*
    - *Restructure the NNPC and the petroleum industry*
    - *Launch reconstruction in the northeast*
    - *Seek foreign loans and investments*
- **Political Change**
    - *Insist on financial accountability*
    - *Require government officials to declare their assets*
    - *Separate branches of government*
    - *Focus on electoral lessons and reforms*
    - *Emphasize national unity*

CHALLENGES OF INSURGENCY AND SECURITY

Chapter 17

The War against Insurgency

As 2015 came to an end, the Nigerian and international media reported claims by President Buhari that the war with Boko Haram was "technically over" in terms of reclaiming territory formerly held by the insurgents. The coordinated suicide attacks continued, however, and it would be a long time before Boko Haram was completely subdued. Meanwhile, Minister of Information Lai Mohammed reminded journalists that "Nigeria was at war."

And if Nigeria was still at war, then the same questions that had confronted the new government remained: How should this war with insurgency be prosecuted? What organizational and financial components were needed to win the war? Was the 2016 budget, presented in December 2015, sufficient in the security realm? Was the Nigerian military up to the task? What should be the role of the local vigilantes? How could police be "localized" (recruited and deployed in ways that reflected local linguistic and cultural realities) while at the same time remaining "federal?" What should be the role of the minister of interior in transforming his ministry more broadly to deal with homeland security? What about relations with international partners?

The insurgency situation in the northeast was complicated in December by two events involving the security forces: a violent clash between the military and a Shi'ite group in Zaria, and pending trials regarding military procurement scandals. The most troubling, in terms of international perceptions, was the clash between the military and Shi'ite followers in Zaria.

Nigeria was facing other security challenges, too, including herdsmen fighting with local farm communities; cattle rustling; kidnappings; low morale and restiveness in the military; and increasing low-level violence in the South-South and South East.

In the South-South, a new group, the Niger Delta Avengers (NDA), claimed responsibility in mid-May for blowing up the Warri and Kaduna refinery pipelines, as well as numerous flow stations in the Delta. This was a direct attack on the Nigerian economy and clearly had political implications. Later in May, the Movement for the Emancipation of the Niger Delta (MEND) dissociated itself from the NDA, which MEND claimed was trying to destabilize the Buhari government. As the group announced in a statement reported in the press:

> [MEND] wishes to condemn and dissociate itself from the recent activities carried out by a group known as the "Niger Delta Avengers." Their sudden emergence has absolutely nothing to do with the Niger Delta struggle but rather is a tool by certain elements to destabilize the current government. Going by their actions and subsequent statements, it has become very apparent who the sponsors of this group are. (http://saharareporters.com/2016/05/22/niger-delta-avengers-formed-destabilize-buharis-government-mend)

This chapter (1) assesses the challenge posed by Boko Haram as it changed its tactics; (2) updates defence and security resource projections, as they impact domestic security and threats of insurgency; (3) reviews the Shi'ite clash with the military; and (4) assesses the behavior of the military with regard to possible human rights abuses.

The following chapter, chapter 18, examines efforts to restructure the internal security apparatus, especially the roles of the police and the Interior Ministry.

The Challenges Posed by Boko Haram's New Tactics

By the end of December 2015, with the territories it once held in the northeast largely recovered by the military, Boko Haram resorted to hit-and-run attacks and suicide bombings. Although the formal military posture was to harden obvious targets, the real need was for ground-level intelligence: the eyes and ears of the public. A big question concerned the future role of the Civilian Joint Task Force (C-JTF) and its coordination with the military.

With the festival of Maulud (marking the Prophet Muhammad's birthday) approaching on December 24, and Christmas on December 25, the number of possible soft targets increased exponentially. Successful Boko Haram attacks would send a powerful message that the insurgents were not defeated.

In several locations—for example, Kaduna—attacks were prevented. In Kaduna, the military arrested seven people suspected of being Boko Haram bombmakers and specialists in improvised explosive devices (IED). An Army spokesman attributed the arrests to extensive grassroots intelligence, and requested that the public continue to alert security agencies about suspicious persons and activities.

Sometimes social media would spread elaborate rumors, which were then picked up by the broader media. In the city of Maiduguri, the Vigilante Group of Nigeria (VGN) was reported in the national media to have forestalled an attack on the Abulfathi mosque, which was about to host between five and ten thousand members of the Tijaniyya Sufi order for Maulud ceremonies. VGN operatives noticed five food carts being moved toward the mosque, and many bystanders assumed that the food in the carts was to be handed out to the needy. But on inspection by the vigilantes, the carts were found to contain bombs. The security forces were alerted and the Boko Haram culprits apprehended. Had it not been prevented, this attack might have claimed more lives than any previous Boko Haram attack.

Yet, surprisingly, the imam of the Abulfathi mosque, Khalifa Aliyu Ahmad Abulfathi, insisted this incident never happened. He further insisted that his mosque had never been the target of Boko Haram even though it was only five kilometers from the original location of the Muhammad Yusuf mosque in Maiduguri.

Not all such attacks, real or imagined, could be prevented. In Maiduguri, on December 28, over sixty people were killed in multiple attacks by female suicide bombers. On December 28, in the town of Madagali in Adamawa State, at least thirty were killed in twin suicide bombings at a motor park. Again, the bombers were women.

The vital role of verifiable local, grassroots intelligence in preventing attacks—something that had been thin on the ground during the Jonathan administration—prompted the announcement of a new counterinsurgency policy. On December 24, Defence Minister Mansur Muhammad Dan-Ali announced that certain civilian vigilante groups fighting Boko Haram would be integrated into the armed forces. He further commented: "Since President Muhammadu Buhari's assumption of office, we have gained more ground against Boko Haram terrorists. And I assure you, the menace of Boko Haram will soon be over" (http://saharareporters.com/2015/12/24/civilian-vigilante-groups-fighting-boko-haram-be-integrated-armed-forces%E2%80%94defense-minister).

Such optimism was premature. Over the next few months, the Boko Haram insurgents increased their use of female suicide bombers. This became front-page news in the Western media, where it was noted that the police found it difficult to search females because of heavy clothing and taboos about women being touched by strangers.

Women who had escaped from Boko Haram told harrowing tales of being sex slaves. Those who escaped with children fathered by Boko Haram fighters faced being ostracized in the camps for internally displaced persons (IDPs), where they were moved.

Borno was facing food shortages because of the hiatus in planting and the insecurity of access roads. This was a problem that affected not only local people and IDPs but also the Boko Haram fighters, who raided villages to steal whatever food remained. Many young men in such villages began to set up defensive capacities, often in an organizational form called "vigilantes."

The cooperation of local vigilantes with the Nigerian authorities was beginning to provide new sources of intelligence. In addition, the DSS counterinsurgency authorities were beginning to show successes.

The most notable success by the DSS occurred on April 1, when it captured the number two leader of Boko Haram, Khalid al-Barnawi, in Lokoja, Kogi State. He had been one of the founders of Boko Haram, and also led the breakaway group Jama'at Ansaru Musulimin Fil Biladis Sudan (JAMBS). He had been a key link with al-Qaeda in the Islamic Maghreb (AQIM), and had been implicated in terrorist attacks throughout northern Nigeria, including the bombing of the UN building in Abuja in 2011, the kidnapping of Europeans, and attacks on Nigerian troops.

President Buhari, on his return from the global summit on nuclear terrorism in Washington, DC, in early April, began to emphasize the need to combat terrorism along parallel tracks: cultural, logistical, and military. In Abuja, on April 5, in a farewell address to a departing Kenyan High Commissioner, he said, "We need a whole cultural orientation in order to succeed against terrorism" (http://www.dailytrust.com.ng/news/general/-wants-insurgents-sponsorship-alliances-investigated-reversed/141097.html). This was in line with his earlier statements that Boko Haram did not represent Islam but was the product of local socioeconomic forces. Buhari also noted that "terrorist activities always have financial sponsorships and this can be seen in their acquisition of weapons and other logistics. Here in Nigeria, we saw that Boko Haram had strong material resources and they had a close link to ISIL [Islamic State]" (ibid.).

On the military front against Boko Haram, Buhari had said in private meetings in Washington, DC, that when the armored vehicles provided by the United States (see the next section) were ready for use, and as soon as Nigerian forces had been properly trained in their use, the strategy would be to use those vehicles to encircle the portions of the Sambisa Forest where Boko Haram fighters were dug in, and root them out. The result would be a military defeat of Boko Haram. Then the social reconstruction phase could begin.

By the end of May, the armored vehicles were finally fitted with ventilation systems to reduce the interior heat and humidity, and specialist training of Nigerian soldiers using the vehicles was nearing completion. The race now was to encircle the Sambisa zone before the summer rains made roads impassable.

Implementing such an encirclement strategy, however, depended on Nigeria's partnering effectively with neighboring states that did not have a history of working together, notably Niger, Chad, Cameroon, and Benin. According to a report in the *New York Times*:

> "The big unanswered question right now is how much are all five of those countries that are participating going to collaborate and work effectively," Col. Robert Wilson, who commands American Special Forces in North and West Africa, said in a recent interview here, noting that Boko Haram moves easily across borders. . . . Gen. Donald C. Bolduc, the top United States Special Operations commander for Africa, said that since Nigeria's president, Muhammadu Buhari, instituted military reforms in recent months, "my guys are now coffee-breath close to our partners in the Lake Chad basin. As a result," General Bolduc said in an interview last week, "we have developed relationships of trust."
>
> Since taking office last year, Mr. Buhari has begun a major push to rid the country of Boko Haram. . . . The nations in the Lake Chad region that have become Boko Haram's new stamping grounds—Niger, Chad, Cameroon—have long been distrustful of one another. Mr. Buhari met with their leaders one by one, shoring up support for a campaign to join forces to fight the group. ("Failure to Share Data Hampers African War on Boko Haram," *New York Times,* April 24, 2016, p. 6)

The continuing challenge would be to combine grassroots intelligence with robust military capacity, including high-tech surveillance. Accomplishing this would require not only arranging training and coordination but also ensuring that budget resources were not squandered. Plus, there was the additional imperative of programs for youth employment. The budget challenge was stark, because the 2016 budget announced in December would require steep cuts in all fields.

Military and Security Resources

In mid-December 2015, President Buhari presented his budget for 2016. He proposed a budget of N6.08 trillion, with a revenue projection of N3.86 trillion and a deficit of N2.22 trillion. Of this total amount, defence capital investment expenditures would consume N134.6 billion. The Ministry of Interior would get N53.1 billion. "We will invest to safeguard lives and property," he explained. Buhari signed the budget bill into law on May 6, after months of haggling and delays by the National Assembly.

The amount of money allotted to recurrent and capital funds for defence and interior is significant, given budget constraints in other areas. Clearly, the high proportion of defence-related resources would need to be spent wisely, given the existential challenges facing Nigeria. Finding funds to combat the insurgency made it yet more important to retrieve some of the funds looted during the previous administration. Also, some of the defence and interior resources would need to come, in various forms, from international partners given the need for borrowing to support the deficit spending in the overall budget.

Hence, the violent clash between a Shi'ite group and the military in December (see below) set off alarm bells inside the government, because if the military were seen as having violated human rights, international donors might withdraw their offers of assistance. The challenge would be to train military and security units to avoid committing human rights abuses.

One of the reasons the military had been unable to deter Boko Haram attacks was the use of IEDs and ambush tactics by the insurgents. The United States had provided the military with heavily armored vehicles from the draw-down of US forces in Iraq and Afghanistan. Such vehicles could resist bombs and IEDs, which would allow the Nigerian military to pursue Boko Haram factions into the Sambisa Forest.

The training of Nigerian troops in the use of these vehicles was being done in Bauchi with the help of US military trainers. However, such training would be prohibited by US law if members of the Nigerian military were found to have engaged in clear human rights violations.

The Nigerian military engaged in a careful assessment of units and individual soldiers accused of human rights offenses. The final list of human rights–offending soldiers and officers was almost complete by late May. US training could work with those who did not have a history of human rights abuses. But the assessment of the commission reports on the Shi'ite incidents in December 2015 was not yet complete.

The Shi'ite-Military Clash in Zaria

On December 12, 2015, Chief of Army Staff (COAS) Lieutenant General Tukur Yusuf Buratai was traveling with his convoy from Jigawa State to Kaduna State, and needed to visit Zaria to greet the Emir of Zaria and attend the passing-out parade of the army at Zaria Depot. The road to Zaria, however, was blocked by followers of Sheikh Ibrahim Zakzaky, the leader of the Islamic Movement in Nigeria (IMN, also known as the "Shi'ite sect"), who were brandishing clubs and guns and shouting "Allahu Akbar!" (God is great!).

Military officers tried to arrange for safe passage of the COAS, but the IMN refused to take down the blockade. What happened next is disputed, but according to the military, the troops felt this was an assassination attempt on the COAS and opened fire. Sixty-one bodies were delivered to the morgue at the Ahmadu Bello University (ABU) hospital in Zaria. International sources claimed that as many as three hundred Shi'ites were killed and that the military buried them in a mass grave. Then, within the next day or so, the military returned to Zaria and demolished many of the IMN's buildings and facilities. Sheikh Zakzaky, along with his wife and son, were taken into "protective custody."

The international press described these events as a "massacre" involving the "disproportionate use of force." Some Nigerians called for Buhari to declare a day of mourning. Interior Minister Abdulrahman Dambazau, along with Inspector General of Police Solomon Arase, visited Zaria to assess the situation. Nasir El-Rufai, the governor of Kaduna State (where Zaria is located), set up an independent commission of inquiry.

Shi'ite supporters from throughout the north marched in protest of the "genocide" in Zaria. President Buhari remained silent on the situation, which was highly charged. Iran offered to fly wounded Shi'ites to Tehran for medical treatment, thus escalating the crisis to an international level. The president of Iran telephoned Buhari to demand an explanation.

The background to the IMN crisis may be summarized as follows. In 1978, nine students were expelled from Ahmadu Bello University (ABU) for being part of a radical faction of the Muslim Student Society (MSS). A private charity in Zaria funded them to go for further studies to various Muslim countries in the Middle East. Some students went to Jordan or Saudi Arabia. Later, Ibrahim Zakzaky, who had been an economics student at ABU, went to Iran, where the turmoil that would culminate in the Iranian Revolution in 1979 was brewing.

After the Iranian Revolution, that government reached out to some of the northern Nigerian university youth with training and funding. Zakzaky had returned from Iran and appeared to have been changed by the experience. He emerged as the leader of a group of self-described "brothers" (*Yan Brotha*, or *Ikhwan*). Outsiders described the movement as "Shi'ite." Over time, it became the IMN.

The IMN insisted that it was nonviolent, although it clashed numerous times with the authorities, and Zakzaky spent some time in jail. The IMN established control of the Gyellesu ward area in Zaria, and ran local affairs, including security, with relative autonomy from the Nigerian state. Sheikh Zakzaky held court in his home much as any other northern religious scholar might do. Throughout the north, posters of Iranian religious leaders were distributed, along with Iranian propaganda.

A key to Zakzaky's recruiting success was IMN's extensive funding of social welfare services. Widows and orphans and the poor were fed. Ambulances were available for hospital visits. As poverty levels increased, his ward became a beacon of hope for the destitute. The state and local government authorities, representing the vast majority of Sunni Muslims, tended to stay clear of the Zaria Shi'ites, who were emerging as a state within a state, much as had happened in an area of Maiduguri run by Muhammad Yusuf, before his killing by the police in 2009.

Another recruiting tool for the IMN was its endorsement of the practice of "temporary marriage." At a time when young men could not afford the traditional "bride price" offerings to a young woman's family, the idea of a temporary marriage, with no bride price, was very appealing. The general (Sunni) public frowned on temporary marriage, seeing it as a case of young men wanting sex without responsibility.

By the end of 2015, the Shi'ite crisis in Zaria was far from over. Sheikh Zakzaky appeared to have weathered the storm, although he had lost one eye during the clash with the military and the full extent of his injuries was unknown to the broader Nigerian public. But the incident raised several questions: Could the Nigerian military avoid such crises in the future? Was the military equipped to handle a domestic crisis of this sort? Should new localized police initiatives be developed to preempt such situations? Were the state-level authorities able to deal with such crises, or should the federal authorities be involved?

Larger questions also came to the surface: Were religious enclaves such as the one in Zaria a prelude to demands for autonomy from the Nigerian state? Could clashes with a federal police force (or with the military) produce new forms of insurgency? The "Taliban" groups in Yobe and Borno in 2003 had both demanded autonomy, and the subsequent clashes between them and the authorities had led to the emergence of Boko Haram. Were there lessons to be learned?

President Buhari deferred judgment on the Shi'ite-military clash until the Kaduna State commission of inquiry could be completed. (The military would conduct its own investigation.) Meanwhile, the authorities in Tehran were insisting that the federal government of Nigeria give a full accounting of the clash.

The question of whether a more localized state police capacity would have managed the confrontation peacefully—or even preempted it—was front and center. At the same time, the immediate challenge was crisis management, including managing how the crisis was seen by Nigeria's international partners and the members of the counterinsurgency coalitions that President Buhari had spent so much effort putting together. Complicating the situation was the fact that the international community's concern with possible human rights abuses by the Nigerian military has a long history. Buhari would have to move carefully to ensure that his administration was not seen as just another chapter in that unfortunate history.

Partly in response to the Shi'ite crisis and other perceived human rights abuses by the military, in mid-February the Nigerian Army announced the creation of a "Human Rights Desk" within the Ministry of Defence to investigate complaints. The new body would focus most of its attention on the fight with Boko Haram and collateral damage, but individual complaints unrelated to the fight against Boko Haram would also be investigated. According to one report in the Nigerian media, "the systematic pattern of impunity and human rights abuses from the Nigerian Army, as well as pressure from international human rights groups, has pressured the Nigerian Army to begin addressing some of these issues" (http://saharareporters.com/2016/02/18/army-creates-human-rights-desk-investigate-its-conduct).

The Nigerian Military and Human Rights Abuses

A Judicial Commission of Inquiry was established in mid-January by the Kaduna State government into the clashes between the Nigerian military and the IMN on December 12–14, 2015. The governor of Kaduna State, Nasir El-Rufai, had been a close ally and confidant of President Buhari for many years, which led some observers to wonder if the commission might be biased in the government's favor. However, after the composition of the commission was announced, most national and international human rights groups were satisfied that it was balanced and fair.

The commission was given six weeks after its public hearings to submit its report. The terms of inquiry included the following:

> Determine the immediate causes of the clashes, examine the historical circumstances and contributory factors of the clashes and ascertain the number of persons killed, wounded or missing during the clashes. The commission of inquiry will also identify the actions of persons, institutions, federal and state actors, and determine whether such actions were necessary, appropriate and sufficient in the circumstances in which they occurred. (http://saharareporters.com/2016/01/16/killing-shiites-kaduna-state-government-announces-members-judicial-commission-inquiry)

According to the Kaduna State government, the members of the commission "were chosen for their professional competences as lawyers, jurists, scholars of religion, human rights activists, security experts, and media practitioners" (ibid.). The members (listed in table 17.1) were recognized by Nigerians and the international community as not only outstanding professionals but also people of integrity.

Table 17.1. Members of the Kaduna State Commission on Military-Shi'ite Clashes

- *Chair:* Justice Mohammed Lawal Garba, presiding justice of the Port Harcourt Division of the Court of Appeal
- Professor Salihu Shehu, lecturer at Bayero University, Kano (BUK)

- Professor Umar Labdo, Faculty of Humanities, Northwest University, Kano
- Salihu Abubakar, former director, National Agricultural Extension and Research Liaison Services, Ahmadu Bello University (ABU), Zaria
- Professor Auwalu Yadudu, professor of law, BUK
- Professor Ibrahim Gambari, former minister of foreign affairs, under-secretary-general of the United Nations
- Afakriya Gadzama, former director general, Department of State Security
- Brigadier General Aminum-Kano Maude (rtd), former deputy director, Army Finance and Accounts
- Dr. Jibrin Ibrahim, academic and civil society leader
- Khadijah Hawaja Gambo, gender rights activist
- Bilya Bala, banker, management consultant, and journalist
- Major General Alexander Anjili Mshelbwala (rtd), specialist in civil-military relations and counterinsurgency, former military secretary of the Nigerian Army
- Desire Deseye Nsirim, former commissioner of police, Niger State
- *Secretary:* Dr. Bala Babaji, director, Centre for Islamic Legal Studies, Institute of Administration, ABU

Meanwhile, on February 7, Nigerian federal prosecutors charged 191 members of the IMN with "illegal possession of firearms, causing a public disturbance, and incitement." In addition, there was the issue of the murder of one soldier by IMN crowds. The IMN members charged were detained in a Kaduna prison while their trial dates were being set.

On April 21, the Kaduna State government charged 50 IMN members with the murder of Corporal Yakubu Dankaduna, who was killed as he was getting out of his vehicle to disperse the IMN crowd on December 12. These 50 suspects swelled the ranks of IMN members being held in custody to 265. The government said it would produce 39 witnesses to the murder. The Kaduna High Court judge, in considering the case of culpable homicide, adjourned the trial until late May.

Meanwhile, the Kaduna State Commission of Inquiry was stalled in April because of the unwillingness of the IMN to participate in the hearings while Zakzaky remained in detention. Zakzaky and his wife were detained in upscale facilities near the Presidential Villa in Abuja—in the area where Sambo Dasuki was being held—so that Zakzaky could get medical attention for wounds to his shoulder and eye. His wife had been shot in the abdomen and arm and also required medical attention.

Tensions were high, with IMN followers in various northern cities demanding the release of Zakzaky. (In Kano, the IMN was also demanding to be given land to build a major new mosque near the airport.) Tehran-linked human rights groups in London were threatening to take Nigerian officials to the International Criminal Court (ICC).

In mid-April, Amnesty International published a report on the December clashes. The report included testimony by eyewitnesses (mainly IMN members) of the killings, and the allegation that mass graves had been dug to cover up the extent of the carnage caused by the military. Before-and-after aerial photos of Zakzaky's compound and surrounding area were included, showing the extensive physical damage involved. (The Amnesty International report is available online: http://www.amnesty.org/en/documents/afr01/3883/2016/en/.)

The Nigerian military responded by saying that the Amnesty International report was premature, because the Kaduna State commission had yet to publish its report

Meanwhile, Buhari made a point of not interfering with the commission and of not commenting on its deliberations. He did continue to try to strengthen the counterinsurgency coalition. In February, he had announced that he would cooperate in the fight against Boko Haram with the Economic Community of Central African States (ECCAS). In March, he traveled with his security team to Equatorial Guinea for further consultations regarding both Boko Haram and the continuing challenge of maritime policing in the Gulf of Guinea. And in mid-April, he visited Egypt, Qatar, and Saudi Arabia to rally support.

In this effort, he was helped by the fact that some six weeks earlier, in late February, the United States had made its own assessment of the situation and was willing to move ahead with the provision of training and equipment to Nigeria's military. According to an article in the *New York Times* on February 26:

> The Pentagon is poised to send dozens of Special Operations advisers to the front lines of Nigeria's fight against the West African militant group Boko Haram, according to military offi-

> cials, the latest deployment in conflicts with Islamic State and its allies. . . . About 250 American service members have deployed to a military base in Garoua, Cameroon, where United States surveillance drones flying over northeastern Nigeria are sending imagery to African troops. . . .
>
> [After conducting an assessment review,] among the team's main recommendations was to position "small dozens" of Special Forces in Maiduguri . . . to help Nigerian military planners carry out a more effective counterterrorism campaign. British special forces are already assisting the city. (The American military now maintains only a tiny intelligence cell in Abuja, Nigeria's capital.) ("U.S. Plans to Aid Nigeria in War on Boko Haram: Training Local Troops, A Noncombat Role for Special Operations Members," *New York Times*, February 26, 2016)

By the end of February, Chief of Army Staff Lieutenant General Tukur Buratai could say that the military had entered the "mop-up" phase in Nigeria and would start to release captives and assist in the resettlement of IDPs (http://saharareporters.com/2016/02/25/boko-haram-defeated-chibok-girls-rescue-underway-says-buratai). But Boko Haram was continuing its suicide bombings of defenseless villages in the northeast, leading many people to wonder how the resettlement of IDPs could take place amid such insecure circumstances.

Many people were also wondering how Boko Haram could show such resilience under massive pressure, and whether it was hiding not just in the Sambisa Forest but also farther beyond.

Boko Haram claimed to have international links—a claim that, if true, meant that even broader cooperation would be needed to defeat it. In early March, President Buhari announced that Nigeria had joined the Islamic Military Alliance to Fight Terrorism (IMAFT). This was a coalition whose formation had been announced in Saudi Arabia in December 2015, and which consisted of thirty-four mainly Islamic countries, including Turkey and Egypt. The idea was to share information and train and equip forces to counter Islamic State.

When asked by the Nigerian media about this coalition, Buhari said this:

> We are part of it because we have got terrorists in Nigeria that everybody knows claim to be Islamic. So, if there is an Islamic coalition to fight terrorism, Nigeria will be part of it because we

> are casualties of Islamic terrorism. . . . Boko Haram itself declared loyalty to ISIS. ISIS is basically based in Islamic countries. Now, if there is a coalition to fight Islamic terrorism, why can't Nigeria be part of it, while those fighting in Nigeria claim to be Muslims? But the way they are doing it is anti-Islamic. (http://www.dailytrust.com.ng/news/general/nigeria-joins-islamic-coalition-against-terror/136753.html)

Buhari was quizzed as to whether Nigeria's membership implied that Nigeria had an Islamic identity. This issue had caused tensions in Nigeria in 1986, when Nigeria joined the Organization of the Islamic Conference. Buhari replied that "it is Nigeria that matters, not the opinion of some religious bigots" (ibid.).

Nigeria was evidently part of a broad alliance of African, Western, and Islamic countries fighting a nonstate network spreading in the Middle East and Africa that showed little evidence of weakening. Labels would be less important than concerted regional efforts both in the military-security and the postconflict reconstruction domains.

Many Nigerians hoped the IMN impasse in Kaduna State would not derail these counterinsurgency efforts. But by the end of Buhari's first year in office, it was unclear if the Nigerian military could achieve its goals while respecting the human rights of ordinary citizens. Reforming the military would probably take more time and resources than were available in spring 2016, but there was strong evidence that the problem was recognized and national leaders were determined to fix it.

Those leaders welcomed the news in May that the US government was planning to sell twelve A-29 Super Tucano attack aircraft to Nigeria to assist in the fight against Boko Haram. The United States would also provide more intelligence and surveillance resources, and would assist in the training of infantry troops. This was seen in Nigeria as a sign of confidence in Buhari, who not only was trying to reform the Nigerian military and take on Boko Haram, but also had launched a full-scale attack on corruption by military and political officials that had been sapping the will and ability of the military to counter violent extremists.

In early May, the presidential panel set up by Buhari through the Office of the National Security Adviser announced that its earlier estimate of the extent of arms procurement diversions and fraud was far too low: the amount involved was not $2.1 billion, but $15 billion. Attorney General Abubakar Malami indicated that high-level indictments would follow.

An additional issue was the status of the Chibok girls. Secret negotiations had been held regarding an exchange of Boko Haram prisoners for the girls. On several occasions, prisoners were taken to Maiduguri to facilitate an exchange. But these negotiations stalled when Boko Haram demanded a ransom of 5 billion euros for the girls.

The dilemma for the DSS, which was handling the negotiations, was that a military assault to rescue the girls would almost certainly result in their deaths at the hands of their Boko Haram captors. But the Nigerian government was not going to accede to Boko Haram's extraordinary demand for a vast sum of money, which would no doubt be used to fund future attacks. One or two girls were able to escape their captors in May, but the rest remained captive and the impasse continued.

In late May, the Nigerian (and British) media showed photos of Buhari cradling the four-month-old baby of one girl who had escaped. It was a painful reminder of the consequences of a "forced marriage," yet also a symbolic statement that the president was determined to protect the innocent.

The Chibok girls were not alone in their grim fate. Hundreds, if not thousands, of persons had been captured by Boko Haram in the northeast. Buhari would need to continue degrading Boko Haram until he could tighten the noose around its Sambisa hideouts and bring a close to this painful episode.

Chapter 18

Police and Security Reform

As the military-Shi'ite clash in Zaria graphically demonstrated, many functions normally performed by the police in Western democracies, such as preempting local conflicts, have come to be performed by the military in Nigeria or are not performed at all. There are historical reasons for this enlarged role of the military and for the fact that police functions have constitutionally gravitated exclusively to the federal level. Nonetheless, this overcentralization of police has weakened their ability to serve and protect local communities, and has forestalled the prospect of the police serving as the eyes and ears of the government regarding local conditions.

The APC election manifesto called for the establishment of state and local police. Fulfilling this pledge would require either changing the Constitution or interpreting it in order to localize police while retaining federal control. This latter option seems to have been the path taken by Buhari and his team at the Ministry of Interior.

Creating localized state and local police forces would also require hiring many new police, even in an era of budgetary constriction. Buhari had said that he intended to recruit 10,000 officers, and the inspector general of police had indicated that these recruits would come proportionally from each of the thirty-six states.

This chapter assesses the following issues: (1) police leadership; (2) the range of police reforms; and (3) security reforms.

Police Leadership

The inspector general of police (IGP) is at the top of the police hierarchy. The IGP reports to the president, although the minister of interior plays a supervisory role over police matters. The president and minister, not the IGP, are responsible for policymaking.

Buhari selected Abdulrahman Dambazau, his chairman of security during the presidential election, to head the Ministry of Interior. Lieutenant General Dambazau (rtd) was born in Zaria in 1954, although he was from a Kano family. He trained at the Nigerian Defence Academy (Kaduna), was commissioned in 1977, and in 1979 attended the US Army Military Police School at Fort McClellan in Alabama. He obtained a BA in criminal justice from Kent State University in 1982 and a PhD in criminology from the University of Keele in 1989.

Dambazau rose through the military ranks, including within the military police. He served in the National War College in 1993–99 and again in 2004–6. In 2007–8, he commanded the Second Division, Ibadan. He then served as chief of army staff in 2008–10 under President Umaru Yar'Adua. He was at the center of the crisis over the terminal illness of Yar 'Adua and the handover of power to acting president Jonathan. Dambazau is, in short, familiar with both military and police functions and with high-level policy issues. He is a strong believer in democracy and rule of law.

The Range of Police Reforms

In December 2015, Dambazau met with the members of the Committee on Police Affairs at the House of Representatives and gave a preview of the types of reforms he believed were needed if the police were to be more effective. He laid out a four-part reform agenda: localizing personnel; improving training and equipment; increasing the number of personnel; and creating better terms of service.

"Localizing" the police meant that police would remain federal, as laid out in the Constitution, but recruitment and deployment would reflect local linguistic and cultural realities. In this way, the government hoped to change public perceptions of the police. "Without changing that perception," said Dambazau, "we don't see how the police can be effective. Generally, people look at the police as being brutal, corrupt, unfriendly, and inefficient. So we thought that policing is not just a matter of arrest and prosecution; policing also involves community service. So we want to see how we can change that perception" (http://www.informationng.com/2015/12/minister-urges-nigerians-to-change-perception-about-nigeria-police.html).

Dambazau stressed the need to ensure professionalization of the police through training and recruitment of high-quality personnel. He commented, too, on the importance of giving the police better equipment with which to "tackle the security challenges of the nation" (ibid.). In response, the chairman of the Committee on Police Affairs, Representative Haliru Jika (Bauchi-APC), assured the minister that his committee was fully supportive of the government's police reform program.

The government planned to recruit an additional 10,000 police officers, with an equal intake of cadets from each of the thirty-six states. The chairman of the Nigeria Police Commission, Mike Okiro, himself a former IGP, underlined the "urgent need to recruit constables, cadet inspectors and assistant superintendents of police. . . . With the current staff disposition of 286,901, [an] additional 119,421 personnel are required." He noted that "arrangements are ongoing to commence the recruitment of the 10,000 policemen as directed by the Federal Government" (ibid.).

Other topics discussed by Dambazau, the IGP, and the committee were conditions of service, including the dire condition of police widows whose husbands have been killed in the line of duty.

Given tight budgets and the need for police recruitment and training, results in terms of police reorientation were not to be expected in 2016. However, the Ministry of Interior would be closely watched for signs of progress in reorienting the police away from fulfilling a highly centralized federal mandate and toward serving the public at the state and local levels. This new focus would free up the military to concentrate more on counterinsurgency at home and on UN peacekeeping abroad.

Assessing Security Reforms

The international and local components of confronting violent extremism were coming into place during spring 2016. The major elements of the Buhari team's approach included (1) strengthening military leadership in Nigeria, focused on the northeast; (2) probing corruption by previous military leaders, including procurement practices; (3) building morale within the Nigerian military at the enlisted level; (4) beginning to restructure the police to allow for human resources to be localized; (5) working with West African and Central African states in creating "fusion centers" for intelligence, planning, and joint actions on the ground; (6) working closely with European powers and the United States; (7) working with Saudi Arabia, Qatar, and other Islamic states in confronting Islamic State affiliates; (8) supporting UN peacekeeping efforts; and (9) working with the World Bank on reconstruction plans.

Each of these elements required the personal and ongoing diplomacy of President Buhari. Meetings with heads of state, regional conferences, international gatherings, internal security strategy sessions: all took time and patience. Also, each of the international components required a unique scheduling and start-up process.

In the case of the United States, this meant factoring the US budget process into projected future military capabilities. According to the US Commission for International Religious Freedom (USCIRF), a congressionally mandated body:

> On February 9, President Barack Obama requested $200 million to combat radicalism in northern and western Africa. The funds are part of an FY 2017 $7.5 billion Pentagon budget which did not specify recipient states, although Joint Chiefs of Staff Air Force General Paul Selva listed al-Shabaab, Boko Haram and the Libyan contingent of ISIL, as the primary regional threats. (https://outlook.office/owa/)

This international perspective also meant that Buhari would be invited to participate in broader efforts at countering violent extremism, which had become a global concern. In mid-March, it was announced that Buhari would participate in the three-day Nuclear Security Summit, hosted by President Obama in Washington, DC, on March 30–April 1. (Attending the summit meant Buhari would have to postpone a scheduled state visit to China until a later date.)

According to the Nigerian media, the summit "aimed at addressing the threat of nuclear terrorism to global security through international cooperation to secure vulnerable nuclear materials, break up black markets, and detect and intercept illicitly trafficked materials (http://saharareporters.com/2016/03/09/president-buhari-attend-nuclear-security-summit-washington-end-march).

The global reach of terrorists had clearly lengthened in a new era of high technology. Within the Nigerian context, Buhari announced in early March that Boko Haram had been aided and abetted by the use of cell phones. According to the BBC:

> Mobile phone giant MTN fueled the Islamist-led insurgency in Nigeria by failing to disconnect unregistered sim cards, the Nigerian president has said. Muhammadu Buhari made the comment during a visit to Nigeria by his South African counterpart Jacob Zuma.
>
> Last year, Nigeria fined the South African–owned firm $3.4bn (L2.7bn) for missing a deadline to disconnect the cards. Nigeria believes Boko Haram militants use unregistered sim cards to co-ordinate attacks. . . .
>
> "You know how the unregistered [sim cards] are being used by terrorists, and between 2009 and today, at least 10,000 Nigerians were killed by Boko Haram," President Buhari said at a joint press conference with Mr. Zuma. (http://www.bbc.com/news/business-35755298)

Clearly, the security situation in Nigeria had changed dramatically between 2009 and 2016. What had started as a local reaction against heavy-handed policing in Maiduguri had gone underground and evolved into a sophisticated fighting force. After 2015, with Boko Haram establishing links to Islamic State, an international response was required. This grim reality would consume much of President Buhari's time and strategic thinking during the first year of his presidency.

CHALLENGES OF CORRUPTION

Chapter 19

Corruption and Law

This chapter examines Nigeria's judicial capacities to handle corruption. More specifically, the chapter looks at (1) recent patterns of corruption and the law; (2) the UAE and Gulf connections; (3) four high-profile cases from the battle against corruption; (4) the strengthened role of the EFCC and special tribunals; (5) the Buhari factor; (6) efforts to rally international support; and (7) Buhari's speech at the London Anti-Corruption Summit.

Recent Patterns of Corruption and the Law

Nigeria's dependence on petroleum revenue in recent decades has been profound. These funds are essential to cover budget items, as well as some off-budget items such as security. Unfortunately, oil revenue has also been an irresistible target for corrupt officials, who have misappropriated vast sums. In the past, when the EFCC or the ICPC has charged suspects, there have been cases of prosecutorial selectivity in enforcement, leading to halfhearted cases presented in court and then dropped. In some cases, too, presidential influence has been brought to bear on the judiciary to secure an acquittal.

Sometimes a case has been tried abroad, as in the Halliburton case, which resulted in Halliburton being fined US$1.3 billion. But when the case came back to Nigeria, it was dropped. The case of James Ibori being convicted in London and then released when remanded to Nigeria has already been mentioned.

In other key cases, such as the Abacha stolen funds, the official amount recovered by the Accountant General of the Federation was $2 billion, but the actual amount returned was several times higher, according to informed sources. When Buhari met with Obama in July 2015, he mentioned that approximately $150 billion had been stolen from Nigeria and asked for help to get it back.

If all the corruption cases pending in Nigeria in 2016 were to be given due process of law, they would be unlikely to be resolved within twelve months; they might not even be decided by the time of the next presidential election. Nonetheless, moving the cases forward, and letting Nigerians see the unimpeded and transparent progress of the law would set an important precedent.

For this reason, at the beginning of 2016, Buhari urged the courts to speed up the corruption trials. At the same time, he pledged not to intrude on the legal process. His media assistant, Garba Shehu, left no room for ambiguity: "President Muhammadu Buhari will not influence the decisions of courts in the ongoing high-profile corruption cases in the country" (http://www.dailytrust.com.ng/news/general/corruption-trials-buhari-ll-not-dictate-to-courts--presidency/127102.html).

The key decision for Buhari's attorney general was which cases should be given priority, and whether to insist on criminal prosecution or to accept a plea bargain by the accused that would involve the accused returning stolen funds in return for charges being dropped. Even the foreign ministry was involved. On January 11, Foreign Minister Geoffrey Onyeama reported that the government of Switzerland would transfer $300 million in recovered money from the Abacha family.

In mid-January 2016, the acting chairman of the EFCC, Ibrahim Magu, announced that more influential Nigerians would have their day in court. He requested input from investigative journalists, and assured them that they would be kept abreast of the EFCC processes. Many of those accused were members of the PDP, but he assured the media that they would be dealt with evenhandedly.

The commitment to evenhandedness was demonstrated in early January, when the EFCC arrested one of the leading figures in the APC. He was the former military governor of Kaduna State from December 1993 to August 1996, Lawal Jafaru Isa, and he was arrested in connection with the military procurement scandal. A retired brigadier general, Isa was a close associate of Buhari. Investigators believed he had received N170 million from Dasuki. (Isa later repaid this amount and was released.)

The first real test for an APC senior official was the prosecution of Senate President Bukola Saraki. On February 4, the Supreme Court ruled that Saraki's trial should continue at the Code of Conduct Tribunal. He was charged with thirteen counts of false asset declaration while serving two terms as governor of Kwara State. Buhari made no effort to intervene in the case.

This prosecution of an APC bigwig, however, did not obscure that fact that those who had had the most access to large-scale government funds in the previous fifteen years were members of the PDP. Details began to emerge in the media of elaborate cut-out schemes involving high-ranking PDP officials laundering military procurement funds through London-based companies, such as Leeman Communication.

The UAE and Gulf Connections

In mid-January, Buhari flew to the United Arab Emirates (UAE) for a three-day world energy summit. In addition to discussing energy (and arrangements for the UAE to help upgrade Nigerian refineries), Buhari held bilateral talks with UAE senior officials on Nigeria's war against terrorism and efforts to recover stolen funds. The two countries signed an extradition agreement, which explicitly pledged UAE help on the recovery and repatriation of stolen assets and the extradition of Nigerian fugitives.

Many prominent Nigerians were known to have properties in UAE. These included former attorney general Mohammed Bello Adoke (who had recently moved to The Hague), and former minister of petroleum resources Diezani Alison-Madueke, plus many other ministers from the Jonathan era. In addition, several PDP governors, high-level PDP officials, and even Dame Patience Jonathan had property in UAE. In some cases, fake names were used to hold such properties.

In late January, panic began to grip former officials, who had previously seen no reason to fear that their property holdings in UAE would be exposed and become vulnerable to legal action by the Nigerian government.

Nigerian security sources believed that as much as $20 billion in stolen Nigerian funds had been parked in banks and invested in properties in the UAE's two major cities, Dubai and Abu Dhabi. Some former officials were believed to be hiding out in Dubai, among them the former comptroller of the Nigerian Customs Service, Abdullahi Dikko, and the chairman of the now-defunct Pension Reform Task Team, Abdulrasheed Maina, who was wanted in Nigeria for allegedly stealing $2.8 million.

In late January and early February, Buhari would continue his international travels, with trips to Addis Ababa (Ethiopia) and Nairobi (Kenya). He would then go on to meetings in Paris, London, Qatar, and Saudi Arabia. His agenda throughout was to get cooperation and assistance on his three top priorities: the war on Boko Haram, economic development, and anticorruption.

The Battle against Corruption: Four High-Profile Cases

In February, Buhari vowed that he would do everything in his power to rid the country of corruption. It was a message he wanted the international community to hear as well as Nigerians, and thus he took the opportunity of a speech at a diplomatic reception at Aso Rock Presidential Villa to declare his commitment to anticorruption efforts:

> We are resolved to build a stable and prosperous Nigeria; a country that is inclusive of all her diverse peoples and a country that is at ease with itself. Building such a country will not be possible where corruption is pervasive. Mindful of this, it has become necessary to wage a relentless war against the cancer of corruption. So long as corruption holds center stage in the affairs of Nigeria, the country will continue to suffer incalculable harm.
>
> You are witnesses to the preliminary findings that have emerged in the past few weeks from our investigations into corrupt practices in different sectors of Nigeria's Public Service. I will leave no stone unturned in the efforts to rid Nigeria of corruption. I must, however, stay in the ambit of the law.
>
> In a similar fight in the past, and armed with the might of military muscle, I led a government that required persons presumed to be corrupt to prove their innocence. Today, as committed democrats, and in a culture of deepening democracy, we

> respect the law that presumes all persons innocent until they are proven to be guilty. (http://www.dailytrust.com.ng/news/general/corruption-buhari-vows-not-to-spare-anyone/134294.html)

Buhari's fight against corruption was being waged on many fronts. A number of big fish were in the cross-hairs of the EFCC, including the PDP's Uche Secondus (accused of receiving twenty-three luxury cars plus N300 million), former EFCC chief Ibrahim Lamorde (accused of misappropriating N1 trillion funds), and former PDP spokesman Olisa Metuh (accused of receiving N400 million from the former NSA).

A whole category of financial institutions, bureaux de change (BDC), was accused by Buhari of being "bogus." (These exchanges were set up to allow people to exchange naira for hard currencies.) "We had just 74 of the bureaux in 2005, now they have grown to 2,800. We will use our foreign exchange for industry, spare parts and the development of needed infrastructure. We don't have the dollars to give to the BDCs" (http://www.dailytrust.com.ng/news/general/arms-deal-probe-tip-of-the-ice-berge-buhari/131303.html).

Numerous smaller fish were also being targeted for litigation. Whether the courts were up to this challenge remained to be seen, given their reputation for corruption. In February, EFCC chair Ibrahim Magu claimed that senior lawyers, who had benefited from corruption in the past, were frustrating the legal efforts of the EFCC, and were often complicit in corrupt schemes (http://saharareporters.com/2016/02/16/senior-lawyers-corrupt-journalists-frustrating-anti-corruption-war-%E2%80%93-efcc-chair-magu).

Four high-profile cases help to illustrate the range and types of alleged corruption. The quartet includes cases against the former minister of petroleum resources Diezani Alison-Madueke and others in a London court; the former attorney general Mohammed Adoke and others for misdirecting petroleum funds; the former Delta militant with the nom de guerre Tompolo and others for money laundering; and nine senators being probed for corruption. (The military procurement corruption scandal is examined in the next chapter.)

Diezani Alison-Madueke

A major challenge for the Buhari government was how to track stolen oil. Ships with bunkered oil often have forged NNPC papers. Furthermore, Nigerian oil cannot be "fingerprinted" with precision. Even so, few experts doubted that one destination for bunkered oil was China. The overall nature of light sweet crude coming into China was apparent, and it could only have come from Nigeria. The shipping of stolen oil to China with the connivance of Chinese criminal networks was a subject President Buhari discussed with Chinese president Xi Jinping, who promised to cooperate. China was in the process of cracking down on corruption and began to investigate the Nigerian oil scandals. At the heart of the oil bunkering scandals was the former minister of petroleum resources and her associates.

The arrest of Diezani Alison-Madueke and others in London in early October has been mentioned in chapter 9. Along with the military procurement investigations, this is by far the biggest criminal case pursued by the Buhari administration. Because the case involves overseas assistance, and because of the complicated nature of the offshore oil contracts, the case may take years to be decided.

A general lack of funds appeared to hamper the Nigerian component of the investigation. According to the Nigerian media, in February, "a letter by the Presidential Advisory Committee on Corruption (PACC), to a United Kingdom–based anti-corruption organization, Global Witness, soliciting assistance in raising funds, revealed that due to the fall in crude oil prices and the general economic downturn the government lacked the needed funds to pursue the recovery of loot" (http://saharareporters.com/2016/02/20/why-we-can%E2%80%99t-recover-funds-looted-ex-minister-alison-madueke-others-%E2%80%94-presidency).

While Alison-Madueke was being treated for breast cancer in London, the EFCC arrested her key associate, Donald Chidi Amamgbo, over allegations of financial crimes. He had received permission from the minister to pump billions of dollars of Nigerian oil despite lacking the requisite experience.

In addition, the former minister had approved $24 billion in "crude swaps" (i.e., exchanges of oil for other goods) without a contract, according to former group managing director of NNPC Austin Oniwon. In spring 2016, the National Assembly in Abuja was insisting that Alison-Madueke return to Nigeria and answer questions.

Former Attorney General Mohammed Adoke

Former attorney general Mohammed Adoke has been a key figure in the widespread perception that, until recently, the very highest levels of government have not been interested in pursuing cases of high-level corruption. The attorney general, it may be noted, is appointed by the president and is unlikely to act independently on politically sensitive issues.

In late December 2015, Adoke was questioned by the EFCC regarding his role in the Malabu Oil scandal of 2011. This involved the transfer of $1.1 billion to associates of President Jonathan. In addition to Adoke, the former minister of state for finance Dr. Yerima Lawal Ngama authorized the release of $400 million to an escrow account. (Adoke had been involved in an earlier incident of corruption, the Halliburton scandal, during the Obasanjo administration, when he had bought shares in a private airline company in a blatant display of sudden wealth.)

Tompolo

In late December 2015, a forty-count criminal charge was brought by the EFCC to the Federal High Court in Lagos against a well-known former Delta militant, Government Ekpemupolo (aka "Tompolo"), and a former official of the Nigerian Maritime Administration and Safety Agency (NIMASA). They were accused of converting property stolen from NIMASA into $108 million plus N2.1 billion. They and their associates were accused under the Money Laundering Act of 2011.

By mid-February, however, the EFCC told a federal judge that Tompolo had simply disappeared, and the police and military could not trace him. On February 19, Justice Ibrahim Buba of the Federal High Court in Lagos allowed the EFCC to seize all of Tompolo's extensive properties.

The Senate Nine

By February 2016, 9 senators (out of 109 in the National Assembly) were facing criminal charges:

1. Senate President Bukola Saraki (APC Kwara Central), a two-term governor of Kwara from 2003 to 2011. He is chairman of the National Assembly. As noted earlier, he was indicted on thirteen counts for false declaration of assets by the Code of Conduct Tribunal.
2. Senator Ahmed Sani Yarima, a three-term senator and former governor of Zamfara State. He was indicted in January by the Independent Corrupt Practices Commission (ICPC) for using N1 billion meant for repairs on the Gusau Dam for other purposes.
3. Senator Danjuma Goje, governor of Gombe State from 2003 to 2011. He was facing an eighteen-count charge of corruption and fraud (N25 billion) by the EFCC.
4. Senator Abdullahi Adamu, governor of Nasarawa State from 1999 to 2007. He was arraigned by the EFCC on a 149-count charge of fraud in the amount of N15 billion.
5. Senator Abdulaziz Nyako, the son of a former Adamawa State governor. He was arraigned by the EFCC on a thirty-seven–count charge of criminal conspiracy, stealing, abuse of office, and money laundering. He and others were accused of stealing N15 billion from Adamawa accounts in 2011–13.
6. Senator Joshua Chibi Dariye, governor of Plateau State from 1999 to 2006, when he was impeached. He faced a twenty-three–count charge of money laundering, abuse of office, and corruption. He was accused of embezzling N1.2 billion from ecological funds.
7. Senator Ike Ekweremadu (PDP Enugu West), deputy president of the Senate. He was facing forgery charges in the Federal High Court.
8. Senator Kashamu Buruji (Ogun East). He was facing extradition by the National Drugs Law Enforcement Agency (NDLEA) at the request of the United States.

9. Senator Godswill Obot Akpabio (PDP Akwa-Ibom Northwest), Senate Minority Leader. He was being investigated for corruption and looting from Akwa-Ibom State funds.

The Strengthened Role of the EFCC and Special Tribunals

The EFCC has been functioning since the administration of President Obasanjo, when it was under the direction of Nudu Ribadu, a policeman and lawyer who initially was effective, before political pressures began to intrude. Under President Jonathan, the EFCC was directed by Ibrahim Lamorde and seemed, from the outside, to be functioning well; inside, however, rumors of corruption among EFCC officials abounded.

Under President Buhari, the acting chair of EFCC has been Ibrahim Magu, who seems to have taken his lead from Buhari's determined fight against corruption. The widespread investigations conducted by the EFCC and the number of referrals to prosecutors have been unprecedented in the EFCC's history.

In addition, Buhari discussed his anticorruption efforts with the Chief Justice of the Supreme Court, Mohammed Mahmud, who agreed to establish a set of specialized anticorruption tribunals. These tribunals would cover both military and civilian cases. Creating such tribunals, however, requires special authorization from the National Assembly, which has been slow in coming.

The Buhari Factor

Although a number of senior officials had been tried for corruption prior to the Buhari presidency, the extent of the current corruption court cases in Nigeria is unprecedented. That does not mean that every case will lead to a guilty verdict. All of the accused are entitled to their day in court, and are likely to have high-quality legal representation; and there will surely be appeals and possible plea bargains. Cases may drag on for years. But the fact remains: the law is taking its course.

Importantly, in none of these cases (apart from certain military procurement scandals that impacted national security) has the prosecution been sponsored or encouraged by President Buhari.

He has kept his hands off the judiciary, despite enormous pressure for him to come to the aid of APC allies.

The question will arise when criminal cases are concluded as to whether the Nigerian judiciary is up to the task of being even-handed in such high-level cases. Buhari's attitude is to let the chips fall where they may in particular cases, although reform of the judiciary is one of his larger goals.

Buhari has often said that if any of his own children were accused of corruption, and the authorities did not investigate, he would never forgive the authorities. On numerous occasions, Buhari has urged public officials to do their duty without fear or favor. He has also tried to inspire younger generations to regard public service as an honest calling.

For example, the current acting head of EFCC, Ibrahim Magu, was a schoolboy in Borno when Buhari was military governor in 1975. Buhari gave a talk to a group of boys that included Magu and urged them to do their best. Magu was inspired and became a professional policeman. In 2015, Buhari asked Magu to head the EFCC, a dangerous job if done well. By mid-May 2016, Magu had secured 143 convictions of corrupt officials.

Efforts to Rally International Support

Buhari's support in the international community has been crucial to his policy of zero tolerance for corruption. In April, Alison-Madueke appeared before the Westminster Magistrate's Court in London regarding money laundering and bribery allegations. Her associates in Switzerland were being pursued by Interpol.

In early April, the so-called Panama Papers scandal unfolded. The Panama company of Mossack Fonseca was hacked, and numerous secret accounts were made public. A number of accounts linked to the Saraki family were uncovered and made public, including the accounts of Toyin Saraki, the wife of the president of the Senate. The Nigerian media published many of these details (http://saharareporters.com/2016/04/04/panamapapers-nigeria%E2%80%99s-senate-president-sarakis-secret-and-undeclared-family-assets).

Of special importance to the international coalition confronting corruption in Nigeria has been the friendship Buhari has developed with US secretary of state John Kerry, who explicitly linked the corruption issue to the challenges of economic diversification in Nigeria. At a meeting of the US-Nigeria binational commission in late March, Kerry stressed that the United States would invest $600 million in Nigeria in 2016, chiefly to encourage diversification of the economy. Such support hinged on Buhari's anticorruption efforts.

One report in the Nigerian media observed:

> On the issue of corruption, Kerry said both President Buhari and President Obama identified one of the largest and most stubborn obstacles to economic growth to include the persistence of corruption. "To fight it, the United States strongly supports the efforts of institutions like Nigeria's Economic and Financial Crimes Commission to prosecute corruption cases. And we back the role of civil society and of the media in exposing corruption and in advocating for greater transparency."(http://guardian.ng/business-services/business/why-u-s-is-supporting-nigerias-diversification-anti-corruption-agenda/)

While such lofty anticorruption goals were being articulated at the senior level on both sides, detailed meetings were being held in Washington, DC, between EFCC chair Magu and counterparts in the US government with a deep knowledge of Nigerian corruption. The sharing of such information meant that many of the most serious corruption offenders in Nigeria would have nowhere to hide, in the United States or elsewhere.

It was widely recognized that much of the looted funds had found its way to the United States, the United Kingdom, the UAE, Switzerland, France, the Seychelles, and the Isle of Jersey. Encouragingly, substantial amounts of these funds were beginning to be retrieved.

On March 8, the Swiss government agreed to return $321 million to the Nigerian government. These were monies deemed to have been illegally acquired by Sani Abacha. Much of the work to identify these monies was done by Nigerian and Swiss civil societies. The estimated $20 billion in the UAE was in the process of being recouped. The US federal government returned $480 million. The Isle of Jersey returned £22.5 million (equivalent to $32 million at the time). Additional billions were being identified in Europe,

Asia, and America. In addition to liquid assets, real estate properties were being identified and, where possible, confiscated.

Meanwhile, the estimate of the amount of money involved in the military procurement diversion scandal in Nigeria had ballooned from $2.1 billion to $15 billion. A former chief of defence staff, Air Chief Marshal Alex Badeh, was found with $1 million in cash in his Abuja home. He claimed not to know how it had come to be there and forfeited it to the EFCC. A military account of $500 million was frozen by the EFCC.

The EFCC also targeted the many properties owned by the former minister of petroleum resources Alison-Madueke in Abuja and Lagos. Gold and diamond jewelry worth millions of US dollars were recovered in her homes. It was revealed that the former minister gave $115 million to Fidelity Bank in Nigeria to be distributed to INEC officials in Rivers, Delta, and Akwa Ibom prior to the presidential election.

In May, it also appeared that Alison-Madueke had given Sterling Bank (Abuja) $88 million as a Jonathan slush fund to rig the 2015 elections. In a separate case involving Fidelity Bank, her son Ugonna was the apparent middleman. Ugonna had studied engineering in the United States, and was seen flying in a private jet, drinking champagne in a limousine, and flashing wads of cash on his Facebook page. When Ugonna could not be found in Nigeria, the EFCC launched a full-scale manhunt for him.

Key former political figures in the PDP also went into hiding, some of them in the United States, others in Europe, and several in Singapore.

Former president Jonathan was not on the EFCC wanted list, but many of his closest associates were. Jonathan traveled to the United States in May, but had to cancel some of his public engagements because of protests by Nigerians living abroad. The Buhari attack on corruption was edging closer to the highest levels.

The London Anti-Corruption Summit

The intersection of Nigerian domestic corruption and the international community came to a head on May 12 in London at the Anti-Corruption Summit. Heads of state from sixty countries gathered to consider specific agreements to curb the flow of stolen assets.

Buhari, who was scheduled to give a keynote address, traveled to London with his attorney general and minister of justice Abubakar Malami, the EFCC chair Ibrahim Magu, and other key officials.

Buhari threw down the gauntlet at the London Summit. When David Cameron characterized Nigeria as "fantastically corrupt" in an aside to Queen Elizabeth, Archbishop of Canterbury Justin Welby commented, "But this president is not corrupt." When President Buhari was asked about the episode by the media, he said that he agreed with Cameron's statement. Then he asked for British help in retrieving the Nigerian looted money hidden in Britain.

Buhari's keynote speech at the London conference summarized his perception of the corruption challenge in Nigeria and possible remedies. His speech included the following observations:

> Corruption is a hydra-headed monster and cankerworm that undermines the fabric of all societies. It does not differentiate between developed and developing countries. It constitutes a serious threat to good governance, rule of law, peace and security, as well as development programmes aimed a tackling poverty and economic backwardness. . . .
>
> Permit me to share our national experience in combatting corruption. I intend to do this by placing the fight against corruption within the three priority programmes of our administration. On assumption of office on 29th May 2015, we identified as our main focus three key priority programmes. They are combatting insecurity, tackling corruption, and job creation through restructuring the declining national economy.
>
> Our starting point as an administration was to amply demonstrate zero tolerance for corrupt practices, as this vice is largely responsible for the social and economic problems our country faces today. The endemic and systemic nature of corruption in our country demanded our strong resolve to fight it. We are demonstrating our commitment to this effort by bringing integrity to governance and showing leadership by example. . . .
>
> Tackling the menace of corruption is not an easy task, but it is possible even if many feathers have to be ruffled. Our government's dogged commitment to tackling corruption is also evident in the freedom and support granted to national anti-corruption agencies to enable them to carry out their respective mandates without any interference or hindrance from any quarter, including the government.
>
> Today, our frontline anti-corruption agencies, namely, the Economic and Financial Crimes Commission (EFCC), the Inde-

pendent Corrupt Practices and Other Related Offences Commission (ICPC), the Code of Conduct Bureau (CCB) and the Code of Conduct Tribunal (CCT), have become revitalized and more proactive in the pursuit of perpetrators of corrupt practices, irrespective of their social status and political persuasion. This is a radical departure from the past.

We have implemented the Treasury Single Account (TSA), whereby all Federal Government revenue goes into one account. This measure would make it impossible for public officers to divert public funds to private accounts, as was the practice before. Through the effective application of TSA and Bank Verification Numbers of public officials, we have been able to remove 23,000 ghost workers from our payroll, thereby saving billions that would have been stolen.

We are also reviewing our anti-corruption laws and have developed a national anti-corruption strategy document that will guide our policies in the next three years and possibly beyond.

I am not unaware of the challenges of fighting corruption in a manner consistent with respect for human rights and rule of law. As a country that came out of prolonged military rule only sixteen years ago, it will clearly take time to change the mentality and psychology of law enforcement officers. I am committed to applying the rule of law and to respecting human rights. I also require our security agencies to do the same.

I admit there are a few cases where apparently stringent rules have been applied as a result of threats to national security and the likelihood that certain persons may escape from the country or seek to undermine the stability of Nigeria. It is for this reason that we are seeking the support of many countries for the prosecution of certain individuals residing in their jurisdictions. Of course, we will provide the necessary legal documents and whatever mutual assistance is required to secure conviction of such individuals, as well as facilitate the repatriation of our stolen assets.

Unfortunately, our experience has been that repatriation of corrupt proceeds is very tedious, time consuming, costly, and entails more than just the signing of bilateral or multilateral agreements. This should not be the case as there are provisions in the appropriate United Nations conventions that require countries to return assets to countries from where it is proven that they were illegitimately acquired.

Further, we are favorably disposed to forging strategic partnerships with governments, civil society organizations, organized private sector and international organizations to combat corruption. Our sad national experience had been that domestic perpetrators of corrupt practices do often work hand in hand with international criminal cartels.

This evil practice is manifested in the plundering and stealing of public funds, which are then transferred abroad into secret accounts. I therefore call for the establishment of an international anti-corruption infrastructure that will monitor, trace and facilitate the return of such assets to their countries of origin. It is important to stress that the repatriation of identified stolen funds should be done without delay or preconditions.

In addition to the looting of public funds, Nigeria is also confronted with illegal activities in the oil sector, the mainstay of our export economy. That this industry has been enmeshed in corruption with the participation of the staff of some oil companies is well established. Their participation enabled oil theft to take place on a massive scale. . . .

It is clear, therefore, that the menace of oil theft, put at over 150,000 barrels per day, is a criminal enterprise involving internal and external perpetrators. Illicit oil cargoes and their proceeds move across international borders. Opaque and murky as these illegal transactions may be, they are certainly traceable and can be acted upon, if all governments show the required political will. This has been the missing link in the international efforts hitherto. Now in London, we can turn a new page by creating a multi-state and multi-stakeholder partnership to address this menace.

We, therefore, call on the international community to designate oil theft as an international crime similar to the trade in "blood diamonds," as it constitutes an imminent and credible threat to the economy and stability of oil-producing countries like Nigeria. The critical stakeholders are here and can lead the charge in that regard.

By the end of our Summit tomorrow, we should be able to agree on a rules-based architecture to combat corruption in all its forms and manifestations. . . .

A main component of this anti-corruption partnership is that governments must demonstrate unquestionable political will and commitment to the fight. The private sector must come clean and be transparent, and civil society, while keeping a watch on all stakeholders, must report with a sense of responsibility and objectivity.

For our part, Nigeria is committed to signing the Open Government Partnership alongside Prime Minister Cameron during the Summit tomorrow.

The international agreement mentioned in Buhari's speech imposed severe sanctions on corrupt officials. They would face travel restrictions and denial of visas, rejection of requests for political asylum, possible loss of citizenship, no approval for naturalization requests, and restrictions on bank accounts in all sixty countries. Intelligence on money laundering would be shared.

In addition, six nations—the United Kingdom, France, the Netherlands, Afghanistan, Kenya, and Nigeria—adopted the key provision of public registers of "beneficial ownership." British adherence to this agreement would mean that the ownership of all properties in the United Kingdom would be publicly listed, allowing anticorruption authorities to scrutinize the list for evidence of corruption. The noose was tightening on flight monies and foreign ownership property investments.

Although the United States did not sign the agreement, it was clear that Buhari had close working relations with President Obama, Secretary Kerry, Treasury Secretary Jack Lew, and a number of senior Justice Department officials. The United States would continue to be helpful in providing information and legal support to Buhari's fight against corruption.

Chapter 20

Corruption and Law in Military Procurement

As noted in previous chapters, the military procurement scandal (popularly known as "Dasukigate" and "Armsgate") appeared to reach to the highest levels, because former NSA Sambo Dasuki clearly seemed to have had authorization from President Jonathan for the diversion of weapons procurement funds toward the presidential election of 2015. Given that the stolen funds were probably not recoverable, and given the likely involvement in some fashion of Jonathan, President Buhari's attorney general would need to demonstrate both good judgment and a keen strategic sense if he was to manage the case successfully.

The attorney general had to contemplate prosecuting two major categories of people: former military or security officials, and PDP officials who may have used misappropriated funds to influence the election of 2015. Buhari's team was conscious of the danger in pursuing the former cases: military and security officers have ways of striking back—as Buhari had discovered in 1985.

In the case of PDP officials and beneficiaries of the election moneybags funds, the question for the attorney general was how to prioritize cases without appearing to victimize the opposition. The situation was further complicated by the fact that virtually all major groups in society were in some ways being enticed to support the PDP. These groups included traditional rulers, the business community, professional groups, and even civil society organizations.

Some Muslim and Christian clergy and organizations had refused to accept such inducements. But other religious figures had not been so scrupulous. In March, a former head of NNPC revealed that President Jonathan had spent N2.2 billion on "prayers" to win the war against Boko Haram. According to a report in the media:

> Former President Goodluck Jonathan's administration blew the cash on special prayers in Nigeria and Saudi Arabia to win the war. The cash was disbursed through the Office of the National Security Advisor (ONSA), following a proposal by a former Executive Director of the Nigerian National Petroleum Corporation (NNPC), Aminu Baba-Kusa. . . .
>
> Baba-Kusa said the N2.2 billion was spent on prayers to hasten the defeat of Boko Haram. The cash was released in two tranches of N1,450,000,000 and N750,000,000. Baba-Kusa told EFCC investigators that the contract proposal was verbal. (http://saharareporters.com/2016/03/11/ex-nnpc-chief-ex-president-jonathan%E2%80%99s-govt-blew-n22b-prayers)

It should be noted that the practice of giving money to religious figures to pray for leaders has a long history in Nigeria. A problem arises, however, when that money is meant to be spent on the petroleum industry or the military procurement budget.

This chapter examines (1) military procurement and the Armsgate scandal, (2) and the role of PDP leaders in the diversion of funds.

Military Procurement and the Armsgate Scandal

In mid-January, on the recommendation of his military procurement Audit Committee, Buhari ordered the EFCC to probe seventeen former and serving military officers, many of whom were or had been in the Air Force. These included Air Chief Marshal A. S. Badeh (rtd); Air Marshal M. D. Umar (rtd); Air Marshal A. N. Amosu (rtd); Major General E. R. Chioba (rtd); Air Vice Marshal (AVM) I. A. Balogun; AVM A. G. Tsakr (rtd); AVM A. G. Idowu; AVM A. M. Mamu; AVM O. T. Oguntoyinbo; AVM T. Omenyi; AVM J. B. Adigun; and AVM J. A. Kayode-Beckley; plus a number of air commanders. Most were questioned and released.

Air Chief Marshal Badeh was later charged with ten counts of money laundering, criminal breach of trust, and corruption.

Among other charges, he was accused of taking N1.4 billion from Air Force accounts to buy a mansion in Abuja.

The military procurement Audit Committee's second report also recommended that the EFCC probe twenty-one companies for breaches in contracts with the Air Force or the NSA. These companies included Messrs Societe D'Equipments Internationaux; Himma Abubakar; Aeronautical Engineering and Technical Services, Ltd; and Messrs Syrius Technologies. Breaches included nonspecification of procurement costs and the transfer of public funds for unidentified purposes.

The consequences of such misappropriation could be tragic. For example, "helicopters were delivered without rotor blades and upgrade accessories. Additionally, the helicopters were undergoing upgrade while being deployed for operation in the North East without proper documentation. It was further established that as of date, only one of the helicopters is in service while the other crashed and claimed the lives of two NAF personnel" (http://saharareporters.com/2016/03/11/ex-nnpc-chief-ex-president-jonathan%E2%80%99s-govt-blew-n22b-prayers).

Part of the drama of this procurement scandal was the relationship between NSA Sambo Dasuki and Minister of Defence Aliyu Gusau, which appeared to some observers as estranged and even bordering on hostility. Gusau, it seems, was unhappy that military procurement and other vital functions gravitated to the NSA, who was increasingly regarded by some as a "co-president" to Jonathan.

The Role of PDP Leaders in the Diversion of Funds

In January, former national chairman of the PDP Adamu Mu'azu was wanted by the EFCC for questioning but had gone into hiding. Former PDP spokesman Olisa Metuh, when asked about N400 million paid to a company in which he had an interest, said he would rather starve than pay back the money. He was arrested.

The former director general of the Nigerian Maritime Administration and Safety Agency, Patrick Akpobolokemi, was arrested, but jumped bail. He was later rearrested. The lawyer who stood surety for him was arrested. The six PDP zonal chairmen claimed they did not know where the campaign slush funds had come from.

Acting EFCC chair, Ibrahim Magu, said that the war against corruption had just begun. The question was how high up the probes would go. Magu did tell the media that former president Jonathan "would not be invited [i.e., asked to go to EFCC offices to answer questions] over the $2.1 billion arms deals because memos and documentation on the disbursements of the money were not approved for political campaigns" (http://saharareporters.com/2016/01/12/metuh-efcc-i-would-rather-starve-refund-n400-million).

When asked why EFCC cases have a tendency to get stuck in the legal process, Magu "blamed the lawyers, saying when a politician steals N10 billion, he keeps N5 billion for litigation. He hires Senior Advocates Nigeria. Judges accuse us of not conducting thorough investigations in order to compromise us" (ibid.).

Throughout January, case after case of senior PDP officials was under review by the EFCC and/or the courts. Although some PDP stalwarts claimed that a witch hunt was under way, ordinary Nigerians were keenly aware of realities on the ground, where the corrupt seldom made any attempt to conceal their "new wealth." The fact that Buhari was enlisting the help of the international community in the probes lent weight to the seriousness of his effort— and also meant that alleged offenders had nowhere to hide.

Would the trail lead to former president Jonathan himself? As of the early months of 2016, it appeared that the EFCC was not going after Jonathan. Nor was it going after former president Obasanjo. The question of the stability of the entire political system seemed at stake.

In addition, a number of senior military officers who had served as head of state—from Babangida to Abubakar—seemed off-limits. Indeed, rumors swirled that if the probes went after senior officers, they might push back, because they had extensive networks in the active military services.

At the same time, the knowledge such heavyweights possessed could well be traded for immunity, and would help to illuminate the patterns and sources of corruption. Buhari had letters in his possession showing Jonathan's requests for off-budget funds. But Buhari's larger purpose was not to put former high-level officials in jail. Rather, it was to retrieve stolen funds and to change the political culture of the country.

CHALLENGES OF ECONOMIC DEVELOPMENT

Chapter 21

The First Buhari Budget

As noted previously, *leadership* provides direction; *management* provides capacity for implementation. Both are necessary in any government. In the Buhari administration, economic leadership has been very much a team effort, drawing in particular on the experience of team members from among the Lagos component of the coalition. For example, the vice president was a spokesman on many occasions, addressing a variety of domestic audiences. But the task of articulating Nigeria's economic vision for an international business and policy audience fell to Buhari himself. As ever, he linked economic development strategy to the need to curb corruption.

One of the clearest expressions of Buhari's economic policy for Nigeria in the twenty-first century was given in his statement "All Change in Nigeria," which appeared in *The World in 2016*, an assessment of the prospects for the coming year produced by the *Economist* magazine in early December:

> In 2014, before the election that saw the first change of power in Nigeria by peaceful democratic means in our history, the then government rebased our country's GDP. Now, by internationally recognised metrics, *we possess the largest economy in Africa.* While this should be a source of pride for Nigerians, it goes no way to addressing the deep *structural challenges our economy faces;* nor does it put more money in the pockets or food on the table of millions of our citizens who go without, every day. To achieve dynamic and sustainable economic growth, and to

eradicate poverty, we need as a nation to undertake serious economic reforms. Some will be painful but all will be necessary.

I am determined that if *my government stands for anything it is the complete breaking of the cycle of gross corruption and theft that has caused investors to look first anywhere but Nigeria when considering business opportunities in Africa.* In visits, starting with Britain, America, Germany and France, I have sought and received the support of their governments to *locate and then return missing billions siphoned out of Nigeria by leaders of previous administrations.* Colossal estimates have been bandied about on the amounts spirited out of Nigeria. Whatever can be repatriated of the stolen money must be reinvested in our economy. That process has now begun, and my administration will not rest until the funds are returned, and those who removed them are brought to justice.

This return of our people's money will be combined with a diversification of our economy, and particularly a manufacturing base that has been allowed to wither away in recent years. Our *oil sector, the largest in Africa, has failed to reach its full potential* because past governments failed to maintain our capacity to process and refine raw materials. This is similarly the case for other extractive sectors. In collaboration with international partners and our own leading businesses we are working to ensure this is addressed expeditiously.

Given the fall in oil and commodities prices, we will also seek to rebalance the economy in other areas. Nigeria's fight against Boko Haram and (once it is defeated) our long-term security require a local military manufacturing base. We are already in serious *discussions with partners to build capacity that can supply locally developed equipment for our armed forces* that will, in time, lower our levels of imports of such equipment and improve our balance-of-payments position.

Broader and deeper transformation in the manufacturing sector is of course possible, and essential, but will not flourish without *greater investment in electricity supply.* Nigeria, like much of Africa, remains underpowered, and we are working on a strategy to boost our own electricity production, leveraging, in the first instance, internally available natural gas, water and wind resources.

It has also been seen in other parts of the world, from eastern Europe to Asia, that the *diversification and opening up of competition within a nation's internal market* leads to growth and job creation. Nigeria, again like much of Africa, remains too state-dependent. In certain strategic areas state intervention is necessary, even in the most advanced economies. But we are determined to attract local and international investors by market reform and improving the environment for business.

> *We can see in Lagos, Nigeria's most economically advanced region, that competition lowers prices* for consumers in everything from the retail sector to the supply of public services, and creates jobs. We will take that blueprint and, underpinned by infrastructure investment, we can grow supply and opportunity in products and services.
>
> I know that millions of people in Nigeria are waiting to see signs of economic recovery and most importantly, the chance for a job and the better life and self-respect that employment and a career can bring. I wish my administration could deliver this for each and every Nigerian overnight. But no government anywhere in the world has ever been able to achieve such transformation instantaneously. We look to examples such as *Singapore, which has managed to achieve economic greatness despite having few natural resources beyond the ingenuity of its people.* It is possible for Nigeria, with its surfeit of natural resources, to achieve the same.
>
> Yet we also note that most nations that have achieved rapid economic growth in recent decades have one thing in common: they first addressed their *breakdown in governance, cracked down on corruption and demonstrated to their own people and the world that to invest in that country is safe.* That is where we must begin.
>
> Delivering on that promise to the people and to the world is already under way. It is the only way we will reach the economic greatness Nigerians deserve. (Economist Group, *The World in 2016* [London: Economist Group, December 2015], 84; emphasis added)

This broad statement (equivalent in some ways to a State of the Union address) made plain the government's overall policy directions. Translating those general goals into specific targets would be a task accomplished through the budget process. After all, a budget is an expression of economic priorities constrained by projected revenue income and political realities.

On December 21, President Buhari stood before a joint session of the National Assembly and unveiled his first budget for 2016. This twelve-page proposal came at a time when the price of oil had slipped to below $38 per barrel, the benchmark for the budget.

Just over a week later, on December 30, President Buhari held his first "media chat" on Nigerian television. A panel of journalists asked questions, and viewers called in with their own questions as well. While some people asked about the Boko Haram situation and the tense situation in Zaria, most asked about the budget initiatives and economic development. Buhari's candid replies signified an open and transparent approach to government.

This chapter examines (1) key points in Buhari's 2016 budget; (2) key points in Buhari's earlier media chat on economics; (3) new initiatives; and (4) the controversy over fuel subsidies and NNPC structure.

Key Points in Buhari's 2016 Budget

Buhari's budget presentation on December 21 was preceded by the publication in mid-December of an eighteen-page technical report, *2016–2018 Medium-Term Expenditure Framework and Fiscal Strategy Paper*. This report detailed a wide variety of economic trends, outlined the policy principles of the 2016 budget, and explained the oil production and price constraints. It also dealt with Nigeria's debt management strategy, its debt service, and the issues of budget sustainability in times of uncertainty.

The budget itself had segments on the 2015 budget background, the 2016 budget assumptions, and laying the foundations for sustainable growth. Its concluding section discussed moving away from dependence on oil. Some of the highlights of the budget speech are given below in brief.

> We have set a benchmark price of $38 per barrel and a production estimate of 2.2 million barrels per day for 2016. . . .
>
> With the full implementation of the Treasury Single Account, we expect significant improvement in the collection and remittance of independent revenues. . . .
>
> One of our early decisions was the adoption of a zero-based budgeting approach. . . .
>
> We have directed the extension of the Integrated Personnel Payroll Information System (IPPIS). . . .
>
> We aim to ensure macroeconomic stability by achieving a real GDP growth rate of 4.37% and managing inflation. . . .
>
> This budget will have a job creation focus in every aspect of the execution of this budget. Nigeria's job creation drive will be private sector led. . . .
>
> As an emergency measure, to address the chronic shortage of teachers in public schools across the country, we will also partner with State and Local Governments to recruit, train and deploy 500,000 unemployed graduates and NCE [National Certificate in Education] holders. . . .

We also intend to partner with State and Local Governments to provide financial training and loans to market women, traders and artisans, through their cooperative societies. . . .

Furthermore, through the office of the Vice President, we are working with various development partners to design an implementable and transparent cash transfer program for the poorest and most vulnerable. . . .

We have proposed a budget of N6.08 trillion with a revenue projection of N3.86 resulting in a deficit of N2.22 trillion. . . .

In 2016, oil-related revenues are expected to contribute N820 billion. Non-oil revenues, comprising Company Income Tax (CIT), Value Added Tax (VAT), Customs and Excise duties, and Federation Account levies, will contribute N1.45 trillion . . . we have projected up to N1.51 trillion from independent revenues. . . .

I have also directed the NNPC to explore alternative funding models that will enable us to honour our obligations to Joint Ventures (JVs) and deep offshore fields . . .

To deliver our development objectives, we have increased the capital expenditure portion of the budget from N557 billion in the 2015 budget to N1.8 trillion in the 2016 budget. . . .

This increased capital expenditure commits significant resources to critical sectors such as Power, Works and Housing—N433.4 billion; Transport—N202 billion; Special Intervention Programs—N200 billion; Defence—N134.6 billion; and Interior—N53.1 billion. . . .

In fulfillment of our promise to run a lean government, we have proposed a 9% reduction in non-debt recurrent expenditure, from N2.59 trillion in the 2015 budget to N2.35 trillion in 2016. . . .

We will devote a significant portion of our recurrent expenditure to institutions that provide critical government services. We will spend N369.6 billion in Education; N294.5 billion in Defence; N221.7 billion in Health; and N145.3 billion in the Ministry of Interior. . . .

I am aware of the problems many Nigerians have in accessing foreign exchange for their various purposes. . . . These are clearly due to the current inadequacies in the supply of foreign exchange to Nigerians who need it. I am, however, assured by the Governor of the Central Bank that the Bank is currently fine-tuning its foreign exchange management to introduce some flexibility and encourage additional inflow of foreign currency to help ease the pressure. . . .

We are carefully assessing our Exchange rate regime, keeping in mind our willingness to attract foreign investors, but at the same time, managing and controlling inflation to levels that will not harm the average Nigerian. Nigeria is open for business.

> We are here to serve. And indeed Nigerians will get the service they have longed for and which they rightly deserve. . . . We as a Government cannot do it alone. We will require the support of all civil servants, the organized labour, industry groups, the press and of course our religious and traditional institutions. This is a call for all of us to stand and serve our country. (cnbcafrica./com/news/western-africa/2015/12/22/nigeria-president-buharis-2016-budget-speech/)

With the National Assembly controlled by the APC, there was little doubt that the Buhari budget would be passed in some form or other. The larger question was how it would be regarded by the general public. By late April, the budget had still not been approved by the National Assembly, due to some specific political controversies. Details of the budget were still pending. The public seemed to be losing patience. Buhari himself was frustrated by earlier padding of the budget by bureaucrats in some of the ministries. This was interpreted by the Buhari team as an attempt to scuttle the innovations proposed by the president by inflating their cost. When Buhari found out, he was reported to be angry and ordered a purge of the ministries involved, from the director general down. Twenty-two top officials were dismissed, including the budget director. In all, 184 civil servants were disciplined.

Even with the budget having been adjusted downward by the National Assembly, the country would still have a need to borrow $3.5 billion, given the drop in oil prices. *The Economist* on January 30 had argued that Nigeria should devalue its currency. Buhari had pushed back, arguing that an oil economy does not gain from such devaluation, because its major export is denominated in US dollars (http://www.dailytrust.com.ng/news/general/why-i-won-t-devalue-naira-buhari/134578.html). Fortunately, the delay caused by the padding scandal gave Buhari time to solicit concessionary international loans to meet the shortfall in budget funds. Nigeria began negotiating with the World Bank for $2.5 billion and with the African Development Bank for $1 billion in emergency loans. Buhari would also travel to Saudi Arabia and Qatar to discuss the crisis in world oil prices.

Finally, on May 6, Buhari signed the 2016 budget at the Aso Rock Villa, in the presence of the vice president (Osinbajo), the president of the Senate (Saraki), and the Speaker of the House of

Representatives (Dogara). Notably, the budget set aside funding for the Lagos-Calabar coastal rail system, which previously had been cut by the Appropriations Committee at the National Assembly.

Buhari's formal remarks at the signing of the N6.06 trillion budget clearly articulated his priorities and strategies:

> 1. It gives me great pleasure today to sign the first full-year budget of this administration into law. I thank the leadership of the National Assembly, in particular the Senate President and the Speaker of the House of Representatives, and indeed all members of the National Assembly for their cooperation in making this a reality.
>
> 2. The budget is intended to signpost a renewal of our committment to restoring the budget as a serious article of faith with the Nigerian people. The Administration is committed to ensuring that henceforth the annual appropriation bill is presented to the National Assembly in time for the passage of the Act before the beginning of the fiscal year.
>
> 3. Through the 2016 budget, aptly titled "Budget of Change", the government seeks to fulfill its own side of the social contract. The Budget I have signed into law provides for aggregate expenditures of N6.06trn. Further details of the approved budget, as well as our Strategic Implementation Plan for the 2016 budget, will be provided by the Honourable Minister of Budget and National Planning.
>
> 4. I shall be speaking in more details about the Budget, its implementation and over-all national economic and social policies of the Government in my address on May 29th, God willing.
>
> 5. In designing the 2016 budget, we made a deliberate choice to pursue an expansionary fiscal policy despite the huge decline in government revenues from crude oil exports. This is why *we decided to enlarge the budget deficit at this time, to be financed principally through foreign and domestic borrowings. All borrowings will be applied toward growth-enhancing capital expenditures.*
>
> 6. The signing of the budget today will trigger concerted efforts to reflate the Nigerian economy, a key element of which is the *immediate injection of N350 bn into the economy by way of capital projects.* To illustrate our renewed commitment to infrastructural development, the 2016 budget *allocates over N200 bn to road construction* as against a paltry N18 bn allocated for the same purpose in the 2015 budget.

7. Despite the current difficulties we will work extra-hard to achieve our revenue projections. Our revenue generating agencies are coming under better management and are being reoriented. The *implementation of the Treasury Single Account (TSA)* is expected to contribute significantly to improving transparency over government revenues.

8. Our determined fight against corruption is resulting in improvements in the quality of public expenditure. The *work of the Efficiency Unit,* as well as other public financial management initiatives, are also contributing in this regard. The continuing *efforts to reduce recurrent expenditures* should hopefully free up more funds for capital expenditure in 2017 and beyond.

9. As I said in my New Year message, living in State House does not in any way alienate me from your daily struggles. I read the newspapers and listen to TV and radio news. I hear your cries. I share your pain.

10. We are *experiencing probably the toughest economic times in the history of our Nation.* I want to commend the sacrifice, resilience and toughness of all Nigerians young and old who have despite the hardships continued to have hope and confidence of a great future for all Nigerians. But permit me to say that this government is also like none other. We are absolutely committed to changing the structure of the Nigerian economy once and for all.

11. We are working day and night to *diversify the economy* so that we never again have to rely on one commodity to survive as a country. So that we can produce the food that we eat, make our own textiles, produce most of the things we use. We intend to produce an environment for our young people to be able to innovate and create jobs through technology.

12. I cannot promise you that this will be an easy journey, but in the interest of so much and so many we must tread this difficult path. I can assure you that *this government you have freely elected will work with honesty and dedication, day and night to ensure that our country prospers and that the prosperity benefits all Nigerians.* God bless Federal Republic of Nigeria. (emphasis added) (http://saharareporters.com/2016/05/06/buhari%E2%80%99s-remarks-2016-budget)

Key Points in Buhari's Earlier Media Chat on the Economy

To provide perspective on the economic strategies of Buhari, including the 2016 budget, it is worth recalling his December 30 "media chat" with four well-known media personalities to answer a range of questions on national television. Most questions dealt with budget or economic issues. Some questions also reflected concerns with corruption. A selection of questions, with a summary of Buhari's candid answers, is given below:

> *Question:* How do you think you are doing with the fight against corruption?
>
> *Buhari:* We cannot prejudge what the courts will do. But we are presenting documents to the courts. Money is being recovered. Evidence of stolen money will be presented in court. . . . We have to cross-check our documents [and] records. . . . We are going far. By the end of first quarter next year, we will tell Nigerians how far we have gone. . . . We are not going to put anyone above the law. . . .
>
> *Question:* What about the big issue of foreign exchange, people taking their money out, devaluation of the naira?
>
> *Buhari:* I do not support devaluation. When we came in in 1984–1985, people did not know the foreign reserve. It had disappeared. The situation now is aggravated by the downturn in oil prices, down to $35, $36 a barrel. . . . In developed countries, when they devalue, their currencies become cheaper, their goods and services become cheaper. But in Nigeria, we import even toothpicks. If we devalue, what are we sending out? What we are doing is that we shall make money available to industries, the real sector, those who are going to produce goods and services and employ people.
>
> *Question:* What about the oil subsidy?
>
> *Buhari:* The oil sector infrastructure was destroyed by past regimes. . . . They failed to maintain tank farms, oil depots, refineries, etc. Today, the cost of fuel is low; we are not subsidizing anybody now. Our first priority is to get our refineries working. If we get them working, we can take care of 60 percent of our needs. Then we can swap to take care of the 40 percent. . . . The new permanent secretaries have just taken over; the ministers have just taken over. A lot of things cannot be done overnight.

Question: The budget? What has changed?

Buhari: I will see if I can stop lawmakers from spending over N48 billion on cars. The first thing I turned down was N400 million for vehicles when I came in. The vehicles I have are good enough for ten years. . . . On the money for cars by the National Assembly, I think I will have a closed-door session with them. . . .

Question: Foreign exchange again? People are unable to get forex [foreign exchange] for their kids in school abroad.

Buhari: [We] need to get our priorities right. Fix the infrastructure, insecurity, the economy. It's a very nasty situation we're in.

Question: Borrowing to fund the budget?

Buhari: Government has no alternative, if it wants to create jobs and fix the infrastructure.

Question: Will government sustain the N18,000 minimum wage?

Buhari: Not a question I can answer offhand. When we came [into office,] twenty-seven states could not pay salaries. The CBN [Central Bank of Nigeria] had to use ways and means to get them money to pay salaries.

Question: How will government collect data on unemployed graduates?

Buhari: [I will get the CBN, the Ministry of Finance, and the Ministry of Education involved to find a solution for the foreign exchange needs of Nigerians outside the country, so that they can complete their education.] The standard of our tertiary education is poor. There are a number of things that need to be done in terms of building new classrooms, laboratories. New classrooms have to be built; the teachers have to be comfortable.

Question: Security agencies disobeying court orders?

Buhari: Technically, you can see the kind of atrocities those people committed against the government. The former president just called the CBN governor to give him N40 billion. If they jump bail, it will be a problem for this country. (Drawn from http://saharareporters.com/2015/12/30/what-president-buhari-said-during-his-media-chat)

These questions and answers identified the topics of most concern to Nigerians. How those issues would evolve was the big question of spring 2016. A skeptical public wanted to see Buhari's new initiatives, especially regarding education and help for the poor, take concrete shape.

New Initiatives

Three new initiatives stand out politically among the many in the Buhari budget and statement of priorities: women's projects, education, and help for youth and the poor. (The matter of fuel subsidies was also of pressing concern to people at the grassroots, and is considered in the next section.)

In late January, Buhari spoke to a gathering of the African Union heads of state in Addis Ababa, and he told them that Nigeria had "increased the budget allocation of ministries that have direct bearing on the lives of women, particularly in health and education, with greater emphasis on girl-child education." The *Daily Trust* also reported the following:

> Buhari told the AU leaders that his administration had demonstrated its commitment to women's rights by appointing women of proven integrity to key positions in his cabinet. . . . Welcoming the African Union's decision to declare 2016 as "The Year of Human Rights in Africa with Special Focus on the Rights of Women," Buhari also told the leaders that Nigeria had amply demonstrated her commitment to issues relating to the rights of women by upholding several human rights treaties and conventions specifically targeted at women.
>
> He said in guaranteeing women's economic rights, his government was embarking on massive employment programmes that would promote small- and medium-scale enterprises in order to provide succor to the nation's teeming women and youth populations. (http://www.dailytrust.com.ng/news/general/buhari-we-ll-vote-more-funds-for-women-projects/131523.html)

A staunch advocate for education, Buhari's proposals for reform included hiring 500,000 new teachers. One specific policy that was announced during his budget speech was free education for tertiary-level students in science, technology, and education.

Subsequent reform proposals came from the Ministry of Education in spring 2016, and several excited controversy, including proposals concerning basic education at the primary level. In May, a controversial decision by the ministry was announced that promised to have an impact on efforts to foster national unity. According to one Nigerian media outlet, the *Guardian*:

> Despite its alleged inherent benefits, the decision by the Federal Ministry of Education to reduce the workload of students at the basic level, from 20 to a maximum of 10 subjects, under the extant nine-year basic educational curriculum, has been greeted with diverse reactions.
>
> In the new system developed by the Nigerian Educational Research and Development Council (NERDC) and intended to be in tandem with international models, Christian Religious Studies (CRS) and Islamic Religious Studies (IRS), which were hitherto taught separately, would now merge under Religion and National Values (RNV), which also embodies subjects like Civic Education, Social Studies and Security Education. (guardian.ng/news/furor-over-revised-basic-education-curriculum/)

Although this model had been developed under the Jonathan administration and started operating in some schools in 2014, Christian parents now saw this as an effort to Islamize the country. Assurances were given that Christian and Islamic textbooks would be published separately. The ministry argued that as the "most religious country on earth," Nigeria could "become a model to the entire world" (ibid.) The focus on "religion and national values" was intended to promote national unity. But the sensitivity of this subject was apparent to all. Buhari stayed out of the debate, leaving it to the ministry to respond to its critics

Regarding the poor, in his budget speech Buhari had promised to unveil a conditional cash transfer program to the most vulnerable. During the election campaign, the vice president had mentioned providing a N5,000 stipend to the unemployed poor, but the government's ability to make good on this pledge was threatened by the drop in oil prices. And during a visit to Doha, Qatar, in February, Buhari appeared to back off from the pledge.

However, some of his supporters had suggested introducing microcredit schemes as a way of getting cash to the grassroots levels, as well as creating a multiplier effect on the economy. In mid-March, the Bank of Industry announced a form of microcredit that would help youth start businesses. Describing the new N10 billion Youth Entrepreneurship Support (YES) scheme, the minister for Industry, Trade and Investment, Dr. Okechukwu Enelamah, said that about 36,000 jobs would be created.

An applicant to the YES program could receive up to N10 million with single-digit interest rates, repayable over three to five years. To apply, a youth had to have a National Youth Service Corps (NYSC) certificate or higher education certificate, plus two external guarantors.

Buhari also promised to unveil a public primary school feeding program. One obstacle to such a program was that primary schools are not run by the federal government. But, a "feeding program" might be possible, with the federal government working in conjunction with state and local authorities.

The northern media editorialized about Buhari's commitment to these antipoverty measures. According to the *Daily Trust*:

> Buhari's concern for the poor is apparent not only from the projects included in this budget but also from the key budget decision he tried to shy away from, namely fuel price deregulation. Buhari is not ready to tackle this issue head on because it is the kind of issue that can break his standing with the masses overnight. Nigerians feel deeply about fuel prices and Buhari, who listens to the BBC Hausa Service every morning, is not ready to cross swords with them on this matter. (http://dailytrust.com.ng/news/columns/robin-hood-of-the-21st-century/126305.html)

The Controversy over Fuel Subsidies and NNPC Structure

Fuel subsidies posed a significant dilemma for Buhari. Ordinary people in Nigeria have come to expect a reasonably low price of petroleum at fuel stations as one of the benefits they receive from living in a petro-state. The government of Nigeria makes up the difference between the international price of oil and the subsidy price. This can amount to trillions of naira, which is a major burden on the federal budget.

If the price of domestic fuel in Nigeria is pegged well below the international price of oil, and subventions are paid to suppliers to make up the difference, suppliers may try to pocket the difference while selling their allocation of fuel to neighboring countries at the international price. Or suppliers may hoard their fuel supplies, creating shortages in the retail markets.

The subsidy system had indeed been widely abused in these ways. Yet closing off or reducing the subsidy can result in massive street protests, as happened in January 2012, when President Jonathan tried to remove the subsidy. In January 2016, the price of oil in the international markets was much lower than four years earlier, so the impact on the federal budget was less but still significant.

In late December, State Minister for Petroleum Ibe Kachikwu announced that the price of fuel would be N85 per liter as of January 1, 2016. He also announced that there was no subsidy on imported petrol at present because of the low price of international fuel. The new price was authorized by the Petroleum Product Pricing Regulation Agency (PPPRA).

Kachikwu said that the "pricing modulation" policy of the government was working. "The new price," he was reported to have said, "is below the current N87 per litre and it would now convince Nigerians that the pricing modulation that the Federal Government promised to embark on a few days ago was not a trick. . . . Justifying government's reasons for scrapping the Petroleum Support Fund, otherwise known as oil subsidy, Kachikwu explained that government can no longer afford to subsidize the product following the fraud that has attended its operation. . . . 'So for the first time people will understand that the pricing modulation I was talking about is not a gimmick. It is for real'" (http://saharareporters.com/2015/12/25/nigerian-government-reduce-price-petrol-n85-litre-jan-1-2016).

Unfortunately, Kachikwu's announcement created confusion. The concept of "price modulation" is unknown in the oil industry. The government had promised to keep the price of a liter at the pump to N87 or below. But what implications would pricing modulation have in the future if international prices went up? If the subsidy program was scrapped, were there any real protections for grassroots consumers? The new year began with all eyes on this new pricing program. Would it eliminate the long lines waiting for petrol at the pump?

The larger question was whether it was possible for Buhari to reform the entire energy sector, and to what extent this would entail deregulation of prices. Such reforms would entail a close look at the upstream sources and downstream outlets, plus the possible use of gas to run the electricity turbines—what was known as "gasifying" the electricity needs of the country. At the same time, Buhari wanted to inject a new, strict set of ethics into the energy sector, which would allow fuller cooperation with major international energy providers.

The crisis in oil prices was a major topic for discussion (along with investment in Nigeria) during Buhari's trip to Saudi Arabia and Qatar in late February. When oil prices had plunged in the mid-1980s, Buhari had sent his petroleum minister to Saudi Arabia to negotiate an increase in Nigeria's production allotment with Sheikh Yamani, who was the all-powerful Saudi representative to OPEC. They had also discussed cooperation in arresting the decline in oil prices and the restoration of a higher benchmark. Likewise, in 2016, the key would be direct talks between Nigerian leaders and senior leaders in Saudi Arabia (http://www.dailytrust.com.ng/news/business/buhari-saudi-leader-vow-to-fix-oil-prices/134945.html). The difference this time was that the petroleum minister was also the president.

The controversy over the NNPC structure erupted in early March, when Kachikwu announced that NNPC would be split up into thirty companies. Each company would have its own managing director and was expected by the government to be profitable. Whether this restructuring would simply result in more overhead costs or provide real profit-and-loss accountability of component companies remained to be seen. Indeed, the whole process of financing government seemed to be up in the air (http://saharareporters.com/2016/03/03/nnpc-be-split-30-profitable-companies-says-kachikwu).

The immediate challenge was to get the petroleum industry back on its feet, but the larger issue facing Buhari was how to move the economy away from dependence on oil. On numerous occasions, at home and abroad, Buhari has tried to signal a change toward diversification of the economy. His trip to the United States in March emphasized this point, as did his trip to China in April. Both trips signaled Buhari's recognition that to achieve his economic goals, he would need to work closely with the two largest economies in the world.

Given the low price of oil on the international market, it was clear that during a transition to a diverse economy, the federal budget would depend on overseas borrowing and investment. And that money would have to fund two key components of a diversified economy: an effective electric power generation system and a good transportation infrastructure.

In the United States, Buhari met with US officials who argued on behalf of General Electric (GE), the world leader in electricity generation. GE had experience in Nigeria, especially in Lagos, but now the entire national grid would need to be revamped, especially the gasification component. A company such as GE had the technology and experience to tackle such a megaproject. Babatunde Fashola, the minister of power, works, and housing, would need to focus more of his time and energy on electric power and delegate more responsibility for works and housing to deputies.

During his trip to China on April 11–15, Buhari focused on power, roads, railways, aviation, water supply, and housing. (Note: GE-China was also a leader in electric power in China, as well as other infrastructure projects.) The main focus of his Chinese interlocutors was on railway development in Nigeria. Buhari visited China's "special economic zones" (zones oriented to foreign trade and investment) and met with a range of political and business leaders. He negotiated a $2 billion loan from China to support their renovation of key railway facilities in Nigeria. He also discussed with President Xi the problem of Nigeria's bunkered oil, much of which was alleged to have found its way to China.

From the Nigerian government's perspective, the trip to China was successful. Buhari secured a commitment of $6 billion in credits for critical infrastructure. He arranged for currency swaps between Nigeria's Central Bank and the Industrial and Commercial Bank of China to facilitate trade. (Nigeria announced it would begin to use the Chinese yuan as a reserve currency.) Nigeria also agreed to cooperate with the China Aerospace Science and Technology Corporation. Needing to borrow several billion dollars to cover the Nigerian budget deficit, Buhari made clear that he would not borrow from the International Monetary Fund, because of its strict conditionalities. Hence, it was implied that he would work closely with the Chinese on a range of financial needs.

In April, Buhari was also aware of a new threat at home, the advent of the Niger Delta Avengers, whose declared aim was to attack the gas and petroleum infrastructure in Nigeria. and who possessed the skills in underwater demolition that might enable them to make good on their threat to bring the Nigerian economy to a standstill. There was a strong element of political payback by the out-of-office politicians from the Delta, including erstwhile Jonathan supporters. This threat might be even greater than that posed by Boko Haram, if it began to close the oil fields.

Meanwhile, work was beginning on Buhari's second budget, led by Minister of Budget and Planning Udo Udo Udoma (known affectionately as "Triple U" to his associates). With the National Assembly in turmoil because of the Senate president's legal troubles, he would need to pay careful attention to avoid a repetition of the "padding scandal" of the first budget and ensure a timely process of vetting and approval.

In late May, Buhari would have to keep an eye on the larger economic challenges of diversification and international investment, retrieving looted public funds, and reforming the petroleum sector. At the same time, he would need to be fully engaged in the humanitarian crisis in the northeast and the beginning stages of reconstruction.

President Muhammadu Buhari addressing the 2015 session of the United Nations.

The United Nations General Assembly listens to President Buhari's speech.

During the September 2015 UN General Assembly session, President Buhari made wide-ranging contacts with world leaders and international business icons. Here he is pictured with Prime Minister David Cameron of Great Britain.

Shaking hands with President Xi Jinping of China.

With Mr. Bill Gates. The president took the opportunity to thank Mr. Gates for the contributions being made by the Bill and Melinda Gates Foundation to tackling socioeconomic challenges in Africa.

With former US president Bill Clinton. Buhari discussed the Clinton Foundation's activities in Africa.

At the UN General Assembly session in September 2015. From left to right: President Buhari, UN Secretary-General Ban Ki-moon, and President Obama.

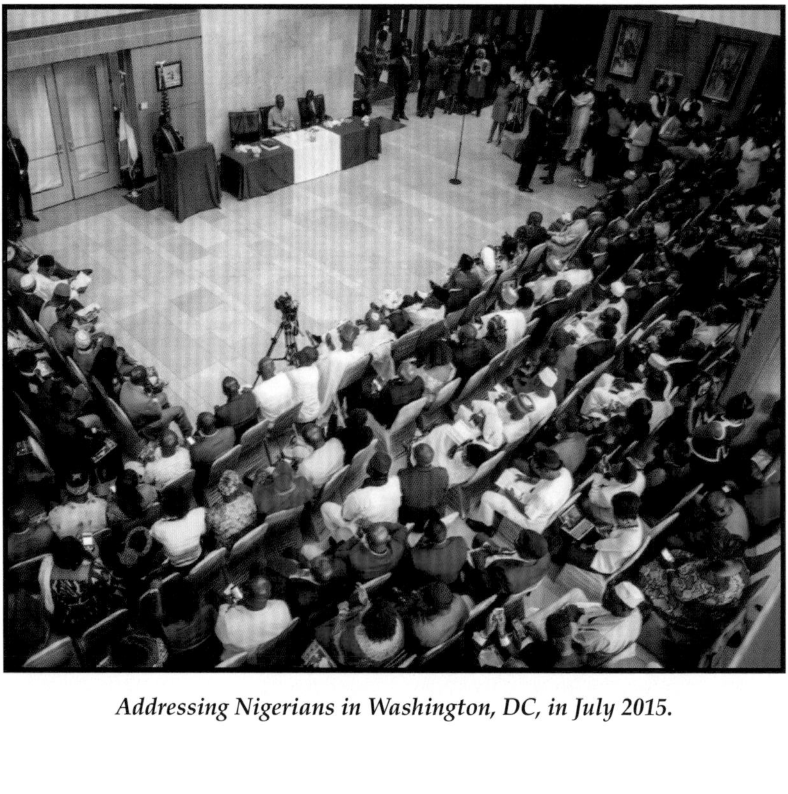

Addressing Nigerians in Washington, DC, in July 2015.

Chapter 22

Reconstruction in the Northeast

A national plan for reconstruction in the northeast began to take shape in October 2015 with the opening by the vice president of the North-East Humanitarian Multi-stakeholder Engagement (NEHMSE), an umbrella organization to coordinate aid and investment in postconflict areas. At that time, the chairman of the Presidential Committee on North East Intervention was General Theophilus Y. Danjuma (rtd), who had been appointed by President Jonathan. Buhari asked Danjuma to stay on as co-chair of the new body to represent the kind of honest leadership that would prevent development aid from being misused.

Danjuma announced budgets for both the short-term and longer-term interventions needed to assist victims of the insurgency. Reference was made to the $2.1 billion commitment by the World Bank for the rebuilding of infrastructure.

With the announcement in late December by President Buhari that the war with Boko Haram had "technically" been won with the reclaiming of lost territories, even though suicide attacks were expected to continue, the question of reconstruction came up again.

At the Buhari "media chat" on December 30, journalists asked if IDPs would be returning to their homes in the northeast in the early months of 2016, and if so, what help they would be given by the government in terms of psychological counseling, reintegration, and personal security. Buhari replied: "We have about 2 million IDPs in various camps. Over 70% of them are children and women. Over 65% of the children are orphans. A committee was set up, the Danjuma committee. Over N25 billion was collected. If you recall, when I went to the G-7 meeting, I raised the issue, and they asked me to send a shopping list. They have come with promises of help. What concerned us most are the orphaned children. We are trying to find out where they come from" (http://saharareporters.com/2015/12/30/what-president-buhari-said-during-his-media-chat).

Evidently, both a short-term humanitarian crisis response and a longer-term reconstruction effort were needed. The reconstruction effort had started under the Jonathan administration, with the publication the previous year of a first draft of the Presidential Initiative for the North East (PINE), *The PINE Long-term Economic Reconstruction and Redevelopment Plan (Initiatives, Strategies and Implementation Framework): 2015-2020.* This 318-page document covered virtually every sector, and detailed sequences for development inputs, with projected costs and "partners" indicated.

This chapter (1) reviews the PINE document; (2) discusses the Buhari-Danjuma approach; (3) examines the Recovery and Peace Building Assessment; and (4) assesses the likely next steps.

Review of the Presidential Initiative for the North East (PINE)

The PINE plan is extremely comprehensive. It lays out short- and long-term targets in the following areas: infrastructure development, agricultural revitalization, health safety and security enhancement, educational transformation, good governance, regional planning and strategic growth management, promotion of entrepreneurship and job creation, and international trade and market development.

For each area, the plan presents the following: vision, prime targets, goals and strategies, and specific projects, plus the types of partners and funding needed. Three- to five-year time frames are indicated per project. The draft report is professionally written. The proposed partners include the Central Bank of Nigeria, the Federal Mortgage Bank, the Federal Housing Authority, housing authorities in individual states, the Federal Ministry of Lands and Housing, state governments, the private sector and private-sector donors, international development banks, and global development partners.

The total budget was N200,100,000,000. Of this amount, N60 billion would come from federal funding, N60 billion from state funding, N20 billion from the Central Bank, and the remainder from other stakeholders. Around N100 million would be used to cover administrative costs.

The concerns of the Buhari administration with the PINE plan were very simple. With billions of naira projected to be spent on the plan, plus hard currency coming in from Great Britain, the United States, the World Bank, and other international sources, the potential for corruption was enormous. Whoever led the PINE program would have to set an example of transparency and accountability, and strenuous efforts would have to be made to monitor every expenditure.

Western donor teams were invited to the northeast to see for themselves the situation on the ground and to make their own assessments of how they could be of most help. The situation was increasingly dire. Not only did the IDPs need help of various kinds (some of them very specialized), but even more worryingly, the specter of starvation was haunting the region, because crops had not been planted for several years and major transit links had been cut.

The Buhari-Danjuma Approach

On January 1, 2016, President Buhari met with women's political groups in Abuja and laid out his vision for the reconstruction of the northeast. According to one report in the Nigerian media:

> President Muhammadu Buhari says that a committee to rehabilitate infrastructure and resettle Internally Displaced Persons, IDPs, in the North-East sub-region is soon to be formally inaugurated. The committee, to be led by a frontline statesman, Lt.-Gen. Theophilus Yakubu Danjuma (rtd), will also include Africa's richest man, Aliko Dangote, GCON.
>
> Speaking at the State House, Abuja, in response to a goodwill message delivered to him by a group, Women in Politics Forum (WIPF), President Buhari announced that all forms of assistance and aid in this respect generated locally and from foreign countries as promised by the Group of Seven, G7, will be channeled through the committee when it is inaugurated.

> He said that he had compiled a list of damaged infrastructure, including schools and bridges, and handed it to the leaders of the G7 and the United States, adding that "I didn't ask for a kobo [i.e., a penny]. It is up to them to choose what they will undertake. Already, some have sent teams to verify our assertions." President Buhari decried the impact of the Boko Haram violence on women and children, declaring that they are its worst victims.
>
> "In the North-East, what I saw for myself and on those clips is a source of concern for people with conscience. They are mostly women and children who are orphaned. Some of them don't even know where they came from. This is the pathetic situation in which the country has found itself." He said that the fight for the return of the Chibok girls is ongoing and "continues to be a most worrying issue" to his government, emphasizing that the administration will do all within its powers in making the best efforts to secure their freedom. (http://www.thetrentonline.com/fg-announces-t-y-danjuma-as-head-of-govt-committee-for-north-east-rehabilitation/)

The public announcement that Danjuma would lead the committee sent a message that the Buhari government was serious about the humanitarian and reconstruction challenges of the northeast. The involvement of Dangote sent a message that private-sector assistance would be needed.

The Recovery and Peace Building Assessment

On January 25, Senior Special Assistant to the Vice President on Media and Publicity Laolu Akande called a press conference to announce the creation of a Recovery and Peace Building Assessment (RPBA) in the northeast. The assessment team would work with the World Bank, the European Union, and the United Nations in rebuilding the northeast. The idea would be to draw on the work of the PINE and other federal and state reports to provide a credible framework for the transformation of the area.

The RPBA team would also work with the IDPs on humanitarian matters and on rebuilding in the six states in the North East zone. In July 2015, President Buhari had met with Jim Yong Kim, the president of the World Bank, and with officials from other donor agencies to discuss reconstruction in the northeast. These meetings led to the establishment of the RPBA, which focused on broad-based public-sector initiatives. It would serve a coordinating function between the government, donors, and private-sector groups.

In mid-February, plans for the composition, structure, and activities of the RPBA were finalized. The *Daily Trust* reported on an arrangement by Akande:

> The team's top-level engagements with stakeholders [are] centered on sector recovery and needs assessment strategy in infrastructure and social services, peace building, stability and social cohesion as well as economic recovery of the affected people in the six states.
>
> [Akande] said that apart from forming the pivot for planning a broad-based public sector recovery programme for the zone, the assessment would also leverage, synchronize and inform the financing initiatives and projects of Nigeria's development partners, civil society organisations and other stakeholders.
>
> He said the team, led by Senior Special Assistant to the President on Internally Displaced Persons (IDPs) Mariam Masha, visited Adamawa, Taraba, Gombe, Bauchi, Borno and Yobe states, where they had engagement with governors, top government officials, civil society organisations, traditional rulers, the IDPs and other stakeholders. The vice president's aide said the team visited several camps and resettlement centres for the IDPs in the different states as well as insurgency-ravaged public institutions like hospitals, markets and military formations.
>
> This assessment programme . . . is a joint, high-level collaboration between the government of Nigeria and development partners—the World Bank, EU and the UN—aimed at supporting government in its short-, medium-, and long-term efforts toward peace building and sustainable recovery in the northeast. It's a follow-up to the agreements reached with the northeast states in respect to the sector and component work plans, data collection modalities and timelines and provision of quantitative and qualitative information by the states. (http://www.dailytrust.com.ng/news/general/boko-haram-northeast-assessment-completed-presidency/133694.html#zgDAoc8HYpsavV2M.99)

The vice president had been designated as the leader of the Buhari economic team for the whole country, not just for the northeast. Reconstruction in the northeast would require a "whole-of-country" and not just a "whole-of-government" effort, as well as close ties with the international community.

Next Steps?

The spring of 2016, before the rains came in summer and planting could begin, was a looming humanitarian disaster in parts of the northeast. It was not clear whether the security situation would even allow for planting in summer 2016. Many areas were without food. The price of maize and rice was beyond the reach of most people. Even a sack of chaff, with no nutritional value, was too expensive for most. Reports of starvation began filtering out.

The Nigerian government and the international community would have to act quickly to prevent mass starvation and a refugee crisis of major proportions. The security situation was far from settled. Yet with 3 million IDPs in camps—including both government camps and some of the informal *zawiyas* run by Muslim Sufi organizations—and many more stuck in villages without resources, major assistance was required.

When President Buhari had inspected some of the camps, tears were seen to stream from his eyes. On one occasion, a two-year-old orphan girl ran up to him and begged "Take me with you." This was not a time for policy debates. Action was needed. But until the security situation was stabilized, humanitarian relief seemed paralyzed.

Buhari had traveled to Egypt, Saudi Arabia, and Qatar in late February looking for financial support for Nigeria's efforts to tackle the humanitarian crisis in the northeast, as well as for allies in the fight against Boko Haram. There was no time to lose.

Meanwhile, the federal government had identified some local government authorities in the North East zone where the reconstruction process could begin. In late March, five hundred students graduated in Hong, Adamawa, from the Youth Empowerment Programme. In that same state, the federal government began reconstruction of schools, police stations, and other infrastructure projects. With Boko Haram still active, however, such reconstruction was a symbol of local (and federal) resilience, and thus a potential target of the continuing insurgency.

Could Buhari mobilize the international community, including the World Bank, to move quickly enough to begin reconstruction in the northeast? Could the insurgents be contained in the Sambisa

Forest so that IDPs could return to their villages? Could Buhari's international engagement strategy put an end to the insurgency within Nigeria?

More urgently, would ordinary people in the northeast be able to plant their farms at the beginning of the rainy season? In Adamawa, some early planting had begun. By late May, it was clear that farmers in Yobe and Borno were also planting. But in the short term, could roads be opened so that foodstuffs from other parts of Nigeria could be transported into the major cities and towns of the northeast? The road from Kano to Maiduguri had been cleared, so foodstuffs from the Kano market began to reach the northeast. But what about the roads to Bama or Mubi? Millions of lives hung in the balance.

Meanwhile, on May 21, the governor of Borno, Kashim Shettima, arrived in Istanbul, Turkey. His mission was to raise $6 billion for reconstruction of the twenty-seven local governments in his state. This amount was based on a Post Insurgency Recovery and Peace Building Assessment report validated by the World Bank. The summit in Istanbul began on May 23, and was organized by the UN Office for the Coordination of Humanitarian Affairs. The United Nations was increasingly trying to use its good offices to facilitate postconflict reconstruction in areas of West Africa devastated by violent extremism.

At last, the international community was paying attention to what the United Nations was calling "one of the most neglected major crises in the world" (http://saharareporters.com/2016/05/21/borno-governor-shettima-travels-turkey-raise-6-billion-reconstruction). The Lake Chad region had been off-limits because of Boko Haram, but it was now time for reconstruction to begin.

The following maps and graph show the scale of the devastation (in terms of numbers of deaths) wrought by Boko Haram since 2011, but they also reveal the extent to which Boko Haram's deadly potency had diminished since Buhari had taken office.

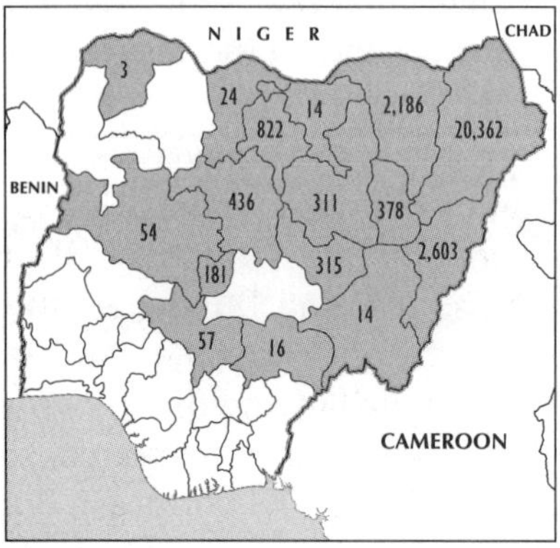

CUMULATIVE DEATHS BY STATE ATTRIBUTABLE TO ALL INCIDENTS INVOLVING BOKO HARAM, MAY 2011–MAY 2016

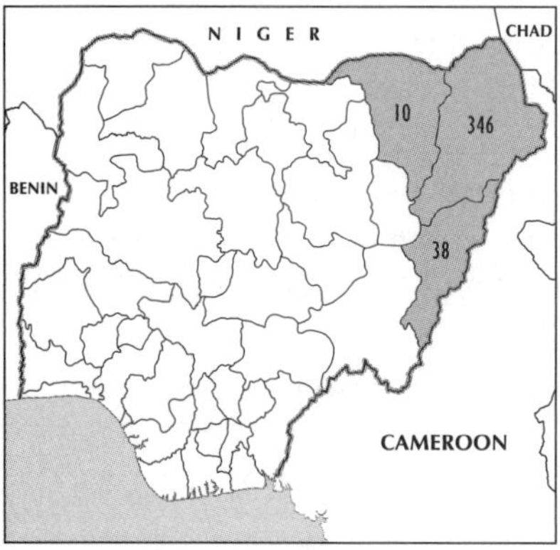

DEATHS BY STATE ATTRIBUTABLE TO ALL INCIDENTS INVOLVING BOKO HARAM, APRIL–MAY 2015

DEATHS BY STATE ATTRIBUTABLE TO ALL INCIDENTS INVOLVING BOKO HARAM, APRIL–MAY 2016

Source: Data for these maps from Council on Foreign Relations, "Nigeria Security Tracker." The author is indebted to Asch Harwood of CFR for his help.

CUMULATIVE DEATHS AND DEATHS PER MONTH, MAY 2011—MAY 2016

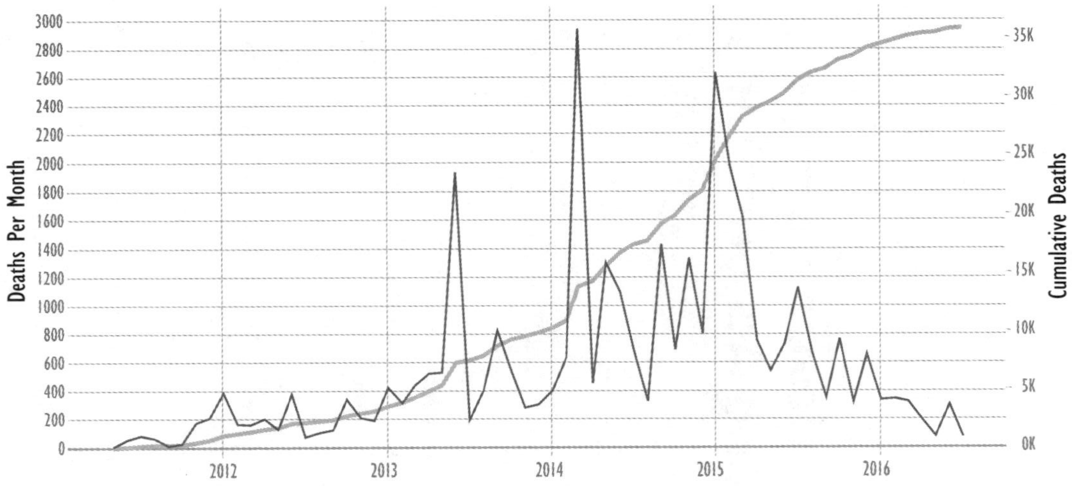

Source: Data from Council on Foreign Relations, "Nigeria Security Tracker." The author is indebted to Asch Harwood of CFR for his help.

CHALLENGES OF POLITICAL CHANGE

Chapter 23

Constitutional Federalism and Accountability

Nigeria is a three-tiered constitutional federation, with the rights and responsibilities of each tier delineated. It is also a petro-state with a legacy of centralization. Since independence in 1960, Nigeria has swung between civilian and military rule, the latter being highly centralized. Hence, one of the major challenges of the Fourth Republic has been to find the appropriate balance between the different levels of government, as well as between the different branches of government.

It may seem counterintuitive that a former military head of state, now a civilian president, should be called on to return Nigeria to a form of democratic federalism that respects both the diversity of the country and the checks and balances inherent in the vision of democratic political life. Yet Buhari has sought to do exactly that—and to do so while introducing significant reforms, for he is a persistent reformer, with little patience for those who bend or break the rules.

He has been able to combine respect for diversity and democracy with a reformer's zeal thanks to two of his defining characteristics: self-discipline and strong political will. In his first year as president, he has withstood both the temptation of imposing his will on others and the pressures to go easy on his ambitious reform agenda. Moreover, the means he has used to pursue his reformist ends do not ignore or overstep the country's constitutional rules or the rule of law; to the contrary, the laws are on Buhari's side and he is on the side of the rule of law. Whether the Nigerian judiciary is up to the task of enforcing the laws, however, remains to be seen.

This chapter reviews Buhari's efforts at ensuring: (1) financial accountability; (2) judicial accountability; (3) electoral accountability; and (4) military accountability. These challenges exist at both the federal and the state levels. (The next chapter, chapter 24, examines the local level, which had long been the missing ingredient in Nigerian democratic federalism.)

Financial Accountability

The challenge of ensuring financial accountability is not just a matter of rewards and punishments in government, although having an effective watchdog is important. It is also a matter of leadership by example. In addition, given Nigeria's history as a petro-state, it is a matter of close cooperation with the international community. In the case of Nigeria, Buhari has worked closely with Western powers, as well as with the authorities in the UAE, in Saudi Arabia, and in China.

Opportunities for financial mismanagement are to be found not only within federal ministries and parastatals but also within the petroleum industry, especially its downstream components, and within state government.

State governors have come under scrutiny by the EFCC because governors have enormous discretion regarding the expenditure of funds. For instance, a state legislature may approve a budget for development purposes—such as repairs to a dam—but the money may be diverted to fund a governor's pet projects, which is clearly an abuse of power.

Cases of misappropriation of funds within the security and military establishments are of special importance, given the existential threats facing Nigeria. Whether such cases are handled through civilian or military courts—or through the proposed anticorruption special tribunals—is less important than the "no immunity" message that is sent when the accused must answer for their actions in court. Since Buhari has been president, very high-ranking figures have been called to account, although prosecutors have as yet not set their sights on the very highest levels of the previous administration.

Judicial Accountability

If an attorney general or a justice on the Supreme Court is seen to be partisan, the whole idea of democratic federalism is undermined. Partisanship has long been a problem in Nigeria, and one that affected Buhari directly in the past. During the first year of his presidency, the court system seems to have functioned reasonably well, in part because the president has insisted that he remain outside the judicial process.

Court processes tend to be lengthy, especially during the appeal phase, so it may be too early to tell if this pattern of judicial independence will prevail. Some uncertainty also surrounds the use of the "plea bargain" system that allows defendants to return stolen money in return for immunity—thereby giving the government the chance to use stolen monies for development purposes.

Buhari has often expressed concern about the integrity and independence of the judiciary, especially in his fight against corruption. In late January, for instance, while addressing the Nigerian expatriate community at a town hall meeting in Addis Ababa, the president "said that far-reaching reforms of the judiciary remained a key priority for his administration." He continued:

> In the fight against corruption vis-à-vis the judiciary, Nigerians will be right to say that this is my main headache now.
>
> If you reflect on what I went through for twelve years when I wanted to be president, I [ran for office] three times.
>
> The first attempt ended up at the Supreme Court and for 13 months I was in court.
>
> The second attempt in 2007, I was in court close to 20 months, and in 2011, in my third attempt, I was also in court for nine months.
>
> All these cases went up to the Supreme Court until the fourth time in 2015, when God agreed that I will be President of Nigeria. (http://www.dailytrust.com.ng/news/general/fight-against-corruption-judiciary-is-my-main-headache--buhari/131553.html)

In short, the personal experience of President Buhari with Nigeria's judicial system has made him realize the importance of rule of law in a democratic system. In Nigeria, the problem with the system lies not in the structure but in the process. Buhari has made strenuous efforts to get the chief justice and others on the country's highest court to turn the page on the past and start afresh in terms of embracing and defending judicial independence.

A definitive test of the Fourth Republic's balance-of-powers system may not occur until Buhari makes new judicial appointments, and until Nigerians see how the president and Senate handle such matters. So far, however, Buhari has shown every indication of wanting not to interfere in court cases or thwart constitutional principles. The APC argument for localizing police in their states of origin or long-term residence was intended to work within a reasonable interpretation of the constitutional provisions on this matter.

The EFCC has been increasingly seen as nonpartisan in its probes, even though the PDP had been the sole party in power since 1999 and thus had exclusive access to government resources.

Military tribunals will always have their separate procedures, but there has been no evidence that the commander in chief is inclined to interfere, except where national security is at stake. The military procurement scandal, with its implications for the northeast insurgency, goes to the very heart of Nigeria's quest for national unity.

Electoral Accountability

The importance of INEC to the legitimacy of elections was demonstrated in the 2015 elections, when the integrity, temperament, and skill of Attahiru Jega and his team helped to produce a credible result. The technical innovations and management techniques deployed in the election also made it more difficult to rig. Jega has written an illuminating account of his experiences (Attahiru Jega, *Election Management in Nigeria: The Evolution of the Nigerian Electoral Process, 2010–2015* [Ibadan: Safari Books, 2015]) and has lectured internationally on the lessons learned from the 2015 election.

As noted previously, Jega stepped down in June 2015 as the chairman of INEC and was succeeded by Professor Mahmud Yakubu. Yakubu's five-year appointment continues the tradition of academic engagement in government and has been welcomed by the international community. Almost immediately after taking office, Yakubu was thrown into the fray by having to organize elections in some of the southern states that required reruns for state officials.

The entire electoral law may need to be reviewed in light of lessons learned during these off-schedule elections as well as in the general election of 2015. In addition, the role of the resident electoral commissioners may need to be reinforced as a nonpartisan function.

If Nigeria cannot hold free and fair elections, it is always likely to suffer from massive social disruption and political instability, especially if the appeals process for candidates contesting the election outcome is seen to be politically slanted. Hence, ensuring that the judicial process is impartial is a key part of electoral reforms. Buhari's painful personal experiences in the elections of 2003, 2007, and 2011 have made him a committed supporter of electoral integrity and judicial independence.

Military Accountability

President Buhari is commander in chief of the Nigerian military, and has been widely seen as capable of taking that role seriously and of respecting the principle of civilian leadership of the military.

Although there will always be groups in the military with grievances, when good governance prevails there is less likelihood of clashes erupting between military and civilian interests. Equally, when the military is not expected to perform police functions, there is less chance of resentment and hostility building between the military and sections of the public. Reforming, localizing, and equipping the police to maintain law and order at the state and local level will thus spare the military from being dragged into every local conflict.

The role of the military goes deep in Nigeria. And that role has been played in ways that range from the good to the bad to the ugly. Yet the military has always been the ultimate guarantor of national unity, despite the ever-present reality of regional factions within the military. And national unity is the cause for which Buhari has been willing to give his life, both as a member of the military and as a civilian.

The $15 billion military procurement scandals uncovered in 2015 and 2016 revealed the extent to which politics had undermined the integrity of the military, including its ability to fight an insurgency in the northeast of the country. Holding high-level officers accountable for such corruption was Buhari's way of sending a message of zero tolerance. Officers both old and young would have to learn that the country would no longer tolerate them putting personal (or political) gain ahead of national service. Of course, this message has been unwelcome in some quarters, and Buhari knows that his approach is not without its perils. The corruption probes of retired officers might provoke their loyalty networks to consider drastic action against Buhari. As the Nigerian saying goes, "When you fight corruption, corruption fights back."

Yet the earlier tension between Buhari and Babangida has gradually been diffused. General Babangida is now elderly and spends most of his time with his doctors in Germany. He has returned to Abuja chiefly for meetings of the National Council—the body on which sit all former heads of state.

Moreover, the Nigerian electorate and the international community have said "never again" both to rampant corruption within the military, which undermines the military's own ability to fight for Nigeria's unity, and to military intervention in the democratic process. Such intervention would lead to civil strife and even war. The Nigeria Project could not tolerate such instability.

Chapter 24

Political Change

A major contribution that President Buhari has made to political change in Nigeria has been to persevere in his electoral challenges to the dominant Nigerian political establishment and demonstrate that opposition parties can win. His victory in the polls seemed to put money politics in its place for once, as a runner-up to constructive policies. Whether he can achieve further political change in Nigeria is hard to predict, but he is trying, and with diminished national financial resources there is in fact little choice but to reset the country's political priorities and introduce good management practices.

The priorities in Buhari's first year as president have been to (1) degrade and destroy Boko Haram; (2) stop large-scale corruption and hold the culprits accountable; (3) restart economic initiatives and diversify the economy; (4) begin reconstruction in the northeast and help resettle IDPs; and (5) set a new tone in politics of probity and playing by constitutional rules.

Much of his first year has been spent acting as an international statesman on behalf of Nigeria's interests in a globalized era. His trips to African countries, the Middle East, Europe, the United States, and Asia have played an important role in helping him meet his domestic challenges. They have also served to demonstrate Nigeria's stature as a credible partner in the international community.

On the domestic front, the Nigeria Project continues as a robust democratic experiment. The powers of executive authority, legislative responsibility, and judicial reach are always in a dynamic state of flux. However, the Buhari influence on following constitutional rules has been profound.

Occasionally, following the rules has meant having to quickly rethink plans. In March, while Buhari was in Equatorial Guinea discussing security measures in the Gulf of Guinea, Vice President Yemi Osinbajo and a high-level Nigerian delegation was scheduled to visit India. But this would have left the Senate president as acting president of Nigeria. Given that the Senate president, Bukola Saraki, was facing criminal proceedings at the Code of Conduct Tribunal regarding his declaration of assets, the vice president canceled his India trip, not wishing to create a situation in which Nigeria's acting president was under indictment.

This chapter examines the key elements of a federal presidential system, looking in turn at (1) the challenges of attaining a federal-state-local balance; (2) the challenges of maintaining an executive-legislative-judiciary balance; (3) the challenges of working with a two-party system; (4) the challenges of preserving national unity; and (5) Buhari's May 29 speech.

The Challenges of Attaining a Federal-State-Local Balance

Nigeria is a three-tiered federation, but although the center is strong, the local government level is weak, and the state level is robust but depends on the center for its finances. With a dominant national party, the subnational levels tend to be reflections of the center, although local personality factors always matter.

Yet with security issues, development needs, and the need for humanitarian relief looming at the local level, the petro-state top-down model has had to be recalibrated. Cross-level cooperation is needed to implement national policies and ameliorate the grassroots crises.

In many ways, this has been a continuing challenge, even under a Buhari administration, brought to power by direct appeals to and support from the grassroots. Given the top-down nature of government funding—from the center to the states and then to local government authorities—one major problem has been ensuring that funds reach the local level without being "chopped" along the way.

It remains to be seen whether a robust local government capacity can be developed. The northeast may be a test case of whether reconstruction can be achieved by drawing on all levels of government. With most funding coming from the top, there may be little Buhari can do to activate local government capacity other than insist on zero tolerance for corruption, especially by governors, who hold the financial whip hand.

The Challenges of Maintaining an Executive-Legislative-Judicial Balance

Throughout the Fourth Republic, the dominance of a single party in the executive branch tended to be reflected in the legislative branch. Under Presidents Obasanjo, Yar'Adua, and Jonathan, the dominance of the presidency tended to overshadow the National Assembly (NASS).

Indeed, presidents often did whatever they wanted without regard to the NASS. The fact that oil revenues came in through the center ensured that the presidency was the most important player in government. Nonetheless, there were some high-profile checks and balances on presidential power. A major example was the Senate's rejection of Obasanjo's efforts to run for a third term, despite the two-term limit.

The judiciary often acted as a reflection of the needs of the powerful presidency. This has clearly changed under President Buhari. His insistence on not getting involved in legislative and judicial matters may be a contribution to a longer-term rebalancing of the federal system.

Buhari has tried to ensure that judges do their duty without fear or favor. With an entrenched legal system in Nigeria, and wealthy defendants well represented by senior advocates, progress toward real legal accountability has been slow. The role of the attorney general has been of special concern, given past practices of serving presidential interests. During his first year in power, Attorney General Abubakar Malami seemed to have acquired a reputation for balance and fair play. Again, time would tell, as prosecutors wrestled with high-level SAN lawyers in the court systems, and judges might still be influenced by financial gratuities.

The Challenges of Working in a Two-Party System

Unlike the brief experiment in 1992–93, when General Babangida mandated "two parties"—one a little to the left and one a little to the right—in most cases party systems tend to reflect electoral systems. Two-party systems usually emerge from the need to put party coalitions together *before* an election. Multiparty systems may exist in electoral systems in which governing coalitions can be put together *after* an election.

In Nigeria, it has made sense to build party coalitions prior to elections, especially for the presidential contest. The Nigerian Constitution mandates that a winning national coalition must receive 25 percent of the votes in two-thirds of the states, plus a plurality of votes cast. If this regional distribution is not achieved, a runoff of the two highest vote-getters occurs, regardless of regional distribution. A runoff election has never occurred in Nigeria.

In addition to the dominant national parties in Nigeria, numerous smaller parties exist, many of them geared to state- or zonal-level politics. On occasion, such smaller parties coalesce with dominant parties for national elections. Yet there are usually several dozen smaller parties on a presidential ballot, and sometimes they are ushered into existence by the dominant party to divide the opposition.

Since the elections of 2015, the former dominant party has been in disarray. Many former PDP officials have resigned from party posts or fled the country, in part because of corruption probes. Buhari has relied on extradition proceedings against the ex-PDP chair Adamu Mu'azu, former minister of state for defence Musiliu Obanikoro, former minister of justice Mohammed Adoke, and several other high-ranking former PDP stalwarts.

In the spring of 2016, the future of the PDP was uncertain. Would it regain its standing as a truly national party? Could it flourish without the moneybags that were part of its past successes? A number of factions in the former PDP seemed to be exploring the idea of creating their own parties.

While it is not the responsibility of President Buhari to rebuild the PDP, it is in the long-term interests of Nigeria to have a viable opposition to enhance transparency and accountability. The old adage that "absolute power corrupts absolutely" is a caution to any Nigerian presidency.

In mid-February, the PDP was hit by another crisis, when Senator Ali Modu Sheriff was sworn in as party chair, replacing Adamu Mu'azu, who had resigned nine months earlier, on May 20, 2015. Many of the stalwarts in the PDP objected, contending that other claimants to the position were better qualified and asking Sheriff to resign (http://www.dailytrust.com.ng/news/general/pdp-crisis-worsens-as-wabara-shagari-juta-others-ask-sheriff-to-resign/134603.html). Indeed, the board of trustees of the PDP told Sheriff, "You can't lead us." According to the media:

> The members of the PDP's Board of Trustees (BoT) stated that Mr. Sheriff, a former governor of Borno State, was unacceptable as their party's national chairman.
>
> Today's meeting was the first time the Board has met since PDP governors, led by Governor Ayodele Fayose of Ekiti and Nyesom Wike of Rivers respectively, last Tuesday foisted Mr. Sheriff on the party as national chairman. . . .
>
> Senator Walid Jibril, acting chairman of the PDP's Board of Trustees read the resolution after today's meeting. He disclosed that the meeting was well attended, with more than 55 members in attendance. . . . Calling the BoT the PDP's conscience, Mr. Jibril stated: "It is of the view that Ali Modu Sheriff is not suitable as national chairman of PDP." (http://saharareporters.com/2016/02/23/you–cant-lead-us-pdp-bot-tells-sheriff)

The backstory on Sheriff is complicated. A wealthy businessman, he was governor of Borno State from 2003 to 2011 on an ANPP ticket. He was a founding member of the APC, but in 2014 switched to the PDP. His appointment as chair stirred controversy, in part because some people have accused him of being a sponsor of Boko Haram in its early days. This charge harkens back to the time when Boko Haram was led by Muhammad Yusuf and apparently was sponsored in part by key Borno politicians. There were even rumors that some political godfathers ordered the police to shoot Yusuf to cover up their own previous involvement.

As the Boko Haram threat increased after the death of Yusuf, and Maiduguri came under siege, the roads became extremely dangerous. Sheriff's apparent purchase of private jet to facilitate his trips to and from Maiduguri, a common practice of many other senior politicians, was noted in the Nigerian media as an example of extreme wealth disparities.

The issue of Sheriff's selection as PDP national chairman engaged the former PDP Ministers Forum, which was sharply critical of Sheriff. Even former president Jonathan kept his distance (http://www.dailytrust.com.ng/news/general/jonathan-has-no-interest-in-sheriff--former-minister-turaki/135650.html). Meanwhile, APC officials were demanding from the sidelines that Sheriff return funds he was accused of having stolen from the PDP (http://www.dailytrust.com.ng/news/politics/apc-to-sheriff-include-return-of-stolen-funds-in-your-master-plan/134296.html).

In late April, the PDP National Executive Committee met in Abuja, although many members refused to attend. The zoning process that emerged gave the national chairmanship to the North East zone. Sheriff was confirmed as chairman, to the dismay of many party stalwarts. Meanwhile, the APC had little in the way of serious opposition.

In late May, this drama took a new turn. The PDP governors staged a mini-coup against Sheriff and removed him as chairman. He was replaced by the former governor of Kaduna State, Ahmed Makarfi. The former governor of Anambra State, Peter Obi, was appointed interim secretary.

With the PDP fracturing, observers wondered if splits were also developing in the APC, given that it is a coalition of recent vintage. As of spring 2016, no serious divisions were visible, although rumors often surfaced when Buhari was out of the country, especially regarding the status of the legal case against Senate president Saraki, a recent convert to the APC.

President Buhari is not a natural party politician. Complaints have arisen within his party that he is a "loner." APC politicians in Abuja were more likely to congregate at night at the home of the vice president than at the Presidential Villa with Buhari.

The fact that Buhari has been perceived as an "outsider" to politics by the general public has been his strength. Still, voices within the APC have suggested Buhari engage such long-term politicians as Abubukar Atiku and Bola Tinubu to rally the APC governors and ensure that the president has closer ties to the state and local levels of the party. Men such as Atiku and Tinubu could provide links to key constituencies, such as traditional rulers and grassroots NGOs.

With economic growth at a dismal level—for reasons largely global—many of Buhari's ardent supporters were losing patience. Expectations were extremely high when he was elected. A year later, many were still waiting for an upturn in economic fortunes.

At least there was a widespread consensus that Buhari was not stealing whatever money remained in the treasury. But with hunger in the northeast and stagnant growth elsewhere, Buhari's political honeymoon seemed to be drawing to a close as he came up on his March 28 election anniversary.

Buhari's answer to such criticism was to emphasize the need to diversify the economy and support indigenous entrepreneurs rather than importers. At the same time, he had been discussing large-sale infrastructural development in Nigeria with international partners, ranging from GE in the field of power generation, to Chinese companies in the railroad construction industry, to the UAE in the upgrading of refineries. But all this would take time to have an impact, and politicians and the public were demanding quick fixes.

The Challenges of Preserving National Unity

Throughout this biography of Muhammadu Buhari, the dominant theme has been his quest for national unity, both when he was in the military and since he returned to civilian life. Looking back on his first year as president, how much has he achieved in the pursuit of this overriding goal?

Although many constitutional provisions are designed to strengthen national unity—such as federal character provisions and regional distribution requirements in the presidential elections—much of what needs to be achieved is in the realm of symbol management. Maintaining a balance of ethnoreligious identities between the president and vice president is an example. Were a president seen to be favoring colleagues from the same ethnic or religious group, national unity would be strained.

The greatest political challenge for Buhari has been in the South East zone, where he received very few votes in 2015. He allocated four senior ministries to that zone: foreign affairs, science and technology, trade and industry, and labor. In addition, his minister of state for petroleum resources, although he is from the South-South, has ethnic ties with the South East. This sent a clear message that the South East is seen by Buhari as a vital part of Nigeria.

The president took advantage of the symbolism of the 2016 Armed Forces and Remembrance Day celebrations in mid-January to make a call for national unity. According to a report in the *Sahara Reporters*:

> President Muhammadu Buhari on Sunday called on Nigerians to build on things that unite rather than divide the country in spite of diverse cultures and religions. He gave the advice at the Inter-Denominational Church Service to mark the 2016 Armed Forces and Remembrance Day at the National Christian Centre, Abuja.
>
> Represented by Vice President Yemi Osinbajo, the President said the nation was proud of the contributions of the armed forces for ensuring peace, justice, freedom and prosperity of the nation.
>
> "Let us renew our determination to build a strong and united nation where freedom, justice, peace and prosperity are easily within reach; a nation where we emphasize those things that bind us rather than those things that divide us.
>
> "We are a country of diverse cultures and even religions but let us tap more into that diversity rather than for strife. . . .
>
> "The armed forces contribute and represent one of the most patriotic institutions in the land and play a leading role in nation building. [They diligently attend] to their traditional duty of defending and protecting our territorial integrity. Their remarkable efforts in particular at this time in combatting insurgency in the north-east is greatly appreciated by the Nigerian people. Boko Haram and insurgency in the north-east [have] now been degraded militarily; the insurgents no longer hold territory and can no longer launch military-style attacks as they have done in the past. . . ."
>
> Mr. Buhari acknowledged the support of foreign partners in the fight against terrorism, adding that their contributions and encouragement had been worthwhile. He said the administration was confident that they would maintain the backing and even step up such support where needed as the nation advanced into the final stage of combatting the insurgency. (http://saharareporters.com/2016/01/10/buhari-urges-unity-among-nigerians-hails-armed-forces)

The basic instinct of Buhari has always been to strengthen and defend national unity. Challenges to that unity might come from regional interest groups or religious fringe groups. How he would manage these challenges could well determine the fate of his presidency.

Buhari's May 29 Speech

Buhari's commitment to national unity was also evident in the national speech he gave on May 29 in Abuja to commemorate his first year in office. His words also sent a message to domestic and international audiences that the days of off-budget looting were over. His passion for change and national unity were evident in his espousal of basic democratic practices, and the need for the country's leadership to be responsive to the concerns of the Nigerian people.

> My compatriots,
>
> It is one year today since our administration came into office. It has been a year of triumph, consolidation, pains and achievements. By age, instinct and experience, my preference is to look forward, to prepare for the challenges that lie ahead and rededicate the administration to the task of fixing Nigeria. But I believe we can also learn from the obstacles we have overcome and the progress we have made thus far, to help strengthen the plans that we have in place to put Nigeria back on the path of progress.
>
> We affirm our belief in democracy as the form of government that best assures the active participation and actual benefit of the people. Despite the many years of hardship and disappointment, the people of this nation have proved inherently good, industrious, tolerant, patient and generous.
>
> The past years have witnessed huge flows of oil revenues. From 2010 average oil prices were $100 per barrel. But economic and security conditions were deteriorating. We campaigned and won the election on the platform of restoring security, tackling corruption and restructuring the economy. On our arrival, the oil price had collapsed to as low as $30 per barrel and we found nothing had been kept for the rainy day. Oil prices have been declining since 2014 but due to the neglect of the past, the country was not equipped to halt the economy from declining.
>
> The infrastructure—notably, rail, power, roads—was in a decrepit state. All the four refineries were in a state of disrepair, the pipelines and depots neglected.

Huge debts owed to contractors and suppliers had accumulated. Twenty-seven states could not pay salaries for months. In the North East, Boko Haram had captured 14 local governments, driven the local authorities out, hoisted their flags. Elsewhere, insecurity was palpable; corruption and impunity were the order of the day. In short, we inherited a state near collapse.

On the economic front, all oil-dependent countries, Nigeria included, have been struggling since the drop in prices. Many oil-rich states have had to take tough decisions similar to what we are doing. The world, Nigeria included, has been dealing with the effects of three significant and simultaneous global shocks starting in 2014:

1. A 70% drop in oil prices.
2. Global growth slowdown.
3. Normalization of monetary policy by the United States Federal Reserve.

Our problems as a government are like that of a farmer who in a good season harvests ten bags of produce. The proceeds enable him to get by for the rest of the year. However, this year he could only manage three bags from his farm. He must now think of other ways to make ends meet.

From day one, we purposely set out to correct our condition, to change Nigeria. We reinforced and galvanized our armed forces with new leadership and resources. We marshaled our neighbours in a joint task force to tackle and defeat Boko Haram. By the end of December 2015, all but pockets and remnants had been routed by our gallant armed forces. Our immediate focus is for a gradual and safe return of internally displaced persons in safety and dignity and for the resumption of normalcy in the lives of people living in these areas.

EFCC was given the freedom to pursue corrupt officials and the judiciary were alerted on what Nigerians expect of them in the fight against corruption. On the economy, in particular foreign exchange and fuel shortages, our plan is to save foreign exchange by fast-tracking repair of the refineries and producing most of our fuel requirements at home. And by growing more food in Nigeria, mainly rice, wheat and sugar, we will save billions of dollars in foreign exchange and drastically reduce our food import bill.

We resolved to keep the naira steady, as in the past, devaluation had done dreadful harm to the Nigerian economy. Furthermore, I support the monetary authority's decision to ensure alignment between monetary policy and fiscal policy. We shall keep a close look on how the recent measures affect the naira and the economy. But we cannot get away from the fact that a strong currency is predicated on a strong economy. And a strong economy presupposes an industrial productive base and a steady export market. The measures we must take may lead to hardships. The problems Nigerians have faced over the last year have been many and varied. But the real challenge for this government has been reconstructing the spine of the Nigerian state. The last twelve months have been spent collaborating with all arms of government to revive our institutions so that they are more efficient and fit for purpose:

- That means a bureaucracy better able to develop and deliver policy.
- That means an independent judiciary, above suspicion and able to defend citizens' rights and dispense justice equitably.
- That means a legislature that actually legislates effectively.
- And above all, that means political parties and politicians committed to serving the Nigerian people rather than themselves.

These are the pillars of the state on which democracy can take root and thrive. But only if they are strong and incorruptible. Accordingly, we are working very hard to introduce some vital structural reforms in the way we conduct government business and lay a solid foundation on which we can build enduring change.

An important first step has been to get our housekeeping right. So we have reduced the extravagant spending of the past. We started boldly with the Treasury Single Account, stopping the leakages in public expenditure.

We then identified forty-three thousand ghost workers through the integrated payroll and personal information system. That represents pay packets totaling N4.2 billion stolen every month. In addition, we will save twenty-three billion per annum from official travelling and sitting allowances alone.

Furthermore, the efficiency unit will cut costs and eliminate duplications in ministries and departments. Every little saving helps. The reduction in the number of ministries and work on restructuring and rationalization of the MDAs is well under way. When this work is complete we will have a leaner, more efficient public service that is fit for the purpose of changing Nigeria for the good and for good.

As well as making savings, we have changed the way public money is spent. In all my years as a public servant, I have never come across the practice of padding budgets. I am glad to tell you now we not only have a budget, but more importantly, we have a budget process that is more transparent, more inclusive and more closely tied to our development priorities than in the recent past. 30% of the expenditure in this budget is devoted to capital items. Furthermore, we are projecting non-oil revenues to surpass proceeds from oil. Some critics have described the budget exercise as clumsy. Perhaps. But it was an example of consensus building, which is integral to democratic government. In the end we resolved our differences.

We have, therefore, delivered significant milestones on security, corruption and the economy. In respect of the economy, I would like to directly address you on the very painful but inevitable decisions we had to make in the last few weeks, specifically on the pump price of fuel and the more flexible exchange rate policy announced by the Central Bank. It is even more painful for me that a major producer of crude oil with four refineries that once exported refined products is today having to import all of its domestic needs. This is what corruption and mismanagement have done to us and that is why we must fight these ills.

As part of the foundation of the new economy we have had to reform how fuel prices had traditionally been fixed. This step was taken only after protracted consideration of its pros and cons. After comprehensive investigation my advisers and I concluded that the mechanism was unsustainable.

We are also engaged in making recoveries of stolen assets, some of which are in different jurisdictions. The processes of recovery can be tedious and time consuming, but today I can confirm that thus far a significant amount of assets have been recovered. A considerable portion of these are at different stages of recovery. Full details of the status and categories of the assets will now be published by the Ministry of Information and updated periodically. When forfeiture formalities are completed, these monies will be credited to the Treasury and be openly and transparently used in funding developmental projects and the public will be informed.

On the Niger Delta, we are committed to implementing the United Nations Environment Programme (UNEP) report and are advancing clean-up operations. I believe the way forward is to take a sustainable approach to address the issues that affect the Delta communities. Re-engineering the amnesty programmes is an example of this. The recent spate of attacks by militants disrupting oil and power installations will not distract us from engaging leaders in the region in addressing Niger Delta problems. If the militants and vandals are testing our resolve, they are much mistaken. We shall apprehend the perpetrators and their sponsors and bring them to justice.

The policy measures and actions taken so far are not to be seen as some experiment in governance. We are fully aware that those vested interests who have held Nigeria back for so long will not give up without a fight. They will sow divisions, sponsor vile press criticisms at home and abroad, incite the public in an effort to create chaos rather than relinquish the vice-like grip they have held on Nigeria.

The economic misfortune we are experiencing in the shape of very low oil prices has provided us with an opportunity to restructure our economy and diversify. We are in the process of promoting agriculture and livestock, exploiting our solid mineral resources and expanding our industrial and manufacturing base. That way, we will import less and make the social investments necessary to allow us to produce a large and skilled workforce.

The Central Bank of Nigeria will offer more fiscal incentives for businesses that prove capable of manufacturing products that are internationally competitive. We remain committed to reforming the regulatory framework for investors by improving the ease of doing business in Nigeria.

Meanwhile, the first steps along the path of self-sufficiency in rice, wheat and sugar—big users of our scarce foreign exchange—have been taken. The Labour Intensive Farming Enterprise (LIFE) will boost the economy and ensure inclusive growth in long-neglected communities. Special intervention funds through the Bank of Agriculture will provide targeted support. Concerns remain about the rising cost of foods such as maize, rice, millet, beans and gari. Farmers tell me that they are worried about the cost of fertilizers and pesticides and the absence of extension services. The federal and state governments are on the same page in tackling these hurdles in our efforts at increased food production and ultimately food security.

I would like to take this opportunity to express my appreciation for the increasing role that our women are playing in revitalizing the agricultural sector. Modern farming is still hard and heavy work, and I salute our Nigerian women in sharing this burden. In this respect I am very pleased to announce that the government will shortly be launching the National Women's Empowerment Fund, which I have approved to provide N1.6 billion in micro-finance loans to women across the nation to assist in rehabilitating the economies of rural communities, particularly those impacted by the insurgency and conflict.

With respect to solid minerals, the minister has produced a road map where we will work closely with the World Bank and major international investors to ensure through best practices and due diligence that we choose the right partners. Illegal mining remains a problem and we have set up a special security team to protect our assets. Special measures will be in place to protect miners in their work environment.

For too long, ours has been a society that neglects the poor and victimizes the weak. A society that promotes profit and growth over development and freedom. A society that fails to recognize that, to quote the distinguished economist Amartya Sen, "poverty is not just lack of money. It is not having the capability to realize one's full potential as a human being."

So, today, I am happy to formally launch by far the most ambitious social protection programme in our history. A programme that both seeks to start the process of lifting many from poverty while at the same time creating the opportunity for people to fend for themselves. In this regard, five hundred billion naira has been appropriated in the 2016 budget for social intervention programmes in five key areas. We are committed to providing job creation opportunities for five hundred thousand teachers and one hundred thousand artisans across the nation. 5.5 million children are to be provided with nutritious meals through our school feeding programme to improve learning outcomes, as well as enrolment and completion rates. The conditional cash transfer scheme will provide financial support for up to 1 million vulnerable beneficiaries, and complement the Enterprise Programme—which will target up to 1 million market women; four hundred and sixty thousand artisans; and two hundred thousand agricultural workers, nationwide. Finally, through the education grant scheme, we will encourage students studying sciences, technology, engineering and maths, and lay a foundation for human capital development for the next generation.

I would like to pay a special tribute to our gallant men and women of the armed forces who are in harm's way so that the rest of us can live and go about our business in safety. Their work is almost done. The nation owes them a debt of gratitude.

Abroad, we want to assure our neighbours, friends and development partners that Nigeria is firmly committed to democratic principles. We are ready partners in combating terrorism, cyber crimes, control of communicable diseases and protection of the environment. Following on the Paris Agreement, COP 21, we are fully committed to halting and reversing desertification. Elsewhere, we will intensify efforts to tackle erosion, ocean surge, flooding and oil spillage, which I referred to earlier, by implementing the UNEP report.

We are grateful to the international community, notably France, the US, the UK and China for their quick response in helping to tackle the recent Ebola outbreak in our sub-region. We also acknowledge the humanity shown by the Italian and German governments in the treatment of boat people, many fleeing from our sub-region because of lack of economic opportunity. We thank all our partners, especially several countries in the EU.

> We appreciate the valuable work that the UN agencies, particularly UNICEF, ICRC and the World Food Program, have been doing. We must also appreciate the World Bank, the Gates Foundation, the Global Fund and Educate a Child of Qatar for the excellent work in our health, education and other sectors.
>
> Fellow citizens, let me end on a happy note. To the delight of all, two of the abducted Chibok girls have regained their freedom. During the last one year, not a single day passed without my agonizing about these girls. Our efforts have centered around negotiations to free them safely from their mindless captors. We are still pursuing that course. Their safety is of paramount concern to me and I am sure to most Nigerians. I am very worried about the conditions those still captured might be in. Today I re-affirm our commitment to rescuing our girls. We will never stop until we bring them home safely. As I said before, no girl should be put through the brutality of forced marriage, and every Nigerian girl has the right to an education and a life choice.
>
> I thank you and appeal to you to continue supporting the government's efforts to fix Nigeria.

Buhari's assessment of his first year as president makes plain how he perceives his role in steering the direction of change in Nigeria. It is a speech that will stand as a benchmark of his accomplishments and his aspirations for the future. At the same time, there are many in Nigeria who were beneficiaries of the old system, and who are adept at slowing down or even thwarting the Buhari reforms.

While the international community applauded the substance of the May 29 speech, the question remained as to how Buhari could implement his policies. Was there time to make the changes required to quell the insurgency, stem corruption, and diversify the economy? Could the political system adapt to the need for democratic practices in addressing these challenges?

Conclusion

Do individual leaders shape history, or does history shape individuals? In the case of Muhammadu Buhari, both are true.

The story of Muhammadu Buhari is a story of the interplay between historical context and the qualities of an individual leader. More specifically, it is the story of how Buhari has exercised leadership at two different periods within the evolving Nigeria Project.

Buhari's own life and the Nigeria Project are closely intertwined. Born in the late colonial period, Buhari has seen his country gain independence, undergo the trauma of civil war, become a major petro-state, and swing between military rule and civilian rule. Throughout, Buhari has done his best to ensure that the Nigeria Project has stayed on track and moved forward. The extent to which he embodies the history of the country he has fought for and worked to develop can be gauged by the fact that he is one of only two people who have served both as Nigeria's military head of state and, subsequently, as its elected civilian president. The extent to which he embodies hopes for Nigeria's democratic future can be gauged by the fact that he is the *only* person ever to win a democratic presidential election as an opposition candidate.

In order to understand how Buhari has been shaped by Nigeria's history, and how he has in turn shaped that history, we need to stand back and see the big picture in terms both of different models of leadership and government and of the evolution of the Nigeria Project.

* * *

In theory, leadership may be based on *power* (the ability to produce intended effects) or on *legitimacy* (the approval of followers). The Buhari phenomenon exemplifies both types of leadership.

Military rule (in Hausa, *mulkin sojoji*) is often characterized as based on power, although in many cases it may also try to acquire popular legitimacy. It may appeal to society's need for order or respond to a need to stem corruption or counter weakness in the face of existential threats. In modern times, military rule is based on the national state, which has exclusive prerogatives to the use of force. In many postcolonial African states, the military has always been the predominant national institution.

As a long-term solution to the need for order, however, military rule is unstable unless it is coupled with a larger sense of national purpose. One such purpose is the promise to transition to civilian rule with clear rules for succession and governing.

Civilian rule takes many institutional forms, but in essence it requires the consent of the governed. This consent may be given through elections or attained in other ways that are considered *legitimate.* Max Weber, the nineteenth-century German sociologist, developed what is now regarded as the classical formulation of legitimacy, or system approval. Legitimacy, said Weber, can take three different forms: charismatic, traditional, and legal-rational.

System founders are often *charismatic*; in other words, their personal qualities command respect as providing societal direction and purpose. Such system founders may be first-generation nationalists or revolutionaries of various sorts. In Nigeria, the founders of the nineteenth-century Sokoto Caliphate were charismatic leaders. Some might argue that Nigeria gained independence in 1960 as a result of charismatic leaders such as Nnamdi Azikiwe, Obafemi Awolowo, Ahmadu Bello, Abubakar Tafawa Balewa, and Aminu Kano.

The successors to original founders are often termed *traditional,* because they follow the traditions established by the system founders. In northern Nigeria, the emirs who were appointed by the Sokoto founders, and their dynastic heirs, are termed "traditional" (*mulkin gargajiya*).

In postcolonial times, such emirs are also termed "royal fathers" or "traditional leaders" and may or may not have power to go along with their legitimacy. (The "chiefs" in other, non-Muslim Nigerian communities are comparable.) The defining quality they possess is that they hold an office that is respected or approved by ordinary people in their communities. The rules for traditional rulers may or may not be clearly articulated.

Finally, as systems emerge or evolve, a clear set of guidelines may determine how leaders are selected and how politics is conducted. These rules are termed *legal-rational* because they are usually articulated in a legal set of *constitutional provisions* and are open to reasoned interpretation.

The United Kingdom is famous for having an unwritten constitution, although parliamentary sovereignty and a deep sense of political culture determine the evolving rules of the game of politics. At the time of Nigerian independence, this British Westminster model had not evolved to its current stage of recognizing devolution of component regions. It was not a *federal* system, and as such was unsuitable for Nigeria, with its regional complexity.

Of course, Nigeria was familiar with the "federal" structures dating back to the colonial era, although they tended to be lopsided in geographic and demographic size, and the reality of overarching colonial rule meant that decentralized decision making was always more of a principle than a practice. The three constitutions introduced in the 1940s and 1950s were at best "quasi-federal."

Nigeria gained independence in 1960, with a parliamentary system at the regional and national levels. In the north, many people still regard this period as a benchmark for probity by leaders across the political spectrum, as referenced by Buhari in his inaugural address.

The breakdown of this First Republic system in 1966 resulted in a long period of military rule. It also resulted in the Civil War, which was the defining experience for junior officers such as Buhari. The slogan "Duty, Honor, Country" was something these officers were willing to die for.

The bonding of junior officers in the heat of battle would last a lifetime, as would the close relationship forged during the war between Buhari and Danjuma. The trauma of losing a wartime comrade—such as the death in prison of Buhari's comrade Shehu Musa Yar'Adua—would leave an indelible scar.

In the postwar military era, the most significant development in terms of national unity was the decision by General Murtala Muhammad to move the capital from Lagos, in the south of the country, to Abuja, in the middle. This set the stage for a new era of efforts to achieve national unity, the pursuit of which was a core principle among those officers who had risen from junior to more senior ranks since the Civil War.

After this military interlude, a new constitution was enacted in 1979 that was *presidential* but remained *federal*. This Second Republic model was an experiment in governance undertaken at just the time that large-scale oil revenues were coming on stream and creating powerful pressures to centralize government, because revenues came in at the top of the federal hierarchy.

Political institutions were not yet fully developed to accommodate these developments. In the absence of strong institutions able to monitor and regulate how politics was played, individual power brokers could interpret the rules of the game to suit their political or individual needs.

Nigeria's senior military officers intervened in December 1983, and made Buhari head of state, in an effort to produce order. This was also a time of experimenting with the use of military power to transform the chaos of the Nigeria Project into a more cohesive whole. The Civil War had tested the external boundaries of Nigeria. Buhari and his comrades tried to make sure that the new petro-wealth was not squandered on fraud and corruption.

After twenty months, General Buhari's rule was brought to an abrupt close by the intervention of other senior officers, who took a more relaxed view of the emerging petro-state, with its inevitable chaos and get-rich-quick culture. General Babangida tried to gain legitimacy by promising to return the country to civilian rule and attempting to guide the emergence of a constitutionally mandated two-party system. (This was the so-called Third Republic.) This effort collapsed in June 1993, and a newer form of tough military rule emerged under General Abacha.

During the Abacha period (1993–98), an effort was made to funnel some of the oil wealth into development projects through the Petroleum Trust Fund. Because of his grassroots reputation for integrity, Buhari was selected by Abacha to head the work of the Petroleum Trust Fund. Abacha was trying to gain popular approval (i.e., legitimacy) by associating himself with Buhari's reputation as a champion of anticorruption.

Abacha's death in 1998 put an end to his efforts to introduce a new constitution that might well have permitted him to continue ruling, but in civilian guise. Abacha's successor, General Abubakar, oversaw the transition to the Fourth Republic, a recognizable version of the Second Republic presidential model.

Nigeria's Fourth Republic (1999–present) has lasted longer than any of the country's other postcolonial political systems. The office of president is central in the Fourth Republic, but the thirty-six states (and their governors) also have powers and control over resources. This presidential system is closer to the US tradition, with its checks and balances, than to the French or Russian models, in which the executive has stronger powers.

Yet checks and balances are often weak in a petro-state. The perceived need for access to de facto strong executive powers in Nigeria had resulted in a do-or-die political culture regarding the presidency. The presidential elections of 1999, 2003, 2007, and 2011 all resulted in victories for incumbents.

The presidential election of 2015 thus stands out as a remarkable departure from the past and an inspiring example for the future. In 2015, for the first time in Nigerian history, an opposition party won the presidency. The reasons for this opposition victory have been discussed in this study, and were due in part to the weakness of the incumbent. But they were also due to the coalition-building skills of the challenging party, the APC, and the personal symbolism of Buhari.

The question in 2015, after the election, was whether Buhari and the APC could *govern,* or simply serve as an expression of *protest.* The capacity to govern was complicated by the depletion of treasury funds, for reasons discussed in previous chapters. It was also a result of having to spend one-fifth of the national budget on security-related endeavors. Despite these formidable constraints, however, during his first year in office President Buhari demonstrated not only that he can govern but also that he has the vision, integrity, dedication, and political common sense to govern effectively.

* * *

The Buhari story is sometimes opaque because Buhari comes from a culture that tends to value modesty. And because it is a culture from the far north of the country, it may be less accessible both to foreigners and to coastal Nigerians. Nonetheless, if we are to assess his leadership accurately, we need to understand the cultural values that have shaped his outlook and actions.

Those values began to be instilled in him at his home in Daura, on the edge of the Sahelian zone, a transition to the great Sahara Desert. The cattle culture in the Sahel gave him a basic appreciation of the realities of nature and outdoor living. Even Qur'anic studies were fitted into the daily needs of a farming-pastoralist community.

At that time, primary and secondary education were still dominated by British teachers, who made a major impression on young Buhari. His own father had died when he was four, which strengthened his bonds with his mother, with surrogate fathers such as his family guardian, and with his schoolteachers.

The major shift in socialization influences occurred in 1961, when the nineteen-year-old Buhari decided to apply for officer candidate training. The Emir of Katsina was encouraging young northern Nigerian men to embark on such careers. Nigeria had just achieved independence, and the north was trying to catch up with the educated elites of southern Nigeria.

The decision to compete for a slot in officer training would shape Buhari's values throughout his life. He had been raised to believe that one's behavior was either right or wrong; there was no moral middle ground where actions were always clouded in shades of gray. Military officer training in Kaduna and the United Kingdom reinforced these values. For example, there was never any doubt in his mind that stealing is wrong. He also learned the value of "appreciation" of complex situations, which was vital to survival and success on the battlefield.

His military training exposed Buhari to fellow officers from throughout Nigeria. Whether they were Muslim or Christian made little difference to him. It did matter, however, that they were of the same generation, which created a strong bond between them. In the Nigerian military, the rank of officers has usually correlated with age groups. Members of Buhari's generational cohort became senior officers and then graduated to become *retired* senior officers who were widely regarded by the public as the country's "elders," even as father figures. They were often seen as stabilizing forces in a chaotic petro-state system.

Buhari's character was tested in officer training and in civil war, but it was given its sternest test in the postwar petroleum economy. Billions of petro-dollars were available for the taking by those in power. Buhari resisted such temptations himself and became a whistle-blower against those succumbed to the lure of easy "new wealth."

Buhari's fearlessness and persistence attracted enemies as well as grassroots supporters. Even some of his fellow officers felt that he was too strict during his term as military head of state. This resulted in his three-year detention, which he endured with as much good grace as he could muster, but which meant a painful separation from family and friends. It was a sobering experience, and one which tested his commitment to public life.

Buhari's work in the military, his term as governor of the North East zone, and his time as minister of petroleum resources, together with his leadership of the Katsina Foundation and the Petroleum Trust Fund, prepared him for his political reengagement.

Buhari's decision in 2002 to reenter public life through partisan politics involved both complex and simple calculations. He still believed in "Duty, Honor, Country," and was convinced that incumbent politicians were ruining the reputation and future prospects of Nigerians. (He felt that Obasanjo was no exception.) Buhari was not a natural fit for politics, however. In particular, he found it hard to go into coalitions with moneybag politicians.

Yet there was tremendous pressure on Buhari from many quarters to return to political life, and public figures from many different perspectives thought that only Buhari could pull Nigeria back from the abyss of failed governance, chaos, or worse. He was particularly conscious of the fact that some junior officers were apparently considering extreme measures to try to put the country back on track.

The decision in 2014 to run for president, and to form a coalition with the "godfathers" of the South West zone, was complex. He had been abused as a "Muslim fanatic" by some of his southern countrymen. His life was often threatened. He barely survived a bomb blast attack on his car in July 2014 (and it remains unclear whether the bombers were from Boko Haram or the ranks of his political opponents). Still, he persisted. The need for reform was too great for him to sit back and enjoy his retirement in Kaduna.

* * *

Buhari's inauguration as president on May 29, 2015, was a milestone, but also just the beginning of the challenges of presidential leadership in Nigeria. Could he put together a team of diverse elements? Could he reengage and cultivate the international community? Could he counter the insurgency in the northeast? Could he thwart regional tensions—sometimes with religious overtones—in the South East and South-South zones? Could he reconstruct the lives and restore the hopes of those who had suffered at the hands of Boko Haram? Could he retain the support of the military while still holding some officers responsible for corruption?

Most important, could Buhari change the political culture of Nigeria to one of accountability and transparency? Could rule of law be revived? Could he set agriculture and education back on track and begin to diversify the country's economy? What about the youth bulge and the need for jobs? Political stability would require not only playing by constitutional rules but also addressing the underlying needs of society. It would mean keeping national unity as a top priority.

As Buhari's administration reached the end of December 2015, the jury was still out on his presidency as to whether change was possible. The early months of 2016 were a formidable test of his leadership.

* * *

The evidence presented in part III of this study suggests that Buhari faced four major challenges in the early months of 2016: combating insurgency and enhancing security, tackling corruption, encouraging economic development, and promoting political change.

It may seem premature as of this writing (July 2016) to assess his response to these challenges. Yet already it is possible to begin to measure progress (or not) along these dimensions during the first year of his presidency.

Regarding *counterinsurgency* in the North East, new military leadership and increased morale among the soldiers has resulted in the recapture of all the territories that had been lost to Boko Haram. Yet the struggle against Boko Haram is likely to continue well into the future, especially as Boko Haram resorts increasingly to hit-and-run tactics and suicide bombings.

The Buhari strategy has been to engage fully with the regional countries in the Lake Chad area: Cameroon, Niger, and Chad. It has also entailed working closely with the international community—notably, Western powers and the United Nations and other international institutions—especially with regard to equipment and training.

Another part of the Buhari strategy has been to win hearts and minds. The rampant corruption of the Fourth Republic had alienated many people in the northeast areas. By sending a strong message of zero tolerance for corruption, coupled with active programs for reconstruction in the area, Buhari may have helped to turn the tide in terms of local support.

Other initiatives launched by Buhari have included working more closely with local ad hoc security forces, such as Civilian Joint Task Force assets. The importance of local knowledge in thwarting an insurgency cannot be overestimated.

The unfortunate timing of the collapse of the international oil market has meant that fewer resources have been available for Buhari's all-of-country counterinsurgency programs than would have been optimal. At the same time, his attempt to instill tighter discipline in the military and prevent the abuse of civilians has meant that international support for Nigeria's counterinsurgency measures is likely to continue. The setting up of a desk at Defence Headquarters to receive complaints of human rights abuses was intended as a significant step toward mitigating these abuses.

Like his counterinsurgency strategy, Buhari's *anticorruption* campaign has come to rely in part on international support. With looted funds banked or invested in cities such as Dubai and London, and in countries such as Switzerland and the United States, efforts to retrieve that money necessarily require international cooperation. So, too, do efforts to prosecute and extradite those suspected of corruption who have fled abroad.

Yet the main effort at stemming corruption—apart from leadership by example—has been to instill new resolve in the EFCC, Code of Conduct Tribunals, and other anticorruption bodies. The proposed special tribunals to be set up by the Nigerian Supreme Court to try corruption cases will add another weapon to the country's anticorruption arsenal. (The use of military courts has yet to be tested in the cases stemming from the procurement scandals.)

The single most important component of Buhari's anticorruption campaign has been the public declaration of no impunity for big fish, including those in the president's own party. The ongoing criminal cases involving nine senators, including the president of the Senate, have sent a clear message of no impunity.

Regarding *economic development* challenges, the collapse of the price of oil to below $30 per barrel made it impossible to introduce a reconstruction budget that emphasized infrastructure. Yet deficit spending and international assistance have allowed for budget priorities to be established, including providing help for the poor and improving electricity infrastructure. Buhari has also emphasized that educational reform is the key to creating a knowledge economy, and that diversification away from oil dependency is critical to the long-term health of the economy.

But unless the youth jobs crisis is addressed, the future will be unstable. Offering better technology training and new agribusiness opportunities are stated priorities. If a conducive investment climate can be achieved, new job opportunities will emerge. Buhari's economic team has been led by Vice President Osinbajo, who has experience with the economic development of Lagos. Each of the individuals appointed to lead the economic-related ministries has brought special strengths to their job, not least the former governor of Lagos, Fashola, who now runs the Ministry of Power, Works and Housing.

Reconstruction in the North East zone requires enormous international input, especially from the World Bank. The numerous trips abroad by Buhari have been inspired in part by the search for international assistance and investment in the reconstruction of areas decimated by Boko Haram. Translating international promises of help into concrete action on the ground takes time, however. Meanwhile, the humanitarian situation in the North East has grown worse, with food in very short supply in some areas as of July 2016.

The fourth of Buhari's top priorities, the need for *political change*, has been pursued by taking the Constitution seriously and creating disincentives for anyone tempted to ignore it. Buhari has promised to respect the different roles of the legislature, judiciary, and the presidency, and during his first year as president did not interfere in the legislature or the judiciary.

In addition, Buhari has recognized the need to respect Nigeria's three-tiered federalism, but has sought to check the frequent pattern of state governors having and abusing absolute control over money matters within their states. Probes into the financial affairs of former governors, many of whom are now in the Senate, have put state officials on notice that they must henceforth use their considerable power wisely and legally.

Regarding electoral reform, the internationally acclaimed standards set by the INEC chair have made it possible to learn lessons from the 2015 election for future elections. The appointment of Mahmud Yakubu as INEC chair augurs well for the future integrity of elections. Although it is not possible for Buhari to shape the future of multiparty democracy in Nigeria, his insistence on free and fair elections will help to level the electoral playing field.

More than a year into his presidency, Buhari has undertaken major efforts in all four priority areas. Whether this will be enough to change Nigerian economic and political cultures remains to be seen. If necessity is the mother of invention, then the collapse of the petro-state monopoly of hard currency revenues might allow a more diversified economy to emerge.

At the same time, as long as the global oil economy is based on a dollar-denominated currency, the management of the Nigerian central banking system will follow different guidelines than exist in developing countries that are not dependent on oil. Despite his personal reservations about the benefits of devaluation to Nigeria's economy and ordinary people, Buhari reluctantly agreed with those politicians, officials, and businesspeople urging devaluation as a way of attracting large amounts of international lending and investment. On June 20, 2016, the Central Bank of Nigeria announced that it was floating the naira against the US dollar, which resulted in a steep devaluation from N197 per US dollar to around N284 per dollar.

It is unclear if such reforms and initiatives will help Buhari retain his support. Buhari has been most popular among the youth, but their expectations have been out of all proportion to the economic realities. Still, to have made progress in counterinsurgency and anticorruption might buy time for other economic and political reforms to take place.

The Nigerian Project often hangs in the balance as events lurch from crisis to crisis. Yet, it may finally become more routinized and institutionalized. By definition, a single person cannot be an institution. But the need for institutions that work and are reliable can be shaped by the transformational efforts of wise and steady leadership.

Buhari's presidency may pull Nigeria back from the brink of failed-state status and give the president's fellow citizens a chance to turn adversity into new opportunities. Leadership by example may not by itself transform the country, but without such an inspiring example change will surely remain elusive.

Despite Nigeria's current economic hardships, Buhari's life continues to be an inspiration to the millions of grassroots supporters who have pinned their hopes on "Mr. Integrity." One of Buhari's major contributions has been to inspire public sector workers to do their best on the front lines of battle with Boko Haram, in the fight against corruption, and in the war on ignorance (*Yaki da Jahilci*), including the major push for girls' education. As in battle, Buhari leads from the front, whether in the fight for national unity, the struggle to clean up the petroleum sector, or the effort to revive confidence in economic recovery.

Yet Buhari remains an enigma to many of his countrymen, and even to some of his close associates. He seems to have no interest in political power for its own sake. He has said on numerous occasions that he would rather give up power than betray the ordinary people of Nigeria.

Meanwhile, the danger remains that corruption will fight back. Rumors abound of rump military elements supporting turmoil in the Delta to provoke an economic crisis and of a possible military coup "to stabilize" the situation.

Buhari will need the confidence and assistance of the international community as he meets these challenges. Fortunately, that help may be forthcoming, because his statesmanship has revived hopes that Nigeria will become a strong contributor to international cooperation and stability.

In his first year in office, Buhari has turned the tide of opinion regarding Nigeria among key world leaders. The leaders he has met include Xi Jinping of China, King Abdullah of Jordan, King Salman of Saudi Arabia, Narendra Modi of India, Angela Merkel of Germany, François Hollande of France, David Cameron of the United Kingdom, and Barack Obama of the United States, as well as Ban Ki Moon of the United Nations and Jim Yong Kim of the World Bank. In each case, Buhari has gained the goodwill and support that will be necessary for Nigeria to take its rightful place in the family of nations.

After one year in office, and despite economic and political challenges, Buhari has helped to put the Nigeria Project back on track. His greatest challenge in the years ahead may be to encourage other Nigerians to strengthen the institutions that can keep it on track.

A strong leader in a democracy needs a relationship of trust and respect with grassroots constituents, even if policy differences are evident. A year into his presidency, Buhari still enjoys such a relationship with a wide range of ordinary Nigerians. He has offered no easy solutions to Nigeria's deep-seated problems, because there are no easy solutions. What he *has* offered is the political will to tackle these problems and the moral courage to take steps that may cause short-term hardships in return for long-term benefits. If he is to make a lasting difference, he needs the Nigerian people to exhibit patience and to focus on what unites them rather than what divides them. The Nigeria Project may stand or fall depending on how his approach to tackling Nigeria's problems aligns with a renewed national vision of "unity with diversity."

Index

About the Author

Dr. John N. Paden is Clarence Robinson Professor of International Studies at George Mason University, which is located in northern Virginia, close to Washington, DC. He was a philosophy major at Occidental College and a Rhodes Scholar at Oxford University in philosophy, politics, and economics. He completed a doctorate in politics at Harvard University. He has served as Norman Dwight Harris Professor of International Studies and director of African Studies at Northwestern University; professor of public administration at Ahmadu Bello University in Zaria, Nigeria; and was founding dean, Faculty of Social and Management Sciences, at Bayero University Kano, Nigeria.

Dr. Paden was part of a team that helped plan Nigeria's new federal "unity" capital in Abuja. He served as an international observer during the Nigerian presidential elections of 1999 (in Kaduna), 2003 (in Kano), and 2007 (in Katsina.) He served for fifteen years on the executive committee of a Ford Foundation U.S.-China scholars exchange program to help set up African studies in China. He has served on review panels and written numerous published reports for the United States Institute of Peace. Between 2002 and 2006, he was a member of the Brookings Institution task force on U.S. policy toward the Islamic world.

Some of Dr. Paden's Nigeria-related books include *Religion and Political Culture in Kano* (winner of the Herskovits Prize); *Ahmadu Bello, Sardauna of Sokoto: Values and Leadership in Nigeria; Muslim*

Civic Cultures and Conflict Resolution: The Challenge of Democratic Federalism in Nigeria; Faith and Politics in Nigeria: Nigeria as a Pivotal State in the Muslim World; and *Postelection Conflict Management in Nigeria: The Challenges of National Unity.*

Other African-related books by Dr. Paden include *The African Experience* (four volumes); *Values, Identities, and National Integration: Empirical Research in Africa; Black Africa: A Comparative Handbook;* and *Understanding Black Africa: Data Analysis of Social Change and Nation Building.*

Dr. Paden has worked closely with colleagues at the Usmanu Danfodiyo University Sokoto (Nigeria), especially at the Center for Peace Studies. In 2012, he received an honorary doctorate in humane letters from that university for "immense contribution to the advancement of the frontiers of knowledge and scholarship."